Touchscreen Archaeology

Touchscreen Archaeology: Tracing Histories of Hands-On Media Practices

Wanda Strauven

μ meson press

Funded by the

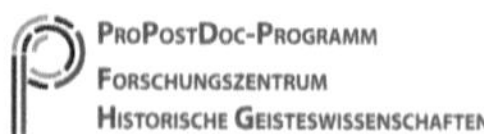

Bibliographical Information of the German National Library

The German National Library lists this publication in the Deutsche Nationalbibliografie (German National Bibliography); detailed bibliographic information is available online at http://dnb.d-nb.de.

Published in 2021 by meson press, Lüneburg, Germany
www.meson.press

Design concept: Torsten Köchlin, Silke Krieg
Cover image: Detail from *Una storia* (2014) by Federica Barbieri
Copy editing: Kyle Stine

The print edition of this book is printed by Lightning Source, Milton Keynes, United Kingdom.

ISBN (Print): 978-3-95796-186-0
ISBN (PDF): 978-3-95796-187-7
ISBN (EPUB): 978-3-95796-188-4
DOI: 10.14619/1860

The digital editions of this publication can be downloaded freely at: www.meson.press

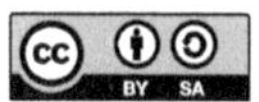

To my daughter

Contents

Foreword

Untimely as it might seem, this book invites the reader to delve into a century-long history of tactility in the arts and media. In these strange times when people are asked to keep distance from other human beings due to the spread of an invisible pathogenic agent and when touching displayed objects in public is considered risky and even transgressive, I propose to study historical and contemporary hands-on media practices as playful and meaningful acts.

I would like to emphasize that the present book was written well before the coronavirus pandemic. Its conception thus predates the safety measurements of social distancing, wearing facemasks and latex gloves, and not touching touchscreens. Yet I revised the manuscript during the early days of the pandemic's outbreak, more precisely during the first strictly regulated lockdown in Italy, and finalized it when so-called second waves hit populations worldwide. Even if these experiences did not affect the overall concept of the book, I cannot circumvent the subject and ignore the current distrust in touching (screen) surfaces and nurturing social contacts.

The pandemic is topical to the content of this book, as it urges us to rethink the activity of screen touching, somehow reversing the logic of the touchscreen as a screen that must *not* be touched. Indeed, as I will briefly address, the global health crisis had direct consequences for the use of touchscreen-based devices in museums. And when discussing manual gestures in terms of communication, I also needed to acknowledge that the handshake, for instance, underwent a change in meaning in response to COVID-19.

On the other hand, the interest of this book lies precisely in the excavation of changing meanings, of topoi that return as unique instances throughout history, with a renewed or altered function. I propose to think of the touchscreen as a low-tech, touchable media object, as a surface and interface that existed long before computers and smartphones. Today's touchscreen, potentially contagious, is only one of the occurrences of what constitutes the object of knowledge for my media-archaeological quest.

January 2021

Introduction:
Is This a Touchscreen?

In the beginning, touch; at the origin,
the medium.
Michel Serres

Three Opening Anecdotes

In the spring of 2012, I visited the then-recently-inaugurated Eye Filmmuseum Amsterdam in the Netherlands and tried out the Video Flipbook machine installed in its basement. This machine allows visitors to make a personalized flipbook by recording a short selfie video, saved as a sequence of still images, that can be printed and assembled for a small fee in the Eye Shop. At that time, the interactive installation consisted of a wall with screens on the front and back: one screen serving as a preview of the recording and another displaying the first images of the videos that various people had just recorded. Above the outward facing screen was a caption that warned: "NO TOUCHSCREEN" (fig. 1a–b). The sign was attached with transparent tape, in a rather provisional way. I assume the staff realized only after the museum opened that the setup was inviting people to touch the screen, probably because the individual images looked like clickable icons.

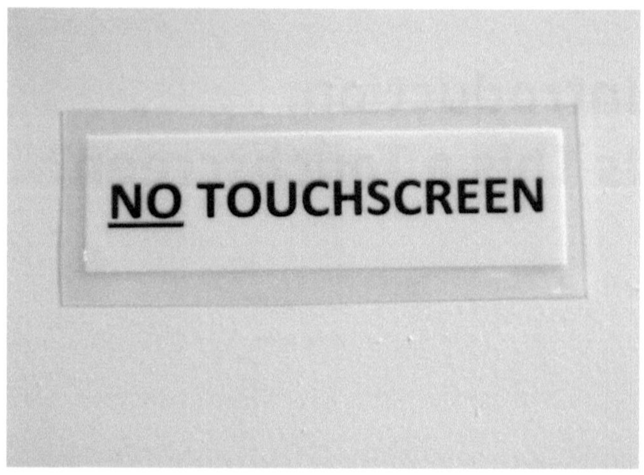

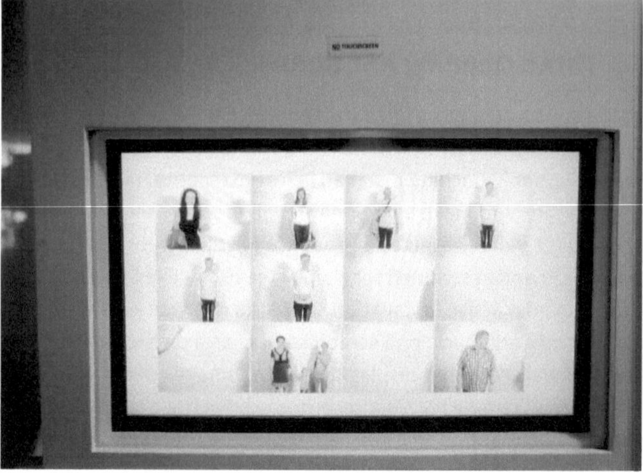

[Figure 1a–b] Video Flipbook Machine, Eye Filmmuseum Amsterdam. From author's personal archive, May 2012.

I was struck by the historically reversed situation, whereby a "high-tech" but not touch-based video screen was incorporated into a setting for creating a "low-tech," century-old media toy, a flipbook, that required active touch to create the illusion of movement. The *kineograph*, as the flipbook was patented in 1868, came also to be known as "thumb cinema" in reference to its manual operation: it can be browsed from front to back with the right thumb and from back to front with the left thumb, while its flipping movement can be stopped at any page, so that a detail can be indicated with the finger. Thanks to its small size, it fits perfectly in your shirt pocket. The flipbook as portable, pocket-sized and hands-on cinema is in stark contrast to the fixed built-in computer screen that cannot be touched. Yet the warning sign of the Video Flipbook machine is also clearly symptomatic of a change in our screen culture, of the fact that the touchscreen is becoming the default technology for screens and that we need a new term to indicate the non-touchscreen or non-touchable screen, which is, obviously, not necessarily obsolete. In a similar vein, after the introduction of the CD in the music industry, the LP was no longer called "record" (or record album) but persisted and made its revival as "vinyl." What could be such a new/old name for the non-touchscreen? Can we think of a comparable connection with its (original) materiality?

In autumn 2014, another museum visit, while not resolving this terminological matter, inspired further reflection on the ontology of the touchscreen. Accompanied by a group of young children, I happened to drop in on a temporary exhibition organized by the independent artist collective Casagallery at the Resistance Museum of Bologna in Italy. At the entrance of the exhibition, entitled *Infiltrazioni* (Infiltrations, October 7–17, 2014), stood a huge round cactus covered with cutout paper eyes, which were all pierced, one by one, by the cactus spines. It was fascinating to see how the kids were immediately attracted by this spiky artwork, entitled *Una storia* (A story, 2014), by Federica Barbieri. Two little girls could not resist touching it. They did so in a very delicate way, as if they wanted to caress the cactus (fig. 2). Or maybe they were just curious to find out if it was a real cactus, if it was hurting despite its "huggable" appearance. And, of course, it did hurt. But it was not an ordinary cactus they were touching: it was a cactus with innumerable eyes that were looking back at them. When I posted a picture of this "encounter" on Facebook, one of my friends, besides referring to *Un chien andalou* (1929) by Luis Buñuel, also made the following astute observation: "Touch screens that look back at you."[1]

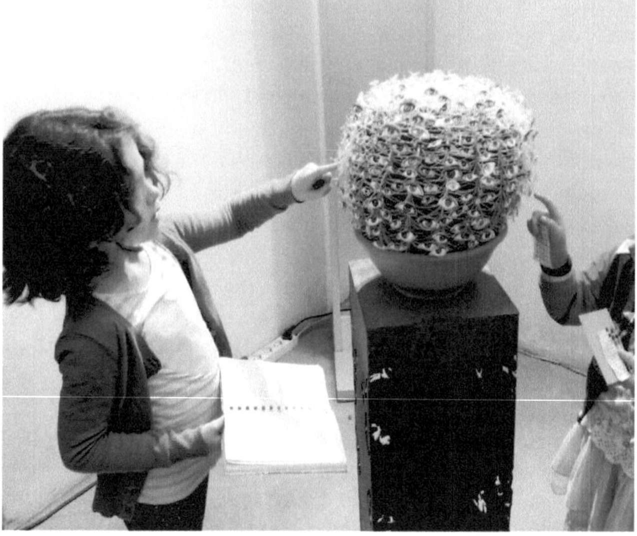

[Figure 2] *Una storia* (2014) by Federica Barbieri, Museo della Resistenza, Bologna. From author's personal archive, October 2014.

Are these cutout paper eyes indeed touchscreens? Why would one call them that? Because of their materiality and the fact we can touch them? Or rather because of their (painful) feedback and the fact they are looking back at us? To be sure, the artwork questions—even pokes at—the culturally established hierarchy

1 Jan Teurlings on my Facebook wall, October 16, 2014.

of the senses, that is, Western ocularcentrism. In fact, over the course of not only Western history but also each human life, the first and primal sense of touch is constantly disciplined by and subordinated to the other senses and, in particular, vision (as the mind's eye). Yet here the eye is literally pierced, evoking indeed the indelible image of the razor cutting the eye in *Un chien andalou*. In Buñuel's film, seeing becomes painful, it becomes (again) an embodied act; likewise, in Barbieri's artwork, seeing becomes a form of touching, with each eye functioning as a screen—a screen to get your finger pricked.

The last and most personal of my three opening anecdotes goes back to the summer of 2011, when my husband gave me a first-generation iPad as a "symbolic" gift, that is, as a companion and hands-on study material for my historical research on the touchscreen.[2] However, this "true" touchscreen device did not survive the journey, turning out obsolete and dysfunctional before I even started writing this book. Yet it served its purpose and triggered the Dutch working title for my ongoing research project: "aaienpet." This untranslatable term was coined by my then three-year-old daughter, who almost instantly "confiscated" the iPad from me. At first, she called it the "present you got from Daddy," but very soon it became her "aaienpet." Morphologically speaking, the term can be split in two parts: "aaien" and "pet."[3] Yet the language-game, which functions only in Dutch, is limited to the first segment: for my daughter, it was not evident to connect the "i" of iPad to the first-person singular of English grammar which she was not yet familiar with at that age, but instead it resonated well with the verb "to caress," which in Dutch is *aaien* (pronunciation: /ˈaːi̯ə(n)/). Because of the phonetic similarity between the English "I" and the Dutch "aai," it is very likely that

2 Elsewhere, I have used this third anecdote in an anonymous way as an illustration of Wittgensteinian language-game (Strauven 2019, 37).

3 As for the latter part of the term, there is no connection to be made with the English noun "pet," since a *pet* in Dutch means "cap."

 the little girl gave her own interpretation to Apple's name for the electronic tablet, namely: it is something to caress.

Objects, Users, Gestures

Of the three opening anecdotes, only the last tells us about what is generally considered today to be a touchscreen: a display screen of an electronic device (computer, tablet, smartphone) that registers a user's input by detecting the touch of a finger or stylus on its surface. While *Merriam-Webster* and the *Cambridge Dictionary* still disagree on the correct spelling of the term, "touch screen" vs. "touchscreen," its meaning is undeniably connected to computer technology. According to *Merriam-Webster*, it is "a display screen on which the user selects options (as from a menu) by touching the screen,"[4] while the *Cambridge Dictionary* defines it even more unequivocally as "a computer screen that you touch to get information, buy something, etc."[5] The challenge of the present book lies largely in opening up this restricted interpretation of the term, by exploring connections, in particular in terms of hands-on usage, between "low-tech" (nonelectronic) screens and "high-tech" (digital) screens. In response to this provocation, one might object that I should not confuse the "touchscreen" with the very broad notion of "touchable screen," the latter indicating a screen that *can* be touched and the former specifying, more precisely, one that *must* be touched. As media scholar Nanna Verhoeff points out,

> The aspect that most clearly distinguishes the touchscreen from other screen devices such as the cinematic screen, or the television screen for that matter, is the fact that spatial proximity of the screen not only *can* involve the user's body, the screen *must* be touched in order to navigate within the screen interface. (2012, 24)

4 https://www.merriam-webster.com/dictionary/touchscreen#h1.

5 https://dictionary.cambridge.org/dictionary/english/touchscreen.

Yet, as I would like to argue, the same can be said about the flipbook, which *must* be activated to generate a short moving image sequence. If no act of touching is taking place, the series of consecutive still images will remain immobile—even more, unseen. And even though the image carrier here is made of paper, its close connection with early cinema and viewing machines such as the Mutoscope places it in a history of visual display devices, if not directly of "media screens," a notion that will be further explored, both etymologically and historically, in this book.

As I will explain in more detail later in this introduction, my scholarly engagement with century-old and up-to-date tactile media devices, which I propose to consider under the common heading of "touchscreens," is embedded in a media-archaeological framework that operates both backward (into the past) and forward (into the future). By combining a McLuhanian method of seeking the old in the new with Siegfried Zielinski's "anarchic" approach of hitting upon the new in the old, my aim is to bring about a productive dialogue between the early and late history of tactile media, not in terms of a one-to-one equation but rather as mutual transparency. Critically arguing against a linear and teleological conception of history, as well as the notions of old media's obsolescence and new media's newness, this study focuses on a wide variety of objects that function as "nonhuman actors" in the act of touching. Even if this study is not conducted intentionally in light of science and technology studies, I follow here Bruno Latour's definition of "actor":

> An "actor" in ANT [actor–network theory] is a semiotic definition—an actant—, that is something that acts or to which activity is granted by others. It implies *no* special motivation of *human individual* actors, nor of humans in general. An actor can literally be anything provided it is granted to be the source of an action. (1996, 373)

The flipbook, to continue with the same example, is the source of an action that consists in using our thumbs to turn its small pages; it directly inspires such a hands-on action and also has a certain impact insofar as it makes something happen: it turns a series of still images into one continuous moving image. This potentiality (or agency) is inscribed in the object itself.

In this book, I am interested in interactions between human and nonhuman actants that constitute concrete actions of touching, whereby it is often technological devices that invite and incite human actions. As for instance in the second opening anecdote, it is the cactus artwork that exerted a force of attraction on the two girls, who, at their turn, became part of the artwork as a live experience or "encounter." The cutout and pierced paper eyes became "touch screens that look back at you" through the (inter)action of touching. In this context, I am less concerned with the artist as actor, in this case Barbieri, who, present during our visit, witnessed and luckily tolerated the girls' "illicit" act of touching the artwork on display. The "encounter" that matters for my argument is between the artwork and the museumgoer, or more generally between the object (as nonhuman actant) and the user (as human actant).

Such a dyadic model is chosen on purpose with a view to a "thick description" (Geertz 1973) of object–user encounters as meaningful events, which all take place in a larger Foucauldian *dispositif*—ranging from a disciplining instance such as the museum or the movie theater to the governmentality of digital, data-based media. The book's scope is not to offer a critical analysis of today's control society and the algorithmization of "computational capitalism" (Stiegler 2019), even if the last chapter will propose a redefinition of the image in terms of data information, operation, and surveillance. At the risk of being too naïve, I want to counterbalance the typical doomsday scenarios of digital media's impact on society and culture, by focusing on the playful dimension of hands-on media practices.

As will become clear throughout the book, I am especially inspired by children's mischievous actions of touching screen-based media and art installations. Instead of making too quick assumptions about a cause-and-effect relationship with their early familiarization with touchscreens, I believe it is more productive to see in the child's approach a reversal of the "look, but don't touch" rule—a typical adult exhortation that children prefer to ignore in favor of an ingenuous exploration of the borders between touchable and non-touchable, interactive and noninteractive. The child is a seemingly naïve user, who is in fact an expert in the pretend play and who shares some behavioral patterns with the so-called rube figure of early cinema, to which is dedicated the first chapter of the book. The rube is a clumsy countryman who does not know how to behave in the modern city and who, when visiting a moving picture show, jumps on stage and touches the film screen. What makes the rube a comical character is that he has failed to internalize the "look, but don't touch" norm and is not only acting like a man of dubious judgment, but like a child. But this is precisely the reason why I take the rube figure as my guiding thread in order to recover the tactile potential of cinema as a screen-based media experience. My sympathy for this apparently unsophisticated character is the basis of *Touchscreen Archaeology*, because it is the rube's "undisciplined" attitude that prompts a change of mindset or perception. Just as children adopt and expand the paradigm of the touchscreen to other media and non-media environments in their forms of play, the rube extends a nineteenth-century tradition of hands-on interaction and manual operation of media devices, ranging from optical toys to coin-operated viewing machines. To be sure, this early cinema figure also had a different "disciplining" function, as I will discuss in Chapter 1, but for the moment I would like to stress the concreteness of the rube's act of screen touching. I consider both the child and the rube as users (or human actants), whose hands-on gestures become in this study the guiding principle for shifting from (a history of) *visual* media to (a history of) *tactile* media.

Their hands-on, touchscreen-like gestures are processes, that is, actions that take place. These gestures can range from tender caressing, as suggested by the term "aaienpet" coined by my daughter, to quick page thumbing, as in the case of the flipbook, to curious poking or pricking, as in the cactus art interaction, to tearing down the calico film screen, as in the case of the rube films. Pointing, pinching, scrolling, swiping, zooming, zapping, clicking, etc., are all actions to be added to a lexicon of screen touching gestures.[6] My interest lies, thus, in touching as a gesture, a process or an action. While the technicity of gestures will be at the center of Chapter 3, it can already be stated that the book is less about touch as one of the fives senses and more about the active verb "to touch." Belonging to the "sphere of action," as Giorgio Agamben argues, gestures show us the process of the action; they mediate concrete encounters, among human beings (which is not the scope of my research), as well as between objects and humans, between artworks and children, between screens and rubes, and so on (as is the central topic of this book). In his *Notes on Gesture* (originally published in French in 1991), Agamben defines the gesture as the "communication of a communicability" (2000, 58). Following distinctions made by ancient Roman writer Marcus Terentius Varro, he suggests that the gesture is not an end in itself, like making (*facere*) or acting (*agere*), but rather reveals or carries out (*gerere*) the process of such actions and therefore functions as a form of pure mediality. Agamben writes: "*The gesture is the exhibition of a mediality: it is the process of making a means visible as such*" (57).

Defining Media

As Dieter Mersch has put it, following Aristotle's theory of perception, "it is the medium that enables perception, but at the same time the medium also evades perception," which makes it

6 Such a lexicon can be seen as a variation on, or sub-corpus of, Jean-Luc Nancy's "corpus of tact" (2008, 93); see also Chapter 3.

extremely difficult, if not impossible, to give an accurate definition of the term (Hoffmann 2014, 20). Since my corpus contains many art(istic) examples, I want to point out from the very beginning that I am not concerned here with what distinguishes art from media, or what turns art into media or media into art. I consider artworks as well as films, toys, and apps as integral parts (or actors) of media insofar as they establish an "encounter" with other actors; and as such they offer or even become a means of an experience, of a communication. This might seem to come close to the definition of media as channels for communication, as in the verbal communication model of the American political scientist Harold Lasswell.[7] Describing unidirectional communication systems from transmitter (author, broadcast company) to receiver (reader, audience), this 1948 model can appear dated in that it does not account for interaction or feedback. However, it is still useful for grasping Agamben's above definition of gesture as "communication of a communicability," which points to a more open notion of media, clearly based on a bidirectional or interactive model of communication.

As already suggested, I prefer to think in terms of "encounter," which implies a physical contact, not necessarily between the author (artist, filmmaker, etc.) and the audience (museumgoer, film spectator, etc.), but rather between the human and the artwork (or media device) itself. For it is the artwork (or media device) that looks back at us. "The medium is the message," as Marshall McLuhan famously proclaimed in the 1960s to emphasize that not only the content but also the (technological) characteristics of the medium mattered. In this context, McLuhan defined television as both a cold medium (requiring high participation from the viewer to "complete" the missing information) and a tactile medium that involves the whole body. As Klemens Gruber (2017, 225–26) points out, tactility has two

7 According to Lasswell's model, communication can be described in terms of "who says what to whom in which channel and with what effect" (Briggs and Burke 2005, 4).

different meanings for McLuhan: on the one hand, its stand for the unity (or interplay) of the senses; on the other, it refers to the line-by-line composition of the TV image which is transferred to the viewer's perception. Notably, the Canadian media theorist described how the "scanning finger" traces the contours of things as if it were actually touching or stroking the dotted TV image (McLuhan 1964, 334). Besides the technical aspect of the cathode ray tube's scanning system, one should not forget that the TV set was still rather small in the 1960s, and therefore the viewer needed to get close.[8] This is exactly what I mean by "encounter" between media device and user—an encounter not only in terms of artistic or aesthetic appreciation but also and especially in terms of physical and often hands-on interaction.

The open notion of media also fits into the book's general framework of media archaeology. The main concern of media archaeology is not to establish what media are but rather how to deal with them. Scholars in media archeology take an interest in diverse questions, including dead and imaginary media, media artifacts and apparatuses, media (art) installations, materiality and microtemporality, media ecology, and "zombie media" (Hertz and Parikka 2012). Most media-archaeological thinkers want to open up the concept of media beyond its institutionalized borders, without however turning its definition into a debate on its own. The question *What Is Media Archaeology?* that Jussi Parikka gave as the title of his comprehensive introduction to the field points not so much to a matter of ontology as to issues of methodology. That is, the primary consideration is the meaning of the term "archaeology," or *how to do it*. From the very first

8 This close encounter between viewer and TV set turned out to be hazardous for patients of photosensitive epilepsy, causing potentially harmful bodily effects such as dizziness, nausea, and epileptic seizures, which some experienced as not entirely unpleasant. On the practice of self-induction of seizures as a new form of visual pleasure, see Jancovic 2020. In Chapter 3, I will briefly discuss another less harmful example of close and hands-on TV viewing, prompted in the 1980s by the French interactive TV series *Télétactica*.

pages of *What Is Media Archaeology?*, Parikka sets the methodological agenda: "[The book] offers an insight into *how to think media archaeologically* in contemporary culture, and maps the various theories, methods and ideas that give us guidance on how to do that" (2012, 2).

As I will discuss in more detail below, "thinking media archaeologically" is, to a large extent, an exercise in *rethinking temporalities*. The present book wants to rethink the history of the touchscreen as a nonlinear, nonprogressive study of old and new media. Alluded to also by Parikka is the importance of historical layers (and entanglements between past, present, and future): "Media archaeology is introduced as a way to investigate the new media cultures through insights from past new media, often with an emphasis on the forgotten, the quirky, the non-obvious apparatuses, practices and inventions" (2012, 2).

Tactile vs. Haptic

My aim to shift perspective from *visual* media to *tactile* media concurs with W. J. T. Mitchell's appeal to think of all media as "mixed media." As one of the great theorists of the image, who in 1992 coined the expression "the pictorial turn" to indicate the predominantly visual culture of the twentieth century, Mitchell declared at the beginning of the twenty-first century that, "There Are No Visual Media."

> "Visual Media" is a colloquial expression used to designate things like TV, movies, photography, painting, and so on. But it is highly inexact and misleading. All the so-called visual media turn out, on closer inspection, to involve the other senses (especially touch and hearing). All media are, from the standpoint of sensory modality, "mixed media." (Mitchell 2007, 395)

Mitchell elucidates his point with various examples from both the media and the arts. For instance, the locution "silent cinema" to indicate the first period of cinema's history seems to imply that cinema was once a "purely visual" medium, but we know that this is a misconception: cinema was never totally silent, as films were accompanied by live pianists, orchestras, and lecturers. Sculpture is the art of touch par excellence. It is the only visual art that is directly accessible to the blind, and even if the sculpture remains untouched, there is a tactile dimension that we cannot grasp with our eyes alone. Photography as a medium that can reveal what the eye alone cannot see, translating the unseen or unseeable into a picture, is also not a "visual medium in any straightforward sense" (Mitchell 2007, 398). Even painting, according to Mitchell, is a mixed medium because it recalls the hand of the artist. When contemplating a painting, we imagine touching the canvas like the painter did. Or as Mitchell formulates it: "Seeing painting is seeing touching, seeing the hand gestures of the artist, which is why we are so rigorously prohibited from actually touching the canvas ourselves" (397). Mitchell pushes his argument even further by suggesting that vision itself is not purely visual, since it takes place through material and multisensory processes. He claims: "There are no purely visual media because there is no such thing as pure visual perception in the first place" (403).

If there are no purely visual media, are they all to be considered tactile media? What are tactile media? Deriving from the Latin *tactus*, the past participle of *tangere* (to touch), the term "tactile" implies the potential of being touched, of being perceived by the sense of touch, or even better, of being involved in a concrete act of touching. Other related notions are "tangible," "touchable," "touch-sensitive," and "touch-based." When I use the term "tactile" in this book, I refer to concrete acts of touching. Departing from Mitchell, I would not use it in relation to an untouched painting or photograph, or an untouched film screen. As a film scholar, I deliberately use the term "tactile" to distance myself from film theories about the "haptic" (or "haptical") dimension of the viewing experience. I am referring here in particular to theories of embodied film spectatorship, which constitute a different yet very valuable line of thought, following Vivian Sobchack's phenomenological approach adopted first in *The Address of the Eye: A Phenomenology of Film Experience* (1992) and developed subsequently in *Carnal Thoughts: Embodiment and Moving Image Culture* (2004).

In this context, (feminist) film scholars have revisited Alois Riegl's notion of the "haptic" in relation to early cinema (Antonia Lant), video art (Laura Marks), and contemporary cinema (Jennifer Barker), insisting on how the viewing process activates the memory of touch. Riegl's *haptisch* (haptic) refers indeed to the sensation of touch rather than the actual act of touching, which he originally indicated with the term *taktisch* (tactical/tactile), in opposition to *optisch* (optical), when distinguishing two different regimes of perception in *Die spätrömische Kunst-Industrie* (*Late Roman Art Industry*, 1901). To put it very schematically, according to Riegl's art theory, the haptic is the visual regime of closeness, and therefore of fragmentation, typical of Egyptian art; the optical, on the other hand, is the visual regime of distance, wholeness, and overall view typical of Roman art. It should be stressed that both the haptic *Nahsicht* and the optical *Fernsicht* are modes of *visual* perception, determining the spatial position of the beholder. However, Riegl did not use the term "haptic" in *Late Roman Art Industry*, but adopted it only afterward, borrowing from the field of physiology, as I will further discuss below.

In her seminal essay "Haptical Cinema" (1995), Lant discusses early cinema's spatiality in terms of layered flatness, which comes into full play thanks to the use of painted and movable décor pieces, transparent curtains, and bas-relief-like superimpositions. Lant's essay is inspirational for my research as it opens the path for a touch-based analysis of the early cinema screen, which Lant herself does not carried out explicitly. Instead she focuses on the Egyptian motifs of early cinema's hapticity, which allows her to connect back to Riegl's theory of art and visual perception.[9] Then, in 1998, Marks introduced the term "haptic visuality" in relation to video aesthetics characterized by low-resolution, graininess, and lack of focus. This notion has been most instrumental in reinforcing the visual dimension of the haptic: "haptic visuality" is a form of embodied vision, where all the senses are involved, but no actual touching takes place. In *The Skin of Film: Intercultural Cinema, Embodiment, and the Senses* (2000), Marks somehow reverses Riegl's teleological approach, by suggesting that we are moving away from the optical regime of Hollywood cinema toward a more haptic (and more intimate) regime, as identified in various intercultural film practices. Finally, in *The Tactile Eye: Touch and the Cinematic Experience* (2009), Barker has pushed Marks's vision even further, from the skin to the guts of the film, according to three modes: tactile (or haptic), kinesthetic, and proprioceptive. Barker talks in phenomenological terms about the film's body as a "lived-body" and the film experience as a "tactile embrace." But she warns from the start:

> The film's skin must not be reduced to the screen, for example; if it were, to touch the film would be simply to mimic the child's caress of his mother's face on the film screen in *Persona* (Ingmar Bergman, 1966), which is too literal a touch to account for the full range of tactility we experience while watching a film. (Barker 2009b, 28–29)

9 From May 2011 to July 2014, Lant co-conducted with Klemens Gruber the research project *Texture Matters: The Optical and the Haptical in Media*, which took its cue, among others, from Riegl's art theory. This joint research between the University of Vienna and New York University led to two key publications that appeared as special issues of the journal *Maske und Kothurn*. The first volume (Gruber and Lant 2014) is dedicated to the sense of touch in cinema and contains the German translation of Lant's seminal article as well as an embryonic version of this book (Strauven 2014). The second volume (Herwig and Seibel 2017) collects various contributions on tactile media, including a text by David Parisi on "computer haptics" (Parisi 2017) and Gruber's "prehistory of tactile media theories," which covers ideas by László Moholy-Nagy, Walter Benjamin, and Marshall McLuhan (Gruber 2017).

It is precisely this very literal path, against which Barker advises, that I propose to take with my book. Against the tradition of sensuous (or embodied) film theory, *Touchscreen Archaeology* is less about the spectator's or user's body and what happens to this body during the film or media "encounter." Therefore, the discussion will not revolve around erotics, sexuality, and consent, nor around contagion and virality through touch, even if these are urgent items on the agenda of our contemporary society. I will touch on issues of gender, especially when discussing screenic devices that, traditionally speaking, belong to the female sphere (e.g., fans), as well as the depiction and representation of female bodies on screens that are touched. Yet the female body in the flesh is not the focus of my research, which instead aims to contribute to scholarship on the materialities of screen media.[10] Along the same lines, this book will not offer an extensive discussion of the sense of touch, which I propose to address exclusively in relation to the practice of touching media. Yet I want to bring about a major rupture in the overall organization of the senses, by putting the sense of touch, which has largely been neglected by media and art historians, in the limelight at the expense of the other senses, in particular sight and hearing. Following Jacques Derrida, who questions Jean-Luc Nancy's inclusion of listening and looking in his tactile corpus, I am not interested in gestures "which rather than touching seem, on the contrary, literally to signify noncontact, interruption, spacing, a hiatus at the core of contact—tact, precisely!" (Derrida 2005, 70).

We need to distinguish between feeling and touching, that is, between sensations felt by the human skin and operations made by our chief (if not only) prehensile organ which is the hand.

10 *Tactile poetics* (2015) by Sarah Jackson pledges to do the same for written media, by considering writing as an act of touching on the skin of paper. Most of its chapters, however, delve into the representation/evocation of skin and touch in novels, assuming the possibility of tactile interchanges between the writer and the reader, in a similar way as theories of embodied spectatorship make claims about the relationship between the filmmaker and the viewer.

Even if the gesture of screen touching can be extended to other body parts, such as the feet and even the buttocks (as will be briefly discussed in Chapter 2), it is most commonly restricted to the hand, and even more specifically to the index finger and the thumb. Vilém Flusser has emphasized how our way of thinking is shaped by our hands and fingers, "by way of the gesture of making" (2014, 32). He writes:

> To understand how we think, we must look at our hands: the fingers and the way the thumb opposes the other fingers; the way the fingertips touch; the way the hand opens as a plate and closes as a fist; the way one hand relates to the other. (33)

Likewise, Michel Serres in *The Five Senses* (originally published in French in 1985) reflects on very concrete manual actions: the hand cutting nails, handling tapestry, moving rapidly on the loom, and making papier-maché puppets. In his discussion of Pierre Bonnard's paintings, Serres reminds us how the latter was involved in the stage production of Alfred Jarry's *Ubu roi* (*King Ubu*) and how he "loved all sorts of media: stage sets, posters, papers, materials, fans, vellum in books, cardboard covers, sheets or screen panels" (Serres 2008, 35). It is precisely in this passage that Serres suggests equating touch with the notion of medium:

> Before the eye sees, there is the texture of the canvas. The eye has no weight to impose, it imprints nothing. On the subject's front line is the skin. Everything is enveloped in a film. In the beginning, touch; at the origin, the medium. (35)

I will come back to Serres's study on the senses and in particular to the first chapter, entitled "Veils," when I discuss the various meanings and types of screens in Chapter 4. At the moment, I want to retain the importance of the hand, its role in the tactile gesture, which I consider, as already repeatedly stated, a gesture of actual touching media devices. To stress this manual dimension of the gesture, that is, the action by the hand that provides a practical experience (as well as an operative pragmatics), I have opted for the term "hands-on" in the subtitle of the book—the hands-on gesture being a specific case of tactile gesture.

It is this full focus on hands-on gestures that distinguishes my research from other historical studies of the screen as material object, such as Giuliana Bruno's *Atlas of Emotions* (2002) and Erkki Huhtamo's "Elements of Screenology: Towards an Archaeology of the Screen" (2004). With both authors I share numerous research objects as well as a materialist, media-archaeologically oriented approach, but in order to counter the dominant narrative of visual media I often push my tactile reading further. On the other hand, I believe my book can be read as supplementary to their work; for instance, my tactile investigation of optical toys for domestic use seeks to complement Huhtamo's discussion of the manually operated slot machines in the public sphere (Huhtamo 2005), while my reading of the screen as an interface for hands-on operations departs from Bruno's notion of the screen as a material surface, that is, as a surface that matters, as thematized in her recent book *Surface: Matters of Aesthetics, Materiality, and Media* (2014). In an interview with Sarah Oppenheimer, Bruno observes:

> There is a tendency in our culture to denigrate surfaces. People say something is superficial when they want to put it down. But, in fact, surface matters. It's so sensual and central to our lives. Surfaces are a primary form of habitation and they are everywhere in artistic expression. (Oppenheimer 2014)

In the same way that Bruno's *Surface* places the superficiality of the surface at the core of its research, the main objective of *Touchscreen Archaeology* is to reflect on very banal gestures, by examining the banality of those gestures and by putting into question what is taken for granted.

Hands-On vs. Haptics

The use of the term "tactile," deriving from the Latin *tactus*, is in this book always connected to the notion of "hands-on" practice, of putting your hands literally onto the art object or media device and of creating a physical, concrete con-*tact*. As explained above, I prefer the term "tactile" over "haptic," because the latter in Riegl, and subsequently in embodied film theories revisiting Riegl, is not about direct contact: instead of actual touching, Riegl's haptic is an evocation of touch through the sense of sight, through the position of "close vision" (*Nahsicht*). Yet, as pointed out by David Parisi, Riegl's interpretation of the "haptic" at the beginning of the twentieth century is problematic, if not erroneous, since it referred, in the 1890s, to a very specific field of "lab experimentation" with electric shocks (Parisi 2018, 6–7).

As already mentioned, Riegl acknowledged borrowing the term "haptic" from the field of physiology. The explanation for this new word choice appears in a footnote to the polemic essay "Spätrömisch oder orientalisch?" ("Late Roman or Oriental?"), published in 1902 in response to the attacks of the rivaling Polish-Austrian art historian Josef Strzygowski:

> It has been objected that this designation [in German: *taktisch*] could lead to misunderstanding, since one could be inclined to comprehend it as a borrowed word from the Greek, quite like the word "optical" which is used as its opposite; and my attention has been drawn to the fact that physiology has long since introduced the more fitting designation "haptic" [in German: *haptisch*] (from *haptein*—to fasten). This observation seems to me justified and I intend henceforth to use this proposed term. (Riegl 1988, 190)[11]

11 The original reads: "Man hat beanstandet, daß diese Bezeichnung zu Mißverständnissen führen könne, da man geneigt sein müsse, sie gleich dem dazu in Gegensatz gestellten 'Optischen' als Lehnwort aus dem Griechischen zu fassen, und hat darauf aufmerksam gemacht, daß die Physiologie dafür längst die passendere Bezeichnung 'haptisch' (von ἅπτειν) in Gebrauch

This 1902 essay summarizes the general arguments of his 1901 book *Late Roman Art Industry*, in which Riegl had used the German term *taktisch*, intended as a derivation of the Latin *tactus* (pertaining to the sense of touch) but, apparently, misinterpreted as being borrowed from the Greek *taktikos* (pertaining to arrangement). In other words, Riegl's use of the term had caused confusion between "tactile" and "tactical," which he hoped to solve with the new term *haptisch*.

Parisi suggests that Riegl opted for the term "haptic" to avoid a strict opposition between vision and touch. The term "implicated touch in a harmonious rather than antagonistic relationship with the visual; haptic vision, in comparison to tactile vision, indicates a synergistic coupling of the touch and vision, a vision capable of becoming like touch" (Parisi 2018, 35). Interestingly enough, Gilles Deleuze and Félix Guattari seem to follow this (mis)interpretation of Riegl's determination in giving preference to the term *haptisch* over *taktisch*. In *Mille Plateaux* (*A Thousand Plateaus*), they write:

> "Haptic" is a better word than "tactile" since it does not establish an opposition between two sense organs but rather invites the assumption that the eye itself may fulfill this nonoptical function. It was Alois Riegl who, in some marvelous pages, gave fundamental aesthetic status to the couple, *close vision–haptic space*. (Deleuze and Guattari 1987, 492–93)

Of course, both Parisi and the authors of *A Thousand Plateaus* are right about the fundamental coupling of vision and touch in Riegl's thinking, about the assumption that the eye can operate beyond the optical in a touch-like way, but this has little to do with choosing the word "haptic." Riegl could have settled the problem of the misunderstanding by opting for the German term *taktil* ("tactile"), or *tastbar* ("palpable"), the latter appearing

gesetzt hat. Diese Beobachtung scheint mir gerechtfertigt, und ich gedenke mich künftig dieses vorgeschlagenen Terminus zu bedienen" (Riegl 1902, 155).

indeed in the 1902 review essay. It seems to me that the main point of Riegl's choice of the term "haptic" was to make sure that his theory of tactile vision was not mistaken for a manifesto about arranging military forces (or "tactics").

Riegl's reference to the contemporary, that is, late nineteenth-century, field of physiology has led, however, to another misunderstanding. The German noun *Haptik* ("haptics"), coined in 1892 by the German psychologist Max Dessoir, did indeed pertain to the sense of touch, albeit in terms of a new research paradigm, defined in *The Dictionary of Philosophy and Psychology* (1911) as the "doctrine of touch."[12] The term "haptic" had, thus, very specific scientific and experimental connotations in that it was "designating the vast research being carried out on the psychophysiology of tactual perception" (Parisi 2018, 35). Applying it to art theory, Riegl modified its original meaning: the "haptic" no longer referred to the isolation of touch in the laboratory but to the regime of "close vision" in a scheme of visual art perception.

These radically different interpretations of the term "haptic" have resulted in two opposing traditions to this day. As Parisi summarizes it,

> For media theorists, "haptic" is a model of touch that can operate without touching, where the senses are capable of becoming synesthetically active in one another. For psychologists and engineers, the material act of touching is fundamental to the formation of haptics as an accumulated body of knowledge; they do not seek to differentiate the senses, but instead to radically and intensely differentiate touch itself through the application of experimental techniques and apparatuses. (2018, 36)

12 Partially quoted in Parisi (2018, 6), the full definition of "haptics" reads: "The doctrine of touch with concomitant sensations and perceptions—as optics is the doctrine of sight, and acoustics that of hearing" (Baldwin 1911, 441).

Clearly, Parisi wants to position himself in the second tradition, by opposing his "haptic subject" to the embodied film spectator (and in particular to Marks's notion of "haptic visuality"). He recuperates the original meaning of "haptics" as psychophysiological lab experiment, which allows for a line of continuity with today's notion of "haptics" as the tactile feedback of computer and media design.

As a consequence, in Parisi's study, the terms "haptic" and "tactile" are used in the exact reversed way as I propose. For Parisi, the term "haptic" involves the actual mode of touching, while the term "tactile" refers more broadly to the sense of touch located in the skin. Whereas I am concerned with cultural practices of touch-based media, he offers a thorough study of touch-based media technologies. His book, entitled *Archaeologies of Touch: Interfacing with Haptics from Electricity to Computing* (2018), covers everything I will not treat, ranging from the medical use of haptic devices to cybersex toys, from prosthetics research to vibration-based feedback in contemporary touchscreens. It is a book about the history of "computer haptics," which takes us back to the eighteenth-century experiments with electricity and more precisely to the "cultivation of a practiced epistemology of electric shock" (Parisi 2018, 4). It can be called an attempt to do media archaeology, because it concerns an unwritten history or the history of forgotten aspects of media. In methodological terms, however, Parisi follows a linear path of progression, from simple experiments with electricity to more and more complex haptic designs, which is exactly the type of historiography that media archaeology has been arguing against and which I will also avoid to undertake.

Media Archaeology, Take 1: Rethinking Temporalities

What is media archaeology? Or rather what do we need to do, to rephrase Parikka, to *think media archaeologically*? In methodological terms, very different and even opposing approaches have been promoted by key figures in the field. In brief summary, we can identify at least four dominant methods of how to *rethink temporalities*: 1) discovering the old in the new; 2) uncovering the new in the old; 3) tracing recurring topoi; and 4) focusing on ruptures and discontinuities.[13] In my own research, I do not consider these approaches as mutually exclusive but instead combine the Foucauldian epistemology of discontinuity with Huhtamo's idea of recurrence, or Zielinski's geological deep time with the principle of circuit bending or hardware hacking as hands-on excavation into media.

The first method of seeking the old in the new is directly inspired by McLuhan's law of obsolescence, according to which old media become the content of newer media, losing their initial novelty and effectiveness, without, however, being eliminated. As famously formulated in *Understanding Media*: "the 'content' of any medium is always another medium. The content of writing is speech, just as the written word is the content of print, and print is the content of the telegraph" (McLuhan 1964, 23–24). Jay David Bolter and Richard Grusin's study of remediation, which, not accidentally, carries the subtitle *Understanding New Media*, departs from this McLuhanian law of media. Remediation is defined as the "formal logic by which new media refashion prior media forms," as in the way that television remediated film, which remediated photography, which remediated painting, and so on (Bolter and Grusin 2000, 273). Despite their openly acknowledged Foucauldian inspiration, Bolter and Grusin's method inevitably implies a historical linearity, resulting in an equally inevitable media convergence. According to Zielinski, this is not the appropriate way to do media archaeology: "In [this] perspective, history is the promise of continuity and a celebration of the continual march of progress in the name of humankind. Everything has

13 For an extensive mapping of the field of media archaeology, along with a more detailed discussion of these four dominant methods, see Strauven 2013.

always been around, only in a less elaborate form" (2006, 3).
Zielinski does not explicitly refer to Bolter and Grusin's work, but he makes his point clear by stating that Michelangelo's ceiling paintings in the Sistine Chapel have nothing to do with today's virtual reality environments.

Opposite the method of seeking the old in the new, Zielinski develops his anarchic approach to media archaeology, called "anarchaeology," which consists in uncovering "something new in the old" (2006, 3). Zielinski literally digs into the deep time of media, going all the way back to the fifth and sixth centuries BC to the life and work of Empedocles. The notion of "deep time," borrowed from the vulcanist James Hutton, refers to geological time and its measurement by analyzing strata of different rock formations. What is crucial for Zielinski's conception of media archaeology is that these strata do not form perfect horizontal layers one on top of the other, but instead present intrusions and changes of direction. Thus, the study of our geological past tells us that there were moments when "a considerable reduction of diversity occurred" (5–6); instead of a continuous increasing of complexity, the evolution of nature (including humankind) sometimes takes a step back. This is also true for the history of media, which is "not the product of a predictable and necessary advance from primitive to complex apparatus," meaning that the "current state of the art does not necessarily represent the best possible state" (7).

The third dominant approach of media archaeology is the cyclical view proposed and practiced by Huhtamo. This method is inspired by the work of the literary scholar Ernst Robert Curtius, who in his *Europäische Literatur und lateinisches Mittelalter* (*European Literature and the Latin Middle Ages*, 1948) tried to explain the internal life of literary traditions by the concept of "topos." Deriving from the Greek word for place, a topos is a (literary) convention or commonplace. Media archaeology, then, becomes in Huhtamo's words the "way of studying the typical and commonplace in media history—the phenomena that (re)appear and disappear and reappear over and over again and somehow transcend specific historical contexts" (1996, 300). The result of such an approach is to see media history as a succession of media clichés, or the eternal return of commonplace views concerning new media and their uses. While Curtius explains the recurrence of topoi by referring to the Jungian archetypes, Huhtamo considers them as "cultural, and thus ideological, constructs" (301). They are ideological constructs that can be consciously (re)activated. A topos is—very literally—a place where century-old ideas manifest themselves, even if, at first sight, they might not be recognized as such because they are offered to us in a new (technologically updated) package. The media industry with its advertisement strategies and other means of communication plays an important role in this cyclical mechanism in that it can bring to the surface old dreams of annulling time and space as well as old anxieties about the (supernatural) power of media technologies. This return of both optimistic and pessimistic commonplaces is at the core of Huhtamo's media-archaeological project, which looks back into the past from the perspective of the present and seeks to explain what Tom Gunning has described as "an uncanny sense of *déjà vu*" (1991, 185).[14]

In his media-archaeological approach to film history, Thomas Elsaesser has been quite skeptical about the cyclical view, more specifically about the return of the "cinema of attractions."[15] He warns us against making "too easy an analogy between 'early' and 'postclassical' cinema" since it might "sacrifice historical distinctions in favor of polemical intent" (Elsaesser 2004, 101). For instance, by overemphasizing the attraction principle of

14 Approaching the end of the twentieth century, Gunning registered the same mixture of anxiety and optimism around new technologies as Freud observed at the end of the previous century, when the telephone was bridging the distance between family members or friends who were separated from one another by other technologies of modernity, such as the railway or ocean liners.

15 The possibility of such a return is explicitly mentioned in Gunning's first article on the "cinema of attractions" (2006, 387).

contemporary feature films in terms of a return to origins, one might forget about the important role played by television's commercial breaks in the development of postclassical narrative cinema. Elsaesser promotes a Foucauldian approach to media archaeology that prioritizes the need to constantly revise our "historiographic premises, by taking in the discontinuities, the so-called dead-ends, and by taking seriously the possibility of the astonishing otherness of the past" (2005, 20).[16] Elsaesser has defined this basic method of media archaeology as the "hermeneutics of astonishment," which, importantly, is not limited to the study of the past but also involves our present:

> Next to an *aesthetics* of astonishment for which Tom Gunning once pleaded, there should also be room for a *hermeneutics* of astonishment, where besides curiosity and scepticism, wonder and sheer disbelief also serve as the impulses behind historical research, concerning the past as well as the present. (2004, 113)[17]

Furthermore, *the* past does not exist; it is always a construction, a selection among many pasts that actually existed or might have existed.

These different methods of rethinking temporalities should be considered as concrete activities, as ways of doing media archaeology. Already in 1996, Zielinski suggested thinking of media archaeology as a practice, or a continual performance, as something that you do or carry out. More specifically, in an essay

16 The point of reference is Michel Foucault's *The Archaeology of Knowledge* (originally published in French in 1969). Anti-historian and anti-humanist Wolfgang Ernst also refers to Foucault's work and notion of epistemic break in his media-archaeological approach: "The archaeology of knowledge, as we have learned from Foucault, deals with discontinuities, gaps and absences, silence and ruptures, in opposition to historical discourse, which privileges the notion of continuity in order to re-affirm the possibility of subjectivity" (Lovink 2003).

17 Elsaesser refers to Gunning's article "An Aesthetic of Astonishment," originally published in *Art and Text* in 1989 (see Gunning 1995).

published in *CTheory* as part of the special section on Global Algorithm, the German media theorist called media archaeology his "form of activity," adopting Ludwig Wittgenstein's notion of *Tätigkeit*. In Zielinski's words, Wittgenstein "adhered to the premise that philosophy is not something to be sat out on a professorial chair, but should be a continuous action of clarification in its very own medium, language" (Zielinski 1996). In the same way that philosophy should consist of clarifying sentences (and not just the sum of "philosophical sentences"), so media archaeology should be thought of as the "continuous action" of excavating the past(s) and future(s) of media, that is, the process of digging, discovering, rediscovering, and rethinking, rather than as the final results of such actions. Adopting Elsaesser's "hermeneutics of astonishment," *Touchscreen Archaeology* lays stress on the process of being astonished, studying both the past and present of touch-based media practices with genuine wonder, taking in the discontinuities, the so-called dead-ends, detours and marginalities, and reflecting on this process.

Media Archaeology, Take 2: The Metaphor of Hacking

Building on these existing methodological traditions, I propose to think of media archaeology as an activity of hacking into history, by countering and altering dominant narratives, unearthing covered evidence and reframing the terms of the debate. Media archaeology, as the "continuous action" of circuit bending the false image of linear history, should somehow remain anarchic, as implied by Zielinski's concept of "anarchaeology," and "unruly" or "undisciplined," as Vivian Sobchack has defined it (Zielinski 2006; Sobchack 2011, 323). In this sense, media archaeology approximates Keith Jenkins's (2003) notion of "disobedient history," as it rejects the authoritative or hegemonic voice of the historian. Yet, as I like to stress, media archaeology is not equal to media history; it is instead the practice of introducing disturbance (or "noise") into media history in particular and into academic discourse in general.

Besides this practice of conceptually hacking into history, I also want to foreground media archaeology as a concrete and literal form of hacking. I am thinking of hacking not as the criminal activity of cracking codes but rather as the form of curiosity (or even creativity) of "exploring the limits of what is possible" (Stallman 2002). According to *The Jargon File*, which contains a glossary of computer programmer slang, a hacker is "a person who enjoys exploring the details of programmable systems and how to *stretch their capabilities*, as opposed to most users, who prefer to learn only the minimum necessary" (Raymond 2004; emphasis mine). Such a notion of hacking is very close to the practice of circuit bending that Garnet Hertz and Jussi Parikka (2012) consider as an artistic media-archaeological method capable of resisting the media industry's planned obsolescence. Circuit bending consists in breaking up battery-powered toys and other similar media devices to manipulate their circuits and repurpose them. Circuit bending is commonly associated with noise music because its techniques often result in generating unusual sound effects and creating experimental musical instruments, as is central to the work of Reed Ghazala, the American circuit-bending artist Hertz and Parikka cite as a reference point.

The metaphor of hacking is also meant to remind media archaeology scholars to hack, constantly and consciously, their own hacking; for instance, to be aware of not wanting to turn the marginal into the dominant, the forgotten "loser" into a new canonized "winner"; to reflect on the possible "ideological bias" of the alternative narrative they are constructing; in order words, to not fall into the common pitfalls. As Huhtamo and Parikka state in their introduction to *Media Archaeology: Approaches, Applications, and Implications* (2011),

> What is it that holds the approaches and interests of the media archaeologists together, justifying the term?

> Discontent with "canonized" narratives of media culture and history may be the clearest common driving force. Media archaeologists have concluded that widely endorsed accounts of contemporary media culture and media histories alike often tell only selected parts of the story. . . . Much has been left by the roadside out of negligence or ideological bias. (2011, 2–3)

But how to avoid telling "only selected parts of the story"? The trickiest aspect seems to be the nature of narrative itself. According to Wolfgang Ernst, media historians should stop telling stories, though he also confesses that he himself sometimes slips back into this convention of recounting media (Lovink 2003; Ernst 2011). How to write a narrative that is not only anti-linear and anti-teleological but also anti-narrative? Possible solutions could be databases, collages, websites (such as Thomas Weynants's *Visual Media Archaeology*), or image libraries (such as Aby Warburg's *Mnemosyne Atlas*) (Weynants 2003; Warburg 2016). Another way could be to regularly interrupt the narrative and reflect on its constructedness and teleological progression, to turn it into a meta-narrative. That is, to create "noise" in one's own academic discourse.

Noise should be understood here in its multiple meanings and implications: in its philosophical sense of "interference" in the dialogue between two interlocutors (Serres 1982, 66-67); in the mathematical notion of uncertainty or "unpredictable perturbation" of a signal during (electrical/electronic) transmission (Shannon 1949, 11); in the postal sense of "interception" and as "tactics of irregularities" (Parikka 2011); in its musical value in Ghazala's circuit bending and Luigi Russolo's Futurist "noise intoners" (Strauven 2015, 36), or more generally in creative terms of avant-garde provocation; and in its behavioral expression of being loud and "unsophisticated," as in the case of the rube or the child. It is the hands-on gestures of both the rube and the child that have guided me in my research into tactile media practices. Taking cue from the rube's transgressive gesture in the movie theater, *Touchscreen Archaeology* seeks to cause a little interference in dominant media discourses on visuality. Equally inspirational for my take on media archaeology as a "noisy" practice is the playful interaction with media by today's children. Children do not need to be instructed on how to become media-archaeological practitioners, because in their play, they often reappropriate old media devices or turn ordinary objects (e.g., stones, crackers, cardboard boxes) into new media devices (e.g., game consoles, smartphones, laptops), exploring—to repeat the definition of hacking quoted above—"the limits of what is possible" and engaging with media's different temporal and historical layers (past, present, future).[18]

Playfulness as Conceptual Framework

As will have become clear by now, I am especially interested in the playful aspect of old and new touchscreen-based or touchscreen-like gestures. Indeed, the book's critique of Western ocularcentrism is, indirectly, inspired by some classic theories of play, in particular Dutch anthropologist Johan Huizinga's *Homo Ludens* (1938; translated into English in 1949 with the subtitle *A Study of the Play-Element in Culture*) and French sociologist Roger Caillois's *Les jeux et les hommes: Le masque et le vertige* (1958; translated into English in 1961 as *Man, Play and Games*). Without going into detail about the merits of these theories in light of contemporary game studies, I want to highlight some insights regarding the so-called pretend play that Huizinga and Caillois formulated in their work and that are particularly productive for my reading of the child's and rube's transgressive behaviors. For Huizinga, it is a kind of performance, a "stepping out of 'real' life" into the temporary

18 Looking at the child's play as a media-archaeological laboratory, considering children as (potential and creative) media-archaeological practitioners, is of course a form of hacking itself: it flips media archaeology upside down, turning the approach against the dominant discourses of media education and media literacy. This is the scope of the book I am currently writing with Alexandra Schneider (forthcoming from meson press).

 sphere of play (2006, 103). Referring to the child's pretend play, he observes:

> The child is *making an image* of something different, something more beautiful, or more sublime, or more dangerous than what he usually is. One is a Prince, or one is Daddy or a wicked witch or a tiger. The child is quite literally "beside himself" with delight, transported beyond himself to such an extent that he almost believes he actually is such and such a thing, without, however, wholly losing consciousness of "ordinary reality." (108)

Children understand, often better than their parents, the rather complex mechanism of the pretend play. Not only do they not completely lose grip of the "real" world, outside their play, but they also know how to pretend they are pretending (or doing "as if"). In other words, the play is about not only pretending to be someone or something else but also playing to pretend. Huizinga writes: "Every child knows perfectly well that he is 'only pretending,' or that it was 'only for fun.'" And he adds:

> How deep-seated this awareness is in the child's soul is strikingly illustrated by the following story, told to me by the father of the boy in question. He found his four-year-old son sitting at the front of a row of chairs, playing "trains." As he hugged him the boy said: "Don't kiss the engine, Daddy, or the carriages won't think it's real." (103)

This anecdote reveals that the boy is not so much trying to fool his father, but rather the chairs that, as the playing child pretends, believe they are real carriages. This double level of pretending is also at stake, as I suggest in Chapters 1 and 2, in several illicit or inappropriate acts of screen touching by rubes and children, whose seemingly naïve practices of media use make much more sense when read as conscious performances or "as if" experiences.

Caillois, who picks up the very same anecdote of playing trains, places the pretend play in the category of *mimicry* or simulation. In his systemic categorization of games and play into the four groups of *agon*, *alea*, *mimicry*, and *ilinx*, Caillois also specifies for each group a scaling between *paidia* (i.e., free, aimless play) and *ludus* (i.e., ruled, goal-oriented game). The child's pretend play is located at the *paidia* end of the scale, while the theater and the cinema, where actors play characters and where spectators lend themselves to such an illusion, are at the *ludus* end of the same category. Mimicry is, for Caillois, the category of "incessant invention" (2001, 23). The child's and rube's playful gestures of touching the screen are, however, not strictly about simulation or "acting as if one were someone or something else" (8), but rather about the pleasure of the (pretended) effect their gestures have on the screen or the image on the screen. There is a certain dimension of dizziness or inebriation, typical of the category of *ilinx* (vertigo). By framing gestures of touch as playful practices, oscillating between *mimicry* and *ilinx*, I hope to shed new light on the attitude of the "unsophisticated" user, whether the child or the rube, and, more generally, to think about touch as an act of play.

Topoi and Anecdotes as Heuristic Tools

Whereas Ernst's recommendation for the media historian is to stop telling stories, I provocatively want to tell many stories, based on anecdotes from my personal life as well as inspired by the storytelling of other media scholars, such as the above anecdote narrated by Huizinga. With the rube as the central figure of this storytelling, I also rely, overtly, on Huhtamo's notion of topos as media-archaeological tool. As discussed above, Huhtamo defines topoi as recurring media clichés. In investigating these topoi, he excavates not only neglected and forgotten media, but also, in a Foucauldian vein, the discourses in which these media emerge. Yet Huhtamo is not aiming at a Foucauldian study of discursive formations. His concept of "discursive objects" is closer to the notion of imaginary media; it is about media that did not really exist but were fantasized about. A good example of such a discursive object is the observiscope, a fantasy device from the 1910s, based on the technologies of the magic lantern, phonograph, and telephone, among other things, that returns as topos at the end of the twentieth century in the form of the webcam, video chat, and online conferencing (Huhtamo 1996, 296).

Other media motifs that can be examined following Huhtamo's approach are, for instance, the visceral impact of special effects (from the phantasmagoria to digital 3D), the family as unit of media consumption (from the stereoscope to the television), the flirting and therefore distracted spectator (from the kaleidoscope to the cinematograph), and so on. The tale of the clumsy countryman who does not know how to behave in the (modern) city fits well into this series. However, while discussing the rube figure as a recurring topos, I will also insist on its discontinuities, that is, its shifts in meaning and function throughout history. Or to put it differently, I am interested in the uniqueness of each occurrence of the rube figure, which I will analyze in the light of its specificity instead of its typicality. As such my approach diverges from Huhtamo's cyclical view, which, even if not chronological, inevitably leads to a linear reconstitution of (media) history, implying not only returns but also "obscure continuities," in a similar fashion as does the history of ideas to which Foucault precisely opposes his "archaeology of knowledge" (Foucault 2007, 154).[19]

Following the tone set by the opening of this introduction, *Touchscreen Archaeology* is permeated by a multitude of anecdotes, which I propose to understand, in line with Sean Cubitt's plea for their use in the humanities, as building blocks of theory-making and history-writing, as "vital form[s] of evidence" (2013, 5).

19 Huhtamo is fully aware of his anti-Foucauldian penchant when he states that his approach is "actually closer to the field characterized by Foucault somewhat *contemptuously* as the history of ideas" (Huhtamo 1996, 302; italics added).

Cubitt's opening statement in the essay entitled "Anecdotal Evidence" is firm: "The core of the anecdote is not its typicality but its specificity" (5). He calls it a "unique instance" or a "specific instance." In media-archaeological terms, one might claim that the anecdote is closer to Foucault's notion of contingency than to Huhtamo's topos. Furthermore, Cubitt considers the anecdote as a laboratory—a conceptual or theoretical laboratory, where claims of others are countered or disputed, where connections are made. He writes:

> Since recounting an anecdote is always a re-versioning, the teller has to recognise that their telling (and any interpretations and connections they offer) forms another anecdote to be pored over by another analyst in another time seeking other relevance. Relevance, another term for "connection," ties anecdotes together. When a researcher has amassed enough anecdotes—read enough poetry, seen enough films, observed enough informants—connections always emerge, and each anecdote can be searched for its relevance to another. This is both how we form theories and how, drawing on counter-examples, we dispute them. (11)

Even if published elsewhere, the anecdote—from the Greek *anekdota* "things unpublished"[20]—will acquire a new, previously inedited dimension. It will be rewritten, rephrased, or "re-versioned," and inscribed into a (hi)story. While Cubitt calls it a "vital form of evidence," Joel Fineman, in his "History of the Anecdote: Fiction and Fiction," defines the anecdote as a *historeme*. Though it manifests itself as literary genre, as something that is narrated (or mediated), the anecdote is "rooted in the real," and therefore we can "think of the anecdote, given its formal if not its actual brevity, as a *historeme*, i.e., as the smallest

20 *Anekdota* is the neutral plural form of *anekdotos*, from *an-* "not" + *ekdotos* "published," from *ek-* "out" + *didonai* "to give." See the *Online Etymology Dictionary*.

 minimal unit of the historiographic fact" (Fineman 1989, 57). Furthermore,

> The anecdote is the literary form that uniquely *lets history happen* by virtue of the way it introduces an opening into the teleological, and therefore timeless, narration of beginning, middle, and end. The anecdote produces the effect of the real, the occurrence of contingency, by establishing an event as an event within and yet without the framing context of historical successivity, i.e., it does so only in so far as its narration both comprises and refracts the narration it reports. (Fineman 1989, 61)

It is precisely this tension between the anecdotes as little (linear) narratives and the larger nonlinear framework in which they can be integrated that turns the anecdote into a productive text-organistic principle for a possible history of the touchscreen. The anecdote as heuristic tool not only represents a challenge to established historiographical methods but also makes my quest into the past of tactile media more topical, or more tangible. It is from concrete hands-on situations that the questions arise—questions that, as I hope, will lead to new questions and further theory formation.

Six Chapters

With this study I want to look into a possible history of the touchscreen, by exploring the tradition of tactile or hands-on practices in cinema, media, and art history, on the one hand, and tracing various screen genealogies, on the other. In other words, I will question, historicize, and rethink both terms: "touch" as media practice (Part 1) and "screen" as touchable object (Part 2). Some fundamental questions that drive my research are: What defines a touchscreen? What is its essence, its unique characteristic, regardless of its function (or functionality) as a media device? Is our notion of the touchscreen bound to the present moment, that is, to today's media technology and usage? Or is it less historically (that is, less presently) determined? Do we look at contemporary artworks, such as *Una storia*, differently because of our familiarity with electronic touchscreens? And what are the grounds to include nineteenth-century optical toys, such as the flipbook, in *Touchscreen Archaeology*?

Part 1 opens with the introduction of the central figure of the rube, for it constitutes the guiding thread of this story. Chapter 1, "A Little History of Hands-On Film Spectatorship," discusses the rube's transgressive gesture of touching what is not supposed to be touched. Here, I discuss filmic (and extra-filmic) occurrences of touching the film screen, pointing out that the practice of touching the screen is nothing new but that its meaning changes over time, as does spectatorship. Apart from the early cinema genre of rube films, I also look at rubes of the 1920s, 1950s, 1960s, and the early twenty-first century. Chapter 2, "Early Museum's Hands-On Ethos," is dedicated to the presence and absence of touch in public exhibition spaces: comparing the hands-on ethos of the *Wunderkammer* and early museum culture to the gradual disciplining of the museumgoer and drawing connections from the provocative touch art of the historical avant-garde to the phenomenon of touchscreen-like gestures in contemporary media art installations. Here, the rube's "undisciplined" attitude is connected to the child, who ignores the "look, but don't touch" order and interacts with noninteractive artworks. Chapter 3, "Sketching, Zapping, Pinching, Clicking, Thumbing," focuses on typical tactile media gestures, related to the chalkboard, the TV remote control, the computer mouse, and the tablet and smartphone touchscreens. Here, the rube is complemented by Michel Serres's "Petite Poucette," a theoretical figure that captures the new generation of media users, addressing their hands-on media interaction, in particular the gesture of thumbing when texting on mobile media screens.

Part 2 groups three object-oriented chapters, in which screens, toys, and images are discussed in terms of tactility or touchability. Chapter 4, "Hands-On Screenology," delves into the etymology of the term "screen" as well as the history of screenic devices to establish a "screenology" (Huhtamo 2004) to be further analyzed in tactile terms: from the military shield to the decorative lady's fan, from the closet to the curtain, from the skin to the sieve, from surface to interface. I also discuss how touchscreen technology has taken significant steps over the last fifty years to allow for more subtle and precise operation, as in the example of the tactile touchscreen launched by Tactus in 2013. In Chapter 5, "Manually Operated Optical Toys," the shift from a history of *visual* media to a history of *tactile* media is explicitly proposed by analyzing nineteenth-century optical toys from a new perspective, that is, no longer for their "pre-cinematic" qualities but instead for their tangibility, their manual operability, and their role as educational tools.[21] Other toys are taken into consideration to question their tactile dimension in relation to property or ownership. Moreover, I look into some philosophical essays on the function of the hand, which I propose to re-read from the perspective of our daily tactile media interactions. Chapter 6, "The Image as Screenic Surface and Interface," proposes to think of the image-on-screen as a touchable object similar to the touchable surface of the screen itself. Here I introduce the notion of "image+"—a term picked up from image processing software by which I refer to today's screenic image that goes beyond its visual appeal by adding an extra, often tactile or hands-on, dimension (e.g., the image as a hyperlink, as a gateway to something else, as a form of play). By bringing the image+ in relation to the film viewing experience of today's youngest generation of media users, I make some speculations about the reinvention of cinema as a true tactile practice, with the post-visual image functioning as both surface and interface.

In my conclusion, I suggest that the act of screen touching is about exploring and understanding the world. If the increase

21 Throughout the book, I will put "pre-cinematic" between scare quotes as a precaution, or warning, against its teleological implications.

of tactile interfaces in our daily life is not enriching our tactile perception, this is partly because *to touch* does not necessarily mean *to feel*. But it is also because we touch screens for different reasons than sensory perception. Today we touch screens to vote, to like a post on social media, to put a still image into motion, to buy products online, to book hotels and flights, to be taken to another place, etc. The motto of the early twenty-first-century media user has simply become: "I touch, therefore I am."

Or so it seems.

PART ONE:
TOUCH AS MEDIA PRACTICE

[1]

A Little History of Hands-On Film Spectatorship

Going to the Feelies this evening, Henry?

Aldous Huxley

Two Founding Myths of the Early Film Spectator

The legend goes that the very first film spectators, at the end of the nineteenth century, ran away from the screen at the sight of an arriving train, supposedly out of fear of being run over, because that is how "real" the moving pictures seemed to be. Such would have been the reaction of the audience at the first public screening of the Lumière brothers' Cinématographe on December 28, 1895 in Paris. However, among the ten films on the program, none depicted the arrival of a train. There is also no historical evidence for the supposed mass panic at the first public showing of *L'Arrivée d'un train en gare de la Ciotat* (*Arrival of a Train at La Ciotat Station*, 1895) in January 1896. The story of the screaming and fleeing film spectator appeared around 1900, not only in the popular press but also as a meta-filmic instance in the so-called rube films, and has persisted in the general knowledge of nonexperts up to this day, despite the demystifying and refuting studies of the facts (Bottomore 1999; Loiperdinger 2004). At the end of the 1980s, Tom Gunning suggested to read the behavior of this mythical figure in terms of an "encounter with modernity," similar to the experience on roller coasters and other fairground attractions. Gunning did not dismiss the possible "shock effect" of the arriving trains on screen but pleaded for a more sophisticated interpretation than that of the credulous spectator:

> The audience's sense of shock comes less from a naive belief that they are threatened by an actual locomotive than from an unbelievable visual transformation occurring before their eyes, parallel to the greatest wonders of the magic theatre. (1995, 119)

Even if the anecdote about the hysterical film spectator is apocryphal, it is nevertheless "rooted in the real" (Fineman 1989, 57); for it highlights the power of the new medium, its incredible liveness and impact as special effect, elicited, in the case of *L'Arrivée d'un train en gare de la Ciotat*, by the film's well-placed camera. Along the same lines, we can place Kendall Walton's tale of Charles, who shrieks during a horror movie, frightened by the green slime that speeds up and comes straight toward the audience (Walton 1978), or my own experience at the theater of repeatedly ducking in my seat during Steven Spielberg's *Jurassic Park* (1993).

In contrast to these bodily reactions of withdrawal (scaring back, ducking into hiding, running away, etc.), there is the tale of the country boy who goes up to the screen to touch it and tries to enter the world of the projected scene. Similar to the film spectator who runs away from the arriving train, the character attempting to enter the screen world mistakes what happens on screen for reality and behaves accordingly. To both of them, the reality of the film screen appears *sur-real*, more real than real. Yet the figure of the rube touching the screen alludes to a richer texture of experience. Instead of being frightened and shying away, he is physically attracted toward the screen, which he touches with his own hands; he embodies an extension and deregulation of the senses through cinema, reversing the traditional hierarchy between sight and touch.

Actually, both reactions—running away from the screen and running toward the screen—are thematized by the early rube films, made around 1900, first by Robert W. Paul in Britain and then by Edwin S. Porter in the United States.[1] In this chapter, I will briefly discuss the disciplinary function of these early rube films, more specifically their function as an example of how *not* to behave when facing a moving image on screen. Yet my real interest is elsewhere. Aiming at recovering the tactile potential of cinema, I will focus on the rube's intervention as a hands-on, touch-based media experience. I will discuss filmic (and some extra-filmic) occurrences of tapping the cinema screen to show that the practice of screen touching is nothing new. Chapter 1 can also be read as a history of changes in spectatorship through the topos of the rube, from early cinema up to the early twenty-first century, following a zigzagging path via the 1960s and 1920s.[2]

The Early Rube Films

As Miriam Hansen points out, the rube was a stock character that early cinema inherited from "vaudeville, comic strips and other popular media" (1991, 25). Hansen cites, for instance, the film *Rube and Mandy at Coney Island* (Edwin S. Porter, 1903), where the term "rube" appears in the title. Unlike other visitors to Coney Island, Rube and Mandy are not "disciplined," as they create chaos when they fail to abide by conventions, such as not exiting the slide on time and causing people to jam on top of each other. Because of their inappropriate behavior, they become an "attraction" on their

1 I would like to thank Vinzenz Hediger for having pointed out the analogy between these two figures of film spectator, the one running away from the screen and the other running toward it, and their role in film history in highlighting the immediacy of the lived-body experience of cinema.

2 Some material of this chapter has been previously published in Strauven 2005a, 2005b, 2012.

own. Indeed, in various scenes, other visitors look at them as a curiosity. Of special interest in tactile terms is the scene at the dog show, where Rube, who by then seems pretty drunk, wants to touch one of the dogs on display and is slapped by the dog trainer as punishment.

Other rube films take place at the movie theater, introducing an early form of self-reflexivity (or meta-cinema). The prototype of such a meta-filmic rube film is Robert Paul's *The Countryman and the Cinematograph* (1901), aka *The Countryman's First Sight of the Animated Pictures*. The surviving footage of Paul's film is incomplete; it lacks both its beginning and, more importantly, its ending. But we know what happened in the film, thanks to the American remake by Edwin Porter for the Edison Manufacturing Company. In Porter's *Uncle Josh at the Moving Picture Show* (1902), the main character is no longer called "rube" or "countryman" but "Uncle Josh," a common name in the late-nineteenth century used to indicate, in a comical sense, elderly rural characters. In Porter's film, Uncle Josh goes to a vaudeville theater where he gets to see three moving pictures, displaying the same scenes as in Paul's rube film, in the exact same order. Moreover, Porter makes use of the Edison trademark by crediting the Kinetoscope and projecting two existing Edison films from 1897, *Parisian Dancer* and *Black Diamond Express*. Uncle Josh, who is seated in a box to the left of the screen, reacts "properly" to these two Edison films: to the first one with joy and imitation (after having jumped out of his box on stage) and to the second with fear and flight (back in his box and then off screen). Then a third and final scene is projected, entitled *The Country Couple*, which was most likely shot for the occasion. It is a courtship scene that takes place in the country-side, that is, in the rube's own territory. According to the Edison catalog, Uncle Josh thinks he recognizes his daughter and decides to intervene (Edison 1902, 81–82). He jumps on stage and, in his attempt to punish the man flirting with his daughter, tears down the film screen and falls into the arms of the projectionist (who is operating behind the screen).

Discussed by many film scholars, Porter's rube film has led to different interpretations.[3] Most commonly, it is considered in "didactic" terms with the rube functioning as a counterexample (Morissette 2002). Uncle Josh's inappropriate behavior serves as a lesson, telling the early film spectator how not to behave at the movies. He acts like a simpleton who does not understand that moving pictures are light projections on a screen and that this screen should not be touched but only looked at. However, the question is whether the early cinemagoer (that is, the early *urban* cinemagoer) still needed such a lesson in 1902. Another possible interpretation is the discipline-through-laughter reading offered by Thomas Elsaesser, who suggests to look at the early rube films as a form of internal (or textual) disciplining (2002, 71–74). Thanks to Uncle Josh's unsophisticated attitude, the attention of the spectator, who might be distracted by extra-filmic actants, is drawn to what happens on the screen. According to this reading, the rube film would have been intended to prevent the spectator from talking and to discipline, through laughter, especially those spectators who were more interested in touching the arms or legs of their neighbors than in watching yet another arrival of a train.[4] In short, Porter's *Uncle Josh at the Moving Picture Show* (like Paul's *Countryman and the Cinematograph*) would have functioned as a farce, as a comedy to amuse rather than to educate the audience.

Besides making the spectators laugh, the early rube film might also have increased their self-esteem. In another text, Elsaesser talks about a "subtle process of internalized self-censorship," which he explains as follows:

3 See among others Barker 2009b, Bruno 2002, Casetti 2008, Elsaesser 2006, Jeong 2012, and Morissette 2002.

4 Touching your neighbor at the movies is a fantasy that haunted the Surrealists in the 1920s. See for instance Robert Desnos's account of his visit to the Marivaux movie theater in 1925 (Casetti 2008, 156).

> Do the Rube films not discipline their audience by allowing them to enjoy their own superior form of spectatorship, even if that superiority is achieved at the price of self-censorship and self-restraint? The audience laughs at a simpleton and village idiot, who is kept at a distance and ridiculed, and thereby it can flatter itself with a self-image of urban sophistication. (2006, 213)

In other words, the citizen would have felt superior in assuming an attitude of ridicule toward the rube.

In my "noisy" reading, which turns the rube into a hero and example to follow, there prevails nostalgia for the tangibility of the screen. By touching the film screen Uncle Josh and the other rubes reactivate old media practices, from manipulating optical toys to touching the calico screen of the magic lantern and the praxinoscope.[5] One could actually claim that, within the context of cinema's emergence, Uncle Josh's intervention is not at all inappropriate. His action of touching the screen and therefore interrupting the projection is, for instance, not so far removed from that of (male) Mutoscope viewers who would arrest the reel to have a better look at a "particularly interesting frame (perhaps a half-naked lady)" (Huhtamo 2005, 9).

I would even suggest that Uncle Josh invites the early (and modern) film spectator to imitate his action. For good artworks encourage imitation, as Leonardo da Vinci has taught us. In his *Trattato della pittura* (*A Treatise on Painting*, 1651), the Renaissance master affirms that a good painting provokes a mimetic impulse in the beholder, an almost compelling need to imitate the scene depicted:

> An artist painted a picture that whoever saw it at once yawned, and went on doing so as long as he kept his eyes on the picture, which represented a person who also was

5 In Chapters 4 and 5, I will come back to these and other nineteenth-century tactile media devices and practices.

> yawning. Other artists have represented acts of wantonness and lust which kindled these passions in the beholders. Poetry could not do as much. (Da Vinci 1949, 66)

Because of this power to directly involve the beholder in a (spontaneous) act of imitation, Da Vinci considers painting superior to the other arts. Applying this line of thinking to his own drawing *Five Grotesque Heads* (ca. 1494), the painter would have aimed not only to "show stages of laughter" but also to "engender laughter in the beholder" (Trutty-Coohill 1998, 185). In other words, a good work of art is contagious! This is precisely what happens in Porter's film when Uncle Josh is watching the first moving picture of the Parisian dancer—he jumps on stage to dance with her, or rather, to imitate her dancing movements. The film-within-the-film might become infectious to the external spectator as well, making him or her want to dance with (or like) Uncle Josh. If we push this reasoning further and apply it to the third attraction, where Uncle Josh grabs the diegetic film screen and eventually tears it down, we could read it as a direct invitation to imitate the action of touching the screen.

Ali Barbouyou and Don Quixote

A more complex rube film is *Ali Barbouyou et Ali Bouf à l'huile* (*Delirium in a Studio*, 1907) by Georges Méliès. The film plays with the historical continuity between living pictures and moving pictures—that is, between three-dimensional theatrical reenactments (or restagings) of well-known paintings and two-dimensional paintings in motion. The film print, also incomplete, tells the story of the oriental artist Ali Barbouyou, who just finished a painting of a courtesan and falls asleep. His servant Ali Bouf accidentally drinks varnish, which narratively motivates the hallucination that follows. The girl on the painting comes to life. When Ali Bouf does not obtain the kiss he requests, he takes a broom and hits the girl, who has turned to lifelessness in the tableau (fig. 3). The canvas acts like a border between hallucination and reality, like an "interface" that prevents the animation of the painted girl, who can only come to life when there is no screen or canvas within the frame. At the same time, the canvas allows Ali Barbouyou (played by Méliès) to vanish at the end of the film, as he jumps into the frame without tearing the screen.[6] In other words, the screen is not a simple surface, but rather a boundary or separation between two worlds. Nevertheless, it is very much a material screen that is touched: first violently by Ali Bouf with the aid of a broom and then tenderly by the artist himself. When Ali Barbouyou wakes up, he first gets rid of his servant by cutting off the latter's head and then runs over to the painting to touch it. At first it seems he wants to ensure that the canvas is still intact, but then he is rather involved in the act of caressing the painted girl, falling in love with his own artwork, as a direct descendant of Pygmalion. The question that inevitably pops up here is: Who is the real rube, the servant or the artist?

With a leap of fifty years, Ali Barbouyou and Ali Bouf can be linked with another couple of screen rubes, the gentleman Don Quixote and the countryman Sancho Panza, filmed by Orson Welles for his unfinished epic film, *Don Quixote*. Originally commissioned by CBS in 1955, the shooting went on till 1972, despite the death of the main actor, Francisco Reiguera, in 1969; the project changed from color TV production to black and white feature film, but the original idea remained untouched: an anachronistic transposition of Cervantes's heroes to modern times. In 1992 an incomplete version of *Don Quixote*, edited by Spanish director Jesús Franco, premiered at the Cannes Film Festival. This version, however, is deprived of the scene where Don Quixote and Sancho Panza visit a movie theater.[7]

6 This is one of the very few examples where Méliès does not reappear on stage after such a "screen exit" (Malthête, Malthête-Méliès, and Quévrain 1981, 288).

7 Franco and his producer Paxti Irigoyen were unable to obtain the missing six-minutes footage held by Italian film editor Mauro Bonanni. The latter was in legal dispute with Oja Kodar, Welles's mistress to whom he left the rights to all his unfinished projects. See http://en.wikipedia.org/wiki/Don_Quixote_(unfinished_film). See also Rosenbaum 2007, 2018.

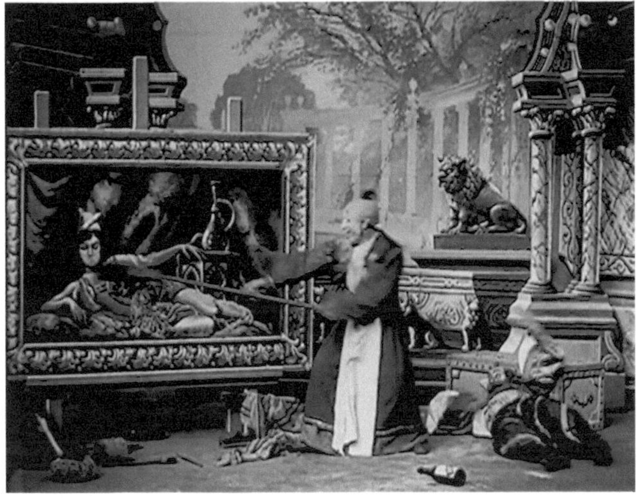

[Figure 3] *Ali Barbouyou et Ali Bouf à l'huile* (Georges Méliès, 1907).

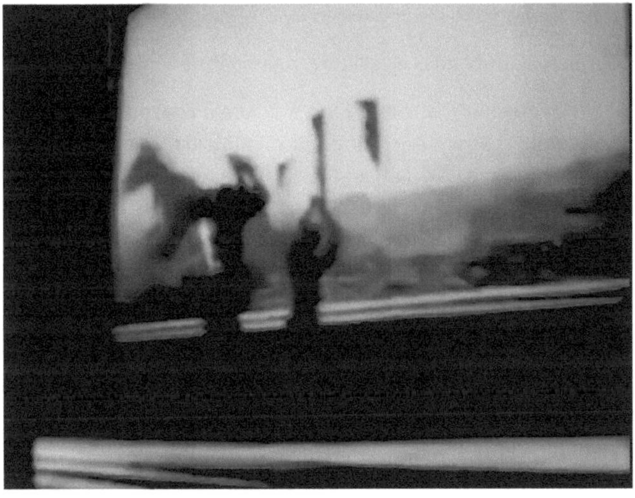

[Figure 4] *Don Quixote* (Orson Welles, unfinished).

For Giorgio Agamben this meta-filmic scene constitutes "the six most beautiful minutes of film history," as he titles the last chapter of his book *Profanations* (originally published in Italian in 2005). He describes Welles's scene-at-the-movies as follows:

> Sancho Panza enters a cinema in a provincial city. He is looking for Don Quixote and finds him sitting off to the side, staring at the screen. The theater is almost full; the balcony—which is a sort of giant terrace—is packed with raucous children. After several unsuccessful attempts to reach Don Quixote, Sancho reluctantly sits down in one of the lower seats, next to a little girl (Dulcinea?), who offers him a lollipop. (Agamben 2007, 93)

The scene was shot in Mexico City, during the postproduction of Welles's *Touch of Evil* (1958), with the girl (Dulcinea?) played by Patty McCormack and Sancho Panza by Welles's favorite actor, Akim Tamiroff. Sancho acts like a typical rube who even does not know how to eat a lollipop. Dulcinea has to calm him down when he get too emotionally distressed by the film projected.

But the real problem is elsewhere. Agamben continues:

> The screening has begun; it is a costume film: on the screen, knights in armor are riding along. Suddenly, a woman appears; she is in danger. Don Quixote abruptly rises, unsheaths his sword, rushes toward the screen, and, with several lunges, begins to shred the cloth. The woman and the knights are still visible on the screen, but the black slash opened by Don Quixote's sword grows ever larger, implacably devouring the images. In the end, nothing is left of the screen, and only the wooden structure supporting it remains visible. (2007, 93)

Agamben's description certainly tries to do justice to this visceral scene, where the guts of the cinema are literally, physically penetrated (in a much more tangible way than Walter Benjamin might have imagined when he compared the cameraman to a surgeon).

I like to stress that the moment of shredding or cutting is rather long compared to the probing of the screen by other rubes. Moreover, Quixote's use of the sword refers to the etymological lineage of screen as (military) shield, as I will discuss in Chapter 4. Yet it is an impossible battle like his (literary) attack on windmills, a scene that Welles never intended to film. Indeed, one could say that the screen battle is the modern (or technologically advanced) version of the windmill duel. Or as Tom Graham (2016) puts it, "Instead of charging windmills, Quixote was bewitched by a film projection."[8]

The sword's stabbing through the screen, however, has also a very plastic (or even artistic) dimension. Especially the first vertical cuts are reminiscent of Lucio Fontana's slashed monochrome paintings (fig. 4). The Argentine-Italian artist started to experiment with this technique in 1949. His most famous works were realized in the second half of the 1950s, precisely in the period when Welles is shooting this scene-at-the-movies with Quixote slashing the film screen and revealing the structure of the scaffolding behind it (as a true painter's canvas mounted on a frame). This is of course a pure coincidence, a nice historical contingency. Still, it problematizes the function of the rube in Welles's film: If Quixote is the real rube (instead of Sancho), what is his role? Is he a warrior, a woman savior, or a cutting-edge artist?

Agamben concludes his chapter on "the six most beautiful minutes of film history" as follows:

> What are we to do with our imaginations? Love them and believe in them to the point of having to destroy and falsify them (this is perhaps the meaning of Orson Welles's films). But when, in the end, they reveal themselves to be empty and unfulfilled, when they show the nullity of which they are made, only then can we pay the price for their truth and

8 According to Jonathan Rosenbaum (2018), it is more likely that the scene derives from Don Quixote's attack on the puppet theater in Chapter 26 of Part 2 of Cervantes's book.

> understand that Dulcinea—whom we have saved—cannot love us. (2007, 93–94)

Is this the true function of the rube Quixote, I wonder, to destroy and falsify our imaginations, to make us understand that true love does not exist? Or is it cinema that falsifies our imaginations that we need to vindicate by cutting the screen, following Quixote's example? Graham (2016) suggests the scene is "a metaphor for both the power of cinema and the film's production: having run out of money, Welles was forced to leave *Don Quixote* unfinished." Apart from a possible auteurist reading, it should be emphasized that we are dealing with a very specific act of screen touching. Like Ali Bouf's broom knocking, Don Quixote's encounter with the screen is an act of violence, in a physical, material sense, which is in stark contrast to the act of love expressed by the rubes of the 1960s (see below). Quixote seems to be blinded by his own ferocious action, not being able, like children in the pretend play, to keep a grip on the "ordinary reality" (Huizinga 2006, 108); he is somehow failing to pretend he is just pretending. In short, what is lacking in Quixote's gesture of screen touching is some form of playfulness.

Michel-Ange's Lure or Pretend Play

Another couple of anachronistic rubes came to the screen in the early 1960s in Jean-Luc Godard's *Les Carabiniers* (*The Riflemen*, 1963). In this war epos, two countrymen, Ulysse and Michel-Ange, decide to join the King's Army in an effort to get rich. This is of course an illusion. The only thing that they will be able to conquer is a series of postcards. Yet, as Susan Sontag writes at the opening of her essay collection *On Photography*, "To collect photographs is to collect the world." Indeed, in discussing Godard's *Les Carabiniers*, Sontag writes:

> The suitcase of booty that Michel-Ange and Ulysse triumphantly bring home, years later, to their wives turns out to contain only picture postcards, hundreds of them, of

> Monuments, Department Stores, Mammals, Wonders of Nature, Methods of Transport, Works of Art, and other classified treasures from around the globe. (1990, 3)

In *Atlas of Emotion*, Giuliana Bruno observes: "Interestingly, for Godard, war is an occasion for sightseeing, a form of tourism that extends to watching films" (2002, 78). It is Michel-Ange who in between war exploits goes to the movies, and as far as one can deduce from his "unsophisticated" attitude, it must be his first visit to a movie theater. His arrival at the cinema resembles Sancho Panza's clumsy entrance. Michel-Ange enters from the back and finds his way toward the front by touch, through the semi-darkness of the unadorned and almost empty movie theater, Le Mexico, which looks like a typical French *ciné-club*. Then he takes his place next to a young woman, after having groped her body all over. Godard's scene-at-the-movies in *Les Carabiniers*, which pays explicit tribute to the early rube films constitutes, in my opinion, the "four most beautiful minutes of film history."

Like Paul's countryman and Porter's Uncle Josh, Michel-Ange gets to see three moving pictures, which are Godardian remakes of early cinema classics: the Lumière brothers' *L'Arrivée d'un train* (1895) and *Repas de bébé* (*Feeding the Baby*, 1895) and Méliès's *Après le bal* (*After the Ball*, 1897), which is retitled *Le bain de la femme du monde* (*The Society Lady's Bath*). During the first attraction, Michel-Ange tries to protect himself from the approaching (and passing through) high-speed train by crossing his arms in front of his face, in conformity with the myth of the early film spectators. The second attraction is an anachronistic slapstick version of early cinema's original, with a spoken soundtrack, an indoor setting, and a grownup baby. Michel-Ange reacts to this little comedy, rightly, if excessively, with loud laughter. The third attraction is the longest and most elaborated of the three and revolves around an instance of actual screen touching, where the interest of analysis lies for me.

First, Godard plays, in a most sublime way, with the off-screen concept: to the amusement of the external spectator, Michel-Ange changes seat twice in order to see what is going on beyond the limit of the frame. He acts like a typical rube, not understanding that the frame is the limit, that there is no beyond. But very subtly Godard fools the external spectator: when the society lady starts taking off her dressing gown, the framing changes from full shot to medium shot; when she steps into the bathtub, the camera lifts slightly up; and when she goes down into the water, the camera lowers. Whose gaze is this, going up and down, preventing us from seeing the entire naked body of the lady? Michel-Ange's? Is he too intimidated, too prudish to look at the full "spectacle"? Very unlikely. According to the logic of early cinema, the framing of the film-within-the-film should be fixed and without camera movement, like in the first two attractions. In this third attraction, Godard reframes the scene for the external spectator! This would mean that Michel-Ange's vision is less limited than ours, that to him the lady's naked posterior is indeed visible.

Then, when lying in the bathtub, the society lady looks briefly into the camera, or, we could say, she looks at Michel-Ange and invites him to join her on/in the screen. This is indeed how Godard's rube interprets her glance. He climbs up the stage, jumps a couple of times to look over the edge of the bathtub, and starts caressing the lady, first her face, then her naked arms and legs (fig. 5). While trying to join her in the bath, he tears down the diegetic film screen. In contrast to Porter's *Uncle Josh at the Moving Picture Show*, there is no rear projection; so, there is no projectionist behind the screen to punish the rube. But more significantly, unlike Uncle Josh, Michel-Ange is not stopping the scene: the projection continues on the wall.

In his psychoanalytical reading, Seung-hoon Jeong suggests a connection between the intrauterine movie theater and the bathtub projected on screen and (possibly) filled with amniotic fluid. After pointing out how Michel-Ange's behavior as rube has led to the exposure of "the raw apparatus of the illusion," Jeong observes that "the figure of womb migrates from the darkened empty auditorium to the bathtub image, the screen really appearing like a skin to rub and caress" (2012, 241). I will come back to the screen as skin in Chapter 4, but for the moment I would like to highlight Michel-Ange's persistence in touching the film projection. Before tearing down the screen, he clearly has no intention to interrupt his action. He goes on touching the projected image of the society lady's leg, as if it were a solid, three-dimensional body, a sculpture (possibly made by his Renaissance namesake). It seems as if, in the 1960s, Godard is trying to convince the film spectator that the two-dimensional film screen is indeed touchable, that Uncle Josh and the other rubes were right, and that the cinema audience has wrongly unlearned the sense of touch.

The key question, then, is: Doesn't Michel-Ange feel that he is touching only a screen and not a flesh-and-blood body? Doesn't he have any sensitivity in his fingertips? I would like to argue that he is pretend playing, that is, *making-believe* that he is feeling a real, solid body. So, he acts like a child who very well knows that the lady is not real but who likes to *pretend* she is. In Roger Caillois's terms, as discussed in the Introduction, Michel-Ange's gesture oscillates between *mimicry* and *ilinx*, between doing "as if" he is touching the lady for real and being delighted, or inebriated, by the fact that he actually does so. Even if the screen image is not reacting to his gentle touch, he continues caressing it as if it were. In Chapter 2, I will discuss some instances of similar screen touching by children, who interact with noninteractive art installations, pretending that they are instead interactive.

For such a playful reading, which turns Michel-Ange into a genuine childlike model, I obviously bracket out the erotic dimension of *The Society Lady's Bath*. In light of gender studies, one could observe that Laura Mulvey's 1975 notion of "to-be-looked-at-ness" is here, prematurely, reinforced by an (even more female-unfriendly) "to-be-touched-ness." It should be recalled that right after Godard finished *Les Carabiniers*, he made *Le Mépris* (*Contempt*, 1963). Shot in Cinemascope format, *Le Mépris* famously opens with the naked body of Brigitte Bardot lying in bed, being touched by the hands of Michel Piccoli.

Allegedly, Godard included this scene at the behest of his American producers who considered Bardot's body the key asset of the film and required a scene where the star could be seen naked. Conversely, we could also argue that the occurrence of the two nudity scenes in the same year is symptomatic of the urge or necessity to attract the film spectator back to the cinema, away from the TV set. For in the 1960s the film spectator was becoming more and more a TV viewer. The introduction of erotic images can therefore be seen as a new form of discipline. As far as the rube is concerned, his function would then consist in telling the (male) spectator of the 1960s that if he would go back to the movies, he would see more than on TV. He would see what the rube sees, that is, the naked posterior of the society lady or Brigitte Bardot.

The Avant-Garde Rube of the 1920s

It is not unlikely that Godard's source for *The Society Lady's Bath* was not Georges Méliès's first "nudity" scene but instead Buster Keaton's *One Week* (1920), where the bride played by Sybil Seely is taking a bath as well. The setting in Keaton's film, a proper bathroom with a tub instead of a bucket in a dressing room, is more like Godard's scene. Yet in Keaton's film, the lens of the camera is covered, literally touched, by an (extradiegetic) hand to block our view when the lady reaches out for the soap that has fallen on the floor (fig. 6). This gesture of covering the lens can be interpreted as a gesture of censorship, which would mean that Keaton's lesson is the opposite of Godard's. That is, at the movies we see less? Or is there something else, more fundamental, at stake in this "disturbing" act of touching the camera lens?

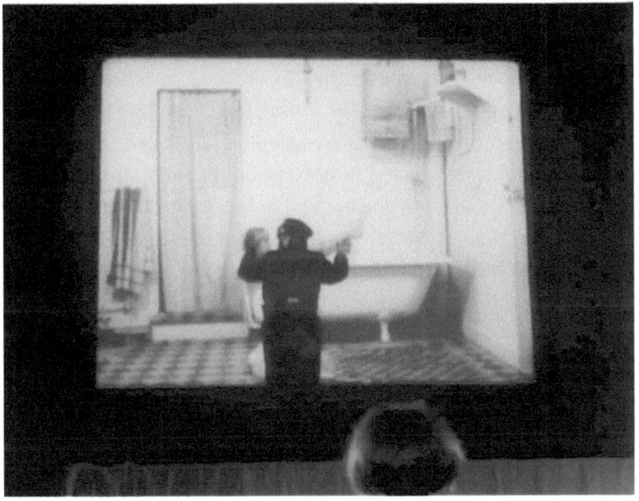

[Figure 5] *Les Carabiniers* (Jean-Luc Godard, 1963).

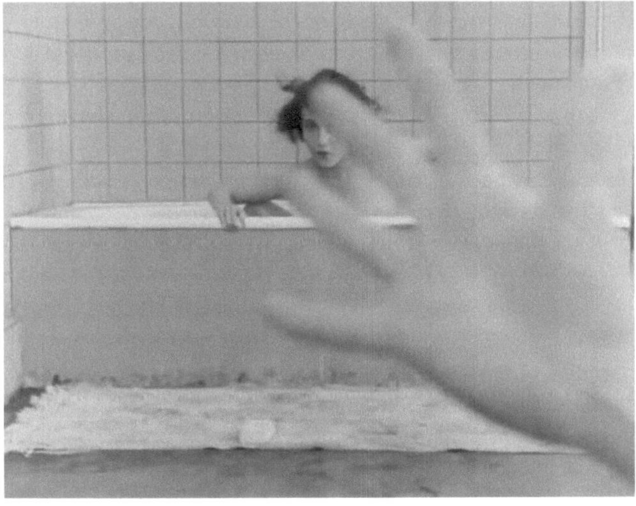

[Figure 6] *One Week* (Buster Keaton, 1920).

In 1924 Keaton offers the film spectator another beautiful meta-filmic experience. In *Sherlock Jr.* the character played by Keaton is a projectionist at the movie theater, while his real dream is to become a detective. One day, during the projection of a film about the theft of a pearl necklace, Keaton falls asleep and his ghost (or double) leaves the projection booth and enters the theater. He tries to enter the screen, or better the screen world, to solve the crime. However, entering the screen is not that easy. First, Keaton enters from the center, after having jumped over the pianist who is playing in front of the screen in a packed movie house. Once Keaton is in the film-within-the-film, his rival kicks him out, and he falls out of the screen onto the dusty stage. He tries again, this time from the side. Now, Keaton finds himself in front of a closed door. He is literally shut out of the diegesis. It seems as if he is imprisoned in an extradiegetic frame from which he cannot exit. Jeong describes the scene as "an inter-facial wonderland whose landscape keeps changing" (2012, 249): from a courtyard to a busy street, to a dangerous precipice in the mountains, to the jungle where he is surrounded by lions, to the desert where he is almost run over by a speeding train, to a boulder in the midst of the wild sea, to a snow landscape, and back to the courtyard. In these two minutes of TV zapping avant la lettre, Keaton changes location (or "channel") seven or eight times, a very bodily operation that has, however, no connection with the narrative told. Compared to the early rube films and their supposedly disciplining dimension, one might wonder if this is a new form of discipline. Perhaps in the 1920s people were getting so used to (and bored by) the narrative tradition that they needed something like a purely meta-filmic moment, the non-narrative within the narrative, to reignite their interest. Likewise, the touching of the camera lens in *One Week*, rather than being a gesture of censorship, is disruptive because the performing hand is situated outside the narrative.

Elsaesser has compared Keaton's *Sherlock Jr.* with a scene from Fritz Lang's *Siegfrieds Tod* (*Siegfried's Death*) of the same year

1924. In this first part of *Die Nibelungen* (*The Nibelungen*), Siegfried meets Alberich (the dwarf with magical powers), who shows him the Nibelungen treasure, inside a cave, projected on the wall. The treasure is "conjured up in the tense of anticipation and in the form of a moving image projection on a rock" (Elsaesser 2006, 214). It is an image to look at, not to touch. However, that is precisely what Siegfried will try to do. Elsaesser continues:

> Stunned by its splendor, Siegfried wants to grasp the image, upon which it disappears like a mirage, pushing and sucking him forward into penetrating further into the world of Alberich. . . . Siegfried shows himself to be the cinematic simpleton, the *Thumbe Thor*, in the Rube tradition. (214)

The projected Nibelungen treasure can indeed be considered, as Elsaesser suggests, a metaphor for the untouchable cinema: "The treasure dangling before Siegfried's eyes acts as a visualization or allegory of the cinema itself as a machine that plants the never-to-be-satisfied desire for palpability in the viewer" (214). On the one hand, Siegfried's gesture toward the projected moving image of the treasure evokes the compulsion we might have to reach out and touch holograms or three-dimensional images. On the other, it also reminds us of the disastrous effect of touching too roughly or too literally the film screen for it might result in tearing it down and making the projection disappear altogether, as happened in Porter's rube film.

Another telling instance of screen tearing occurs at the end of the Dadaist film *Entr'acte* (1924) by René Clair. Here, the character of the magician jumps through the white (paper) screen carrying the word *FIN*. After being resurrected from his coffin and having made all the bystanders disappear one by one with the touch of his magic wand, he conjures also his own disappearance only to reappear again, from behind the screen. He lacerates the screen, first with a hand and then almost diving through it, to end up on the ground. Then, another character kicks the magician back through the screen, which thanks to the trick of reverse motion is restored to its initial tearless state. The function of the rube-magician is double: with his screen exit he not only pays homage to the early cinema master-magician Méliès but also offers a final surprise to the bourgeois audience whose mind was probably already blown away by the irreverent funeral procession with dromedary. It is a last slap in the face of those who thought the film was finally over.

Similar avant-garde film "surprises" that could be further discussed in terms of screen breaking or damaging are, for instance, Luis Buñuel's cutting of a bull's eye in extreme close up in *Un chien andalou* (*An Andalusian Dog*, 1929) and Jean Cocteau's falling through the mirror in *Le sang d'un poète* (*The Blood of a Poet*, 1930). Instead I want to mention here the (mis)fortune of *Vita Futurista* (*Futurist Life*), the Futurist film made by Filippo Tommaso Marinetti and some Florentine Futurists in 1916. The aim was to provoke curiosity and scandal. Yet the first public screening, which took place in Florence, on January 28, 1917, was a big failure because the public was not shocked at all, but instead welcomed the film with enthusiasm. The next day, the newspapers reported: "A few hisses, a few ironic laughs and nothing edible."[9] In June 1917, the film was released in Rome, where its provocation was more efficient and it turned out necessary to suspend the projections. According to the memories of Arnaldo Ginna, who directed the film, "the audience threw objects, stones, etc. against the screen, which proved to be too vulnerable to this kind of performances" (1965, 158; my translation). In other words, the Futurist audience was an undisciplined public, but that was precisely the desired effect of the Futurists.

It is evident that the return of the rube in 1920s avant-garde cinema has another function than the early rube films; the figure no longer embodies a form of (self-)censorship or nostalgia for previous tactile media practices, but instead stands for a

9 This was the report of *Nuovo Giornale*, January 29, 1017. For a more detailed discussion of *Vita Futurista*'s reception, see Strauven 2006 (185–88).

deliberate provocation of the too-disciplined, too-institutionalized film spectator. To shock the bourgeoisie (*épater le bourgeois*), avant-garde filmmakers rely on various strategies, ranging from meta-filmic experimentation to magic tricks, surprises, and violent shock effects, including the destruction of the screen.

Expanded Cinema Rubes

In his discussion of rube films in light of new media and interface studies, Jeong (2012) has drawn attention to another rube figure that appeared on movie screens in the same year as Michel-Ange. His name is Joe and he features in Roberto Rossellini's episode "Illibatezza" ("Chastity"), which opens the omnibus film *Ro.Go.Pa.G* (1963).[10] Joe is a middle-aged American who obsessively falls in love with a beautiful Alitalia flight attendant, Anna Maria. During a stopover in Bangkok, they both end up in the same hotel. The young woman informs her fiancé back home, to whom she regularly sends self-made 8mm films (video messages avant la lettre), about the harassment by the American. The episode starts with the fiancé consulting a psychiatrist, who advises that Anna Maria completely change her look (from brunette to blonde) and attitude (from chaste to slutty). The effect is immediate: Joe loses all interest in this new Anna Maria in flesh and blood but instead tries to hug and kiss her old, "pure" image as he projects an 8mm film on his hotel room wall.

The obvious Oedipal dimension of Anna Maria's maternal image allows for a psychoanalytical reading, as suggested by Jeong, who also points out how the two bodies, Joe's and Anna Maria's, seem to fuse with each other. When standing between the projector and the wall, Joe notes how Anna Maria's chaste body is projected on his own body, which he tries to grab in a surrogate embrace. As Jeong puts it, "when her image is projected onto his body, . . .

10 Acronym of the four directors: Roberto Rossellini, Jean-Luc Godard, Pier Paolo Pasolini, and Ugo Gregoretti.

our attention shifts from her body on screen (screen-as-body) to his body becoming a screen (body-as-screen)" (2012, 238). Skin as "biological interface" and screen as "technological interface" get confused. Jeong writes:

> Walking through transcendental psychoanalysis and acting out of imaginary narcissism, Joe the protagonist of this drama leads us to an embodied phenomenology of the biological interface (skin), whose ambivalent tactility is externalized in the technological interface (screen). (239)

In Chapter 4, I will come back to the notion of interface in relation to both skin and screen. For the moment, I would like to make two additions to Jeong's in-depth analysis of Rossellini's short. First, besides the rube Joe, who is the focus of Jeong's reading, there is also Anna Maria's fiancé who acts like a rube in the vein of Ali Bouf or Don Quixote: at the beginning of the episode he throws a book at the projected image of the American on the wall (out of jealousy, anger, and revenge), and he is even tempted to hurt the projected image of his transformed girlfriend (out of frustration, but probably also because he prefers the angelic one to the new lustful one) but finally manages to control himself. Second, the projected image of the chaste Anna Maria on the body of the American allows for a direct connection with "expanded cinema" practices, especially as explored by Robert Whitman in *Prune Flat* (1965), where live actors perform in front of a film screen on which prerecorded performances are projected.[11] The skin of the live actors becomes here a projection screen as well, which leads to a dense visual, nonnarrative show with a complex and misleading play of projected/live nudity and projected/live costumes.

In this context of expanded media performances, one feels almost obliged to mention Valie Export's street happening *Tapp und Tastkino* (*Tap and Touch Cinema*), that premiered on November

11 It is striking that Jeong himself does not explicitly make this connection, while placing his case studies under the category of "Expanded Rube Cinema."

11, 1968, in Vienna and was repeated a couple of days later in Munich. Famously, the Austrian artist turned her own body into a film screen, not to be looked at but to be touched by (mostly male) hands. With a Styrofoam box attached to her upper body, Export invited passersby on the street to "visit the cinema," allowing them to palpate her naked breasts hidden behind a little cloth curtain. This provocative feminist critique of the male gaze upon the female body, as displayed by the bourgeoisie ideology of classical Hollywood, anticipated by seven years Mulvey's equally provocative "Visual Pleasure and Narrative Cinema."

Reflecting on her expanded cinema performance at the beginning of the twenty-first century, Export explains:

> In *Tapp und Tast Kino* (*Touch Cinema*), which I made in 1968, I examined the breasts as a central theme within the film industry. The *Tapp und Tast* film is a street film, a mobile film and the first real women's film. The performance takes place as usual, in the dark. Only the movie theatre has become somewhat smaller, there is room in it only for two hands. In order, to see the film, which means in this case to sense and feel it, the "viewer" must put both hands through the entranceway to the theatre. . . . Tactile reception counteracts the fraud of voyeurism. (2003)

In *Tapp und Tastkino*, the female body *is* the film—a film which cannot be seen, but which can be, or better, *must* be touched. It is a "true" and very literal touchscreen. Revisiting Export's film in rube terms, one can say that it is the male spectator of the late 1960s who is caught here in action, that is, in his fantasy of being a (shameless) rube at the movie theater.

The Technological Rube of the Twenty-First Century

At the beginning of the twenty-first century, the situation is becoming more complex because of the huge range of (erotic) moving images online, the change in the screen from projection to "transit point" (Casetti 2014), the shift in the image from photographic to algorithmic, and the increasing pervasion of the touchscreen. In a society where everyone is constantly texting and connecting to social networks via their handheld mobile screenic devices, looking down instead of looking up, thumbing instead of speaking, one wonders what today's rube might look like. Most obvious would be to think here of the non-technological user, the one who does not know that the screen is actually supposed to be touched.

Instead I will discuss one specific high-tech, sci-fi case that has been read in rube terms by other scholars as well. It concerns Chief John Anderton, played by Tom Cruise, in Steven Spielberg's *Minority Report* (2002). The film presents two key situations where Anderton touches a futuristic screen device without really touching it. The first takes place at work, in the PreCrime office, where Chief Anderton has at his disposal an immense translucent screen on which appears information concerning crimes not yet committed ("pre-crime crimes") in the form of text, statistics, mathematical formulas, and images of the past, present, and future. Anderton wears special high-tech gloves that allow him to move these data under his fingertips without actually touching the screen. This "virtual" screen touching resembles some sort of choreography, whereby the fingers follow specific (dance) patterns. Or, as Spielberg himself envisioned it, the gestures are "like conducting an orchestra" (Rothkerch 2002).

Released five years before the official iPhone launch, *Minority Report* is a typical "near-future film" (Koeck and Penz 2003) that offers us a prescient glimpse into our actual gadget future. In this respect, the PreCrime transparent glass screen can be seen as a "nonportable version of the iPhone," as proposed by Alexandra Schneider who positions the iPhone user between the early cinema rube Uncle Josh and Spielberg's turn-of-the-millennium rube Chief Anderton. Schneider explains:

> Uncle Josh wants to touch the object but finds out that there is no object, only a screen. Anderton never actually touches the screen . . . yet he reliably obtains the object (or information) he wants. It is therefore perhaps somewhere in between the fictional characters of Anderton and Uncle Josh that one comes close to the figure of the iPhone user: she is part Uncle Josh, part John Anderton. Like Uncle Josh, she actually touches the screen, since the touch screen is a material object, but like Anderton, she can make any object of knowledge appear on the screen at the touch of her finger. (2012, 57–58)

The PreCrime interface was designed by John Underkoffler, who showed a real-life version of it at the 2010 TED conference. His vision was to implement the "spatial operating environment" interface everywhere: "on every laptop, every desktop, every microwave oven, TV, dashboard" (Underkoffler 2010). What should concern us about such a vision, and about Anderton's tele-touching of the translucent screen, is the dimension of data underneath the information and images displayed. The interaction that takes place through sensors is by no means limited to the object–user encounter but embedded in a larger system of corporate data collection and analysis. Indeed, it turns out that agent Anderton has very little agency in the PreCrime office-*dispositif* where he believes he controls the images but is in fact manipulated himself by the Precog program (due to malicious intent on the part of his antagonist Lamar Burgess).

In the home setting of *Minority Report* we witness another moment of technological touching-without-really-touching. Anderton is home, alone and lonely, watching "old" holographic home movies that are stored on small transparent disks. We first see his son running in a forest, on the edge of a lake, and then a short clip of his wife in a nightgown begging him to put down the camera. The little home movies seem interactive, but that is only because Anderton knows his part. This is especially true in the first home movie, where a "real" conversation between father and son takes place. Anderton asks his son for a kiss, which he does not get. He did not get it at the time of recording either, but now he tries to get it from the holographic version of his recorded son. Here Anderton acts like a rube, namely "as if," as also observed by Elsaesser in his discussion of the different diegetic spaces that are created by different forms of media and their users:

> Feature films, too, confront us with characters who "engage" with different diegeses, defined by their temporal and spatial co-presence, activated by a performative or enunciative gesture. One could name *The Matrix* trilogy (1999–2003), but a possibly more interesting example, because of its indirect reference to the Rube complex of "acting as-if" would be Steven Spielberg's *Minority Report* (2002) where the character of Tom Cruise tries to "touch" his missing son, whose (moving) image he projects in his living room by means of a hologram screening system. Cruise acts like a Rube: (he knows) his son is not there, and the hologram is a mere image, yet nevertheless he wants to touch it/him. (2006, 219)

Do we feel pity for this technological rube, whose son was kidnapped and probably murdered, whose wife only stayed with him in the shape of a holographic illusion, and who takes hits from a high-tech pipe to overcome his loneliness? Is his attempt to virtually touch his lost loved ones ridiculous or rather piteous? Or should we see his situation as a warning for the future, for a dystopian world where human relationships are "reduced" to technological interaction?

What matters for my little history of hands-on spectatorship is that *Minority Report* addresses a different spectator from, for instance, the one in Godard's *Le Mépris*: no longer a TV viewer but a computer user, one who will soon discover the possibility of video calls (with the release of Skype in 2003) and the multi-touch smartphone (with the launch of the iPhone in 2007). Or, even better, instead of *addressing* a different spectator, Spielberg's film is *constructing* one. As Gunning claimed in his seminal article on the "cinema of attractions": "Every change in film history implies a change in its address to the spectator, and each period constructs its spectator in a new way" (2006, 387). Through the topos of the rube, I have been dismantling the construction of the "disciplined" spectator. Each period has its own rube figure(s) and each rube figure its own function(s): from silencing the distracted audience to unsettling the bourgeoisie, from destroying our imaginations to stimulating them (erotically), from reminding us of past screen practices to warning us about the future.

Today's Children as Rubes

In the following chapter we will encounter children acting like rubes in a museum context or public exhibition space, ignoring the (unspoken) "look, but don't touch" rule, like the two girls who pricked their fingers on the cactus artwork on display in Bologna (see Introduction). In their capacity as film viewers, at home or in the movie theater, young children often reenact, without knowing, the double founding myth of early cinema: running away from the screen when frightened and running toward the screen when curious, intrigued, eager to know, or anxious to interact. I recall that my own daughter at the age of two jumped up to touch the wall when her favorite movie *Finding Nemo* (2003) was projected in a home cinema setting. Having watched the film over and over again on a computer screen, she was marveled by its bigger-than-life projection on the wall and started to play with the characters she was so familiar with, chasing and being chased by the fish in the ocean. Quite different is the anecdote told by film scholar Malte Hagener about a child touching the screen in a movie theater, at an afternoon screening of Martin Scorsese's *Hugo* (2011) in 3D. This anecdotal instance happened at the end of the film, when the end credits were scrolling across the huge screen-wall and the audience was leaving the auditorium. The child, a little girl, ran to the front. At first a bit hesitant, she reached up and touched the screen. Then she ran to her father who was waiting for her back at the entrance. Hagener wondered when he posted the anecdote on Facebook, is this the "return of the rube in the digital age"?[12]

Why did this little girl want to touch the screen? For sure, she did not want to play with Hugo Cabret and the other characters, like my daughter did during the full-wall projection of *Finding Nemo*, since the images of the movie were already gone. But how did these girls even think about touching the screen? One might question whether their propensity is somehow grounded in (or enhanced by) today's early familiarization with touch-based media devices. Without wanting to suggest that before the advent of the iPhone and the iPad children would not have touched screens, I am nevertheless wondering whether today's children touch projection surfaces for the same reasons as children did, or would have done, before the age of the touchscreen. Are they touching the screen because they expect something to happen? And when it becomes clear that nothing is happening, why do they continue to touch the screen? At the *Hugo* screening the urge to touch the film screen was without doubt prompted by the 3D quality of the images. The girl's familiarity and hands-on experience with touchscreens, if not a direct cause of her attitude as a rube, might have made her more conscious of the materiality of the images, about their tangibility. In any case, it seems she was reflecting on cinema's "work" (or *travail*), trying to find out where the images came from, as Hagener also suggested.[13]

More generally, I like to think that for children movies make much more sense as "feelies," as three-dimensional stories that you can enter (as Buster Keaton does in *Sherlock Jr.*) and where you can touch the skin of the beautiful heroes or heroines (as Michel-Ange does in *Les Carabiniers*), not for the sake of sexual arousal, as envisioned by Aldous Huxley, but just to check out how it feels. In

12 See Malte Hagener's wall on Facebook, March 6, 2012.

13 Here I refer to Jean-Louis Baudry's discussion of cinema's basic apparatus and the "knowledge effect" that is brought about when the work of cinema—that is, the process of transformation of raw materiality into a film—is made evident (Baudry 1974–75, 40–41).

Brave New World (1932), the Feelies are specially equipped movie theaters with knobs on the arms of the chairs that spectators should hold to experience "tactual effects" and "titillations." In the mind (or imagination) of both children and rubes, no special equipment is necessary: for them movies are not only talkies but also always "feelies," and therefore they use their sense of touch without embarrassment. This is precisely why I argued in this chapter against the current consensus that the rube (like the child) serves to discipline the audience and to caution against indulging in a tactile film experience; instead, I defend the rube (like the child) as a positive model, a figure that serves to induce the spectators to enrich their film experience by getting back in touch with the hands-on layer of the "feelies."

[2]

Early Museum's Hands-On Ethos

Do not touch! How many times do children hear this order? No one would ever say: do not look, do not listen.
Bruno Munari

Please Do Not | Touch It

In the spring of 2011, I was staying with my family in the Keio Plaza Hotel in Shinjuku, Tokyo's major commercial and administrative district. In the hotel lobby was an exposition of traditional Japanese decoration consisting of all kinds of little colorful objects hung on long red strings. Very tempting to my then three-year-old, it was strictly forbidden to touch this decorative installation. However, the "Please do not touch it" sign was folded into two parts across the angle of a wooden beam, inviting English-speaking tourists actually to "touch it" (fig. 7a–b). This effect was obviously unintentional, as is the case with many of the typical lost-in-translation signs in this city, but it allowed me to turn a blind eye to my daughter's transgressive act.

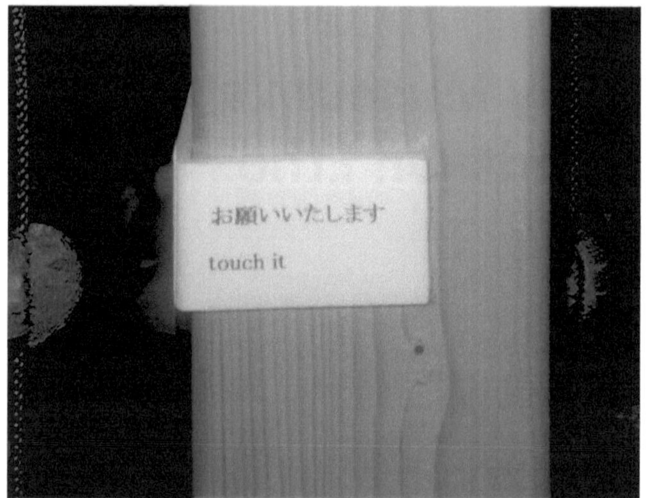

[Figure 7a–b] Keio Plaza Hotel, Tokyo. From author's personal archive, March 2011.

The pendulous decorations looked like a refined form of crib mobiles, or an oriental version of Bruno Munari's "useless machines" or Alexander Calder's "mobiles." Both the Italian Futurist designer and the American sculptor made their first kinetic sculptures in the early 1930s, adding motion to the art of sculpture, which, according to W. J. T. Mitchell, is already "so clearly an art of the tactile that it seems superfluous to argue about it" (2007, 398). Whereas Munari is famous for the initiative of organizing "tactile workshops" in the Italian museum context, it is also well known that Calder's hanging wire sculptures, however fragile they may seem, were meant to be put in motion, either by (breathing of) air or by a touch of the hand, in a gentle tactile interaction. Yet parents will often feel compelled to restrain their children from touching these artworks when on display in a traditional museum or exhibition setting. In May 2012 the Stedelijk Museum Amsterdam posted on Facebook a picture of a mother with son at their Calder Exhibition in 1969. The mother is clearly trying to prevent her child from touching one of the mobiles, as confirmed by the caption: "Niet aanraken!" (Don't touch!).

"Touch with your eyes, not with your hands" is another saying that parents with young children might find themselves repeating aloud, when taking them to an exhibition. It is a typical response of a typical responsible parent, who observes the rules of our (Western) hands-off culture. As Alexandra Schneider notes, "A visit to an art exhibition in a traditional museum space in the company of small kids will teach you not only about art but also about culture more generally. The most striking, and probably also most obvious lesson, concerns the issue of looking as opposed to touching" (2012, 55). Furthermore, she writes:

> In some contemporary art exhibitions you are either explicitly invited to touch the exhibited art work or reminded not to touch it. The basic ethos is still the same: hands off! The invitation to touch the artwork has to be made explicit

> because it is commonly understood that we are not supposed to do that. (56)

This might also explain my perplexity in the lobby of the Keio Plaza Hotel, when, standing at a particular angle, I first read only the second part of the "Please do not | touch it" caption. For it countered my intuition, or rather my knowledge of the tacit (and still dominant) hands-off rule.

Even in exhibition rooms without disciplining parents (or when disciplining parents are maybe not needed), the same unspoken rule is made evident by the behavioral difference between adults and children: the former usually refrain from touching exhibited works (or they do it secretively), while the latter engage very openly, shamelessly, in a tactile interaction with touchable art objects, screen projections, and installations. I remember experiencing this discrepancy at the retrospective of Bill Viola in the Grand Palais, in Paris, in March 2014. The setup of this exhibition impressed me for the way it was organized as a fluid, almost visceral, path in the semi-darkness, from one installation to another. With all of his major works on display, Bill Viola emerged as a monumental artist of intimacy, or better of intimate encounters. Two works in particular attracted me because of the screen's materiality and potential interaction, each revealing the behavioral difference between adults and children in a traditional museum context.

The first, *The Veiling* (1995), was installed in a large room that one entered from the side, almost bumping into a row of nine translucent screens hung as parallel layers between two opposing video projectors (projecting images of a man and a woman respectively). In front of me, an elderly couple literally hit the screens, probably disoriented by the semi-darkness of the room. Furtively, I also touched one of the screens, curious to feel the texture of this stiffened gauze-like cloth. The second installation, *Going Forth by Day* (2002), occupied a vast room allowing for an impressive display of Viola's famous tribute to Giotto's Scrovegni

Chapel with its five "panels" of HD video projected directly onto the wall (that is, the naked, screen-less wall). In the middle of the room, many adult viewers were sitting on the ground. My attention was drawn to a girl of about ten years old, who was casting shadow figures with her hands on the main entrance panel, "Fire Birth," through which visitors enter Viola's "chapel." Then she walked over to "The Voyage" panel, approaching it very closely, and physically touched the slowly moving image, as if to play with its characters. I was spellbound by this moment of screen touching, by its magic and its naturalness. Nobody reacted, nobody intervened. The Bill Viola exhibition did not bear signs saying "Please do not touch." Yet the disciplined (adult) museumgoer knows that this hands-off rule is implicit: in the Grand Palais as in any other major Parisian museum, you do not touch the artworks, even if they are "mere" projections. Yet the girl did so, unabashed and on purpose.

One might wonder if there is any correspondence with the child running up to the movie screen after the projection of Scorsese's *Hugo* as narrated at the end of Chapter 1. Are the two girls driven by the same force of attraction? To what extent are the situations comparable? First of all, we are clearly dealing with two different settings (museum space vs. cinema multiplex), each with a very specific type of "cinematic" experience (fresco-like video panel vs. 3D adventure motion-picture). But also the motivation behind the actions of the two girls may have to be found elsewhere: Whereas the girl at the Grand Palais might have been bored due to the long museum visit (yet creative enough to entertain herself with shadow plays and screen touching), at the *Hugo* show the touching of the screen was most likely motivated by curiosity. And the latter happened at the very end of the screening, when the images had already disappeared. The girl at the Grand Palais instead was engaging with the artwork itself, with the characters of "The Voyage."[1]

In this panel, like in many of Viola's installations, the characters' movements develop very slowly. The tension between motion and stillness, so characteristic for Viola's video art, might trigger even in the adult visitor an impulse to touch the screen. For instance, when facing for the first time the "video painting" *The Quintet of the Astonished* (2000), which shows the unfolding expressions of five actors in extreme slow motion, one might be tempted to touch the group portrait to check out whether its motion can be speed up (or slowed down to a complete standstill), whether any type of interaction is possible or not. Yet our knowledge of the hands-off ethos in the museum context will keep us at a safe distance, causing another type of tension, between our own motion and stillness. As Eivind Røssaak observes in relation to *The Quintet*,

> In a strange way, the barely moving figures in the video lead the spectator to be aware of her own motions in front of the screen. To see the image adequately, the spectator must work with her own body's orientation. The spectator's work with the piece becomes a work with her body and its shifting positions, including, significantly, immobility. (2009, 340)

Later in this chapter I will come back to this notion of shifting viewing positions in front of contemporary media art, pointing out how children in particular are able to interact with noninteractive installations following a hands-on approach, that is, performing actions of concrete screen touching. But first I will delve into the history of museum culture to trace the possible origins of the hands-off ethos. In fact, as the research of cultural historians, such as Tony Bennett and Constance Classen, among others, has indicated, the prohibition against touching artworks arises

1 "The Voyage" displays the cross-section of a house, sitting on a hill overlooking a lake. In the house an old man in dying in bed, whereas at the shore of the lake a boat is being prepared to depart.

as an effect of the gradual institutionalization of the museum that occurred during the long nineteenth century. Before this institutionalization process, touching artworks on display was a rather common practice. When using the notion of "early museum," I am aware of suggesting a possible link with "early cinema" and the figure of the rube discussed in Chapter 1. This is not accidental but deliberate.

The Early Museum

The first museum in the world was reputedly the Museum of Alexandria, with its annex Library of Alexandria. For the origins of the "modern" museum, however, one generally considers as a benchmark the foundation of the Ashmolean Museum of Art and Archaeology in 1677. Upon receiving Elias Ashmole's private collection, the University of Oxford erected a building to house it and make it publicly available. The doors of the Ashmolean Museum opened in 1683. Searching for origins, one can also go back to the early sixteenth century, when Pope Julius II founded the Vatican Museums. After the discovery of the famous Laocoön Group in a Roman vineyard in 1506, the pope decided to purchase the marble statue and put it on public display. His precursor, Pope Sixtus IV, already in 1471, donated a collection of important Roman sculptures to exhibit to the people, which marked the foundation of the Capitoline Museums. If one considers that other significant public museums, such as the British Museum and the Louvre, opened their doors only during the course of the eighteenth century, Italy is the leading example in the sixteenth century.

Precisely in this period, in sixteenth-century Italy, there is an important discussion among artists about the hierarchy of the senses. The so-called *paragone* debate basically turned into a contest between painting and sculpture—a contest about the noblest art form. The central argument in this debate concerned sculptural tactility, which for the defenders of painting (including, above all, Leonardo Da Vinci) was a proof of sculpture's obscenity, while for the defenders of sculpture the tactile dimension was precisely praised as sculpture's most positive and powerful characteristic.[2]

The artistic rivalry between the senses of sight and touch is rooted in the famous painting contest between Zeuxis and Parrhasius, as described by Pliny the Elder in *Naturalis Historia* (AD 77–79). According to this anecdote of Greek antiquity, Zeuxis painted grapes in a manner so realistic that birds came to peck. The victory of the painting contest seemed to be his, so he said to Parrhasius to push aside the curtain that covered his picture, but it turned out to be a painted curtain. The outcome: Zeuxis deceived the birds, but Parrhasius deceived Zeuxis. Seventeenth-century Dutch painters, such as Gerard Dou and Gerrit Houckgeest, played with Parrhasius's trick. In those times it was customary to protect oil paintings from bright light by means of a drape that had to be pushed aside manually. Dou's *Painter with Pipe and Book* (ca. 1645) and Houckgeest's *Interior of the Old Church in Delft* (ca. 1645) are two examples that fool the viewer by adding at the right side of the frame a little curtain painted so realistically that you can almost reach out and touch it.[3]

In the late seventeenth century, the art theoretical discussions on the senses became philosophical questions with the debate around the Molyneux problem (1688). Irish philosopher and scientist William Molyneux, troubled by the blindness that afflicted his wife, proposed to John Locke a disturbing scientific

2 Art historian Geraldine Johnson (2002) outlines three different senses of tactility in these art theoretical discussions: cognitive (referring to touch as the primordial sense for gaining empirical knowledge about the world, more reliable than sight), socio-sexual (referring to touch in terms of desire and differentiation), and magical-illusionistic (referring to touch as a life-giving force, as a power to animate the inanimate as in the case of Pygmalion, or referring to the hand as being in direct connection with the intellect as in Michelangelo's view).

3 I saw both paintings on display in the Rijksmuseum in Amsterdam in June 2006.

question: If one day a blind man finds his sight, would he be able to recognize with his eyes two solid objects, such as a cube and a sphere, which until then had been perceived by touch only? (Crary 1992, 58). Locke's answer, formulated in *Essay Concerning Human Understanding* (1690), was basically no, because he considered sight and touch to be two completely different (and separate) senses. For more than three centuries the Molyneux problem has continued to resurface in the writings of many authors, from Berkeley to Leibniz, from Merleau-Ponty to today's cognitive sciences and discussions on the phenomenon of synesthesia.

Both the *paragone* debate and the Molyneux problem are crucial in understanding and contextualizing the pre-institutionalized museum, which lasted for a rather long period from the mid-seventeenth century to the end of the eighteenth century. Key for constructing my history of tactile media is the recent rediscovery, or revaluation, by scholars such as Constance Classen and Barbara Stafford, of how this period of early museum culture was indeed characterized by a hands-on ethos.

Classen's research has demonstrated that the first public museums inherited the practice of touching artworks on display from private art collections. As Classen puts it, it was an almost mandatory aspect of the guided tour with the curator (or the owner of the museum) acting as "gracious host" and the museum visitors as "polite guests." According to this hospitality logic, the museum visitors were supposed to "show their interest and goodwill by asking questions and by touching the proffered objects" (Classen 2005, 275). And Classen adds: "To be invited to peruse a collection of exotic artefacts or *objets d'art* and *not* touch anything would be like being invited to someone's home for dinner and not touching the food" (275). Important to note here is that this hands-on practice was not limited to three-dimensional objects, but also applied, although in a lesser degree, to paintings. People would like to touch paintings to feel the texture of the canvas and paint, or "simply to exercise their right to touch"

The *Wunderkammer* contained all types of *mirabilia*, objects that generated or inspired wonder, divisible into two main categories: the *naturalia*, or strange objects from the natural world, and the *artificialia*, or strange objects created by the human hand. To mention some typical items: fossils, shells, animals with two heads, rare fish or birds, rare prints and books, collections of dried leaves, diamonds, cameos, filigrees, coral and pearl necklaces, vases, antique coins, etc. In other words, these were curiosities of every imaginable kind, in particular *scientific* curiosities (so cherished in the Age of Enlightenment), not necessarily works of art. What mattered was the rareness, or uniqueness, of an object.

The gradual institutionalization of the museum entailed not only a new selection of objects, according to their representability instead of their exceptionality, but also a new organization of knowledge, a new "order of things" (Foucault 1970), grounded in the modern episteme of the human sciences. As Tony Bennett argues in *The Birth of the Museum* (1995), the three epistemes of Foucault's "archaeology of human sciences" apply also to the history of the museum. The Renaissance episteme is the knowledge of curiosities as displayed in the *Wunderkammer*, that is, according to the logic of analogy, of hidden and distant relations between exotic objects, relations that the "user" needs to explore or to create. I would add that this is the most tactile episteme, since hands-on practice is an integral part of this specific "order of things," which is in continuous reorganization and reactivation. This is the episteme of the early semi-private, semi-public museums. Then follows the classical episteme that founds the knowledge of the scientific taxonomy, according to which trivial, common objects are "arranged as parts of series rather than as unique items" (Bennett 1995, 96). And, finally, the modern episteme constitutes the model (or rather the historical a priori) on which the institutionalized museum is based. It forms the conditions of knowledge of the new human sciences (biology, geology, archaeology, anthropology, history, and art history); objects are no longer arranged as parts of taxonomic tables but instead identified or distinguished according to their position within evolutionary series and arranged as parts of a sequence such as the history of earth, life, or civilization (Bennett 1995, 96). According to Bennett these conditions of knowledge are at the core of the democratization process that drives the institutionalization of the museum: the aim is to make art, or rather knowledge, available to everyone. This is in stark contrast to the private collections that were accessible to a very restricted and elitist public only. However, to make art more democratic, the body of the museum visitor needed to be disciplined. Those who did not respect the new rules of public behavior were excluded from the democratization process.

The Exhibitionary Architecture of the Modern Museum

As Bennett further argues, the new "order of things" goes together with a new museum *dispositif*: the modern museum is a space of observation and regulation with an architectural structure that is inspired not by the *Wunderkammer* or labyrinthine private galleries but by spaces of (public) surveillance. Central to the new museum architecture is the idea of auto-regulation: each museum visitor can watch the behavior of the other museum visitors and therefore knows that he or she is also watched, and therefore behaves "correctly," keeping their hands off the exposed artworks. This is the known principle of Jeremy Bentham's Panopticon, designed in 1791, that is, two years before the inauguration of the Louvre in Paris. Conceived as a circular building, the Panopticon has a central tower from which the guardian can observe all the prisoners. The prisoners, however, are unable to know whether or not they are indeed watched. Yet, knowing that there is the possibility of being watched, due to the particular arrangement of the prison, the prisoners would behave well and maintain order in an almost automatic way.

Bennett refers to the model of the Panopticon in his discussion of the new architectural structure of the museum, pointing out some important differences between the prison and the museum: punishment vs. education, segregation vs. mixture (of people, of publics), closedness vs. openness. Even if the exhibitionary architecture of the museum seems to reverse the Panopticon design, turning a closed system into an open public space, Bennett insists that it incorporates "aspects of [the Panopticon] principles together with those of the panorama, forming a technology of vision which served not to atomize and disperse the crowd but to regulate it, and to do so by rendering it visible to itself, by making the crowd itself the ultimate spectacle." It is all about "to see and be seen" (Bennett 1995, 68–69).

Not all museumgoers will succeed in acquiring (or intuiting) this implicit rule of seeing while being seen, of looking at things on display while being on display themselves. A comparison could be drawn to the rube figure of early cinema. In his essay "Expanded Rube Cinema," Seung-hoon Jeong (2012) discusses two screen performances by Jerry Lewis that are telling in this respect: his mischievous act of pulling a string and causing the fall of a huge Samson statue in *The Errand Boy* (1961) and his clumsy yet creative "encounter" with a woman's clay bust on display in the hotel lobby in *The Bellboy* (1960). While in the former scene Lewis seems to act out of (naïve, childlike) curiosity, in the latter he is incited to touch the artwork by its accompanying sign "wet paint" which leads to a laborious gender transformation, from young woman to old man with monocle and cigarette. Citing Steven Shaviro (1993), Jeong sees in this deforming act of art touching "a masochistic abjection that comes from [Lewis's] hyperdisciplined state; he becomes 'an anarchist not in spite of, but because of, his hyperconformism'" (Jeong 2012, 243). In other words, Lewis perfectly knows that he is not supposed to touch artworks on display, but he cannot resist their force of attraction. I would argue that especially the scene with the clay bust has a playful dimension; besides acting like an avant-garde (and blasphemous) artist, Lewis is clearly having fun.

For this rube, as for children, the Panopticon's (or panorama's) technology of vision remains without effect.

Besides the Panopticon and the panorama, Bennett discusses other forms of exhibitionary architecture that served as direct models for the first public museums. Among these models are shopping arcades, department stores, and fairs (with elevated platforms, galleries around a central hall, display cases, etc.). Like those contemporary public spaces, the museum became a space that organized the gaze. Alison Griffiths has described this context using the notion of "promenade cinema," a form of proto-cinema seen particularly in museums of natural history that exhibited objects along an itinerary (or "promenade") of display cases with so-called life groups. As with early cinema, these nineteenth-century museums allowed the public to travel to remote places, even though such journeys excluded direct contact with the objects on display because they were protected behind glass (Griffiths 1996).

The Museum Touchscreen

Paradoxically, while during the nineteenth century the process of democratization excluded touch, in more recent days, at the end of the twentieth century and the beginning of the twenty-first century, touch is reintroduced into the museum precisely for the same reason. In 1995, Bennett commented on this new hands-on tendency with skepticism:

> In order to attract sufficient visitors to justify continuing public funding, [the museums] now often seek to imitate rather than distinguish themselves from places of popular assembly: interactive computer displays competing with video parlours, for example, "touch and feel" exhibits, [etc.]. While these attempts to democratize the ethos of the museum are to be welcomed, their capacity to substantially alter the visitor profiles of museums is difficult to assess. (1995, 104–05)

More recently, Ulrike Bergermann has questioned the merits of "hands-on knowledge" through the use of tactile devices. Looking at the case of science museums, science centers, and other places of popularization of scientific knowledge, she warns against a too-simplistic assumption that touching leads to a better understanding of things, as if a hands-on approach would give us access to the world "in its most objective form" (Bergermann 2006, 318). This critique of the "aesthetics of immediacy" (*Asthetik der Unmittelbarkeit*) could also be applied to early museum culture, more specifically to the touchable collections of the private galleries and curiosity cabinets. Yet Bergermann aims at the pedagogical validity of haptics for knowledge transfer, rather than at the early museumgoer's right to touch (art) objects on display.

Sometimes the touchscreen interface is chosen as a compromise with the hands-off museum rule, allowing for the indirect touching of the "real" object; for instance, in the first decade of the twentieth century, the New Mexico Museum of Natural History and Science installed a so-called Fossil Viewer that permitted visitors to touch, via the touchscreen, the fossil on display at a safe (hands-off) distance. Viewing and touching are here in a complex relationship, where touching seems to complement or even dominate viewing but only as a surrogate of touch itself. Here again the tactile *dispositif* makes use of the touchscreen for (merely) didactic reasons of knowledge transfer, which requires a focus on the operative side of media use, as opposed to the artistic dimension of tactile art.

As a topical anecdote, I might mention here my visit to the *Van Eyck in Bruges* exhibition at the Groeningemuseum in Bruges, Belgium, in August 2020. Organized around two masterpieces by Jan van Eyck, *Portrait of Margaret van Eyck* (or *Margaret, the Artist's Wife*) (1439) and *The Virgin and Child with Canon van der Paele* (1434–36), the exhibition nicely documented the restoration process of the latter, disclosing the operation of infrared reflectography as it registers the carbonaceous material in the oil painting and reveals Van Eyck's underdrawing, which allows, in various areas of the showpiece, for a comparison between the first sketch and the final result. The didactic explanation was supported by a large touchscreen table, the surface of which the visitor was, absurdly enough, not permitted to touch. As the accompanying sign reads: "Please do not touch this touch table. You are currently seeing a demonstration. The content of this table is available at www.museabrugge.be/closer-to-van-der-paele" (fig. 8a–b). Obviously, the phenomenon of the untouchable touchscreen is a contingency of the COVID-19 times.

Another curiosity for the archaeology of the electronic touch-screen concerns experimentation with the user interface by means of the "museum kiosk," which was one of the earliest applications of the touchscreen in the public sphere, together with sales kiosks and public information services. The logic behind these first implementations was very simple; as Catherine Plaisant, senior research scientist at the University of Maryland's Human–Computer Interaction Laboratory, put it, "Mice were unpractical in public settings, so touchscreens were the natural choice!" (Plaisant 1999). In the late 1980s and early 1990s, research at the University of Maryland focused on so-called high-precision touchscreens for better selection strategies. The museum was used as a test case for one of their experiments in "hypertext exploration": the Guide to Opportunities in Volunteer Archaeology, which basically consisted of an interface to sign up as volunteer for an archaeological project somewhere (according to your hypertext exploration) in the world.[5] Not only did the touch-screen not render the exhibition of archaeological objects more tactile, it also had no direct connection with the museum or its exhibits.

5 This program was tested in 1988 at the Smithsonian Museum. For a video demonstration, see "Overcoming Limitations to Access (1992 University of Maryland UIS Broadcast)," https://www.youtube.com/watch?v=NFpVHGLSDLM.

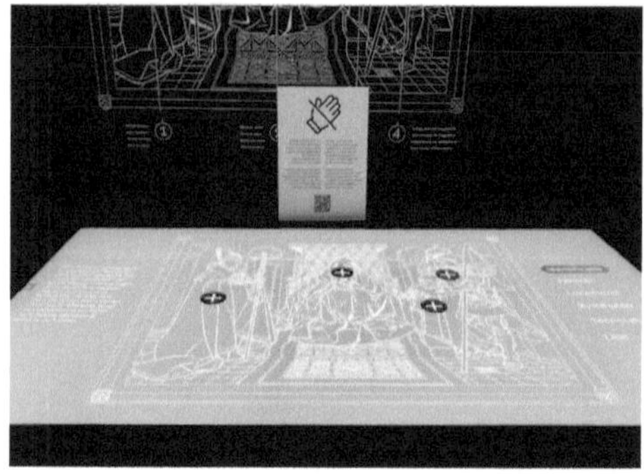

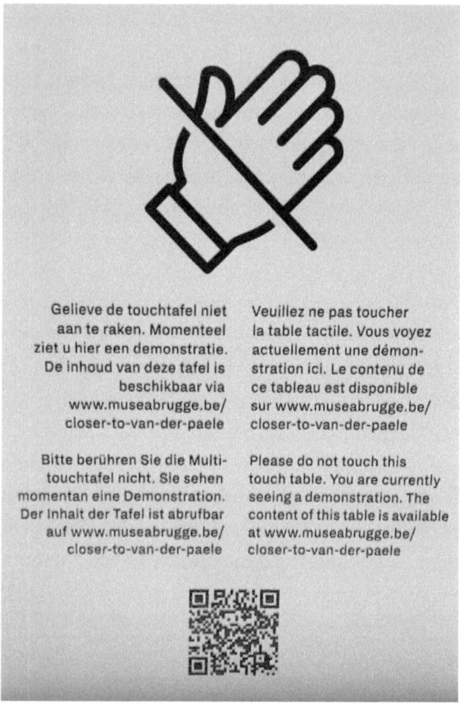

[Figure 8a–b] Non-touchable touchscreen *dispositif*, Groeningemuseum, Bruges. From author's personal archive, August 2020.

Futurist "Tactilism" and Tactile Tables

Going back in time, at the beginning of the twentieth century, the path for touch-based art installations and interactions was explicitly (and provocatively) explored by historical avant-garde movements, such as Futurism, Dada, and Surrealism. The emergence of early forms of tactile art can be connected in particular to the notion of "tactilism" (*tattilismo*), invented by the founder of Italian Futurism, Filippo Tommaso Marinetti.[6] Conceived in the early 1920s, in collaboration with his wife, Benedetta, tactilism signified a decisive (albeit not definitive) turn in the bellicose and virile program of Futurism, a move toward a more gentle or subtle approach to "reality." Central to this new art view was the artist's own fragility and the reeducation of the senses. In the corresponding manifesto "Tactilism," dated January 16, 1921, Marinetti narrates:

> I began my own tactile education by submitting my sense of touch to intensive therapy, localizing the confused phenomena of will and thought on the different parts of my body, and especially on the palms of my hands. This education was slow, but also easy, and all healthy bodies can use this education to get precise and surprising results. (2009, 266)

The manifesto proposes six categories of tactile sensations subdivided according to two scales, planes vs. volumes. Furthermore, it introduces the notion of the Futurist "tactile table." The Italian word for the latter is *tavola tattile*, which would have been a nice term for referring to the electronic tablet if modern Italian had not opted for the English loanword. Its diminutive, *tavoletta*, is even closer to the English term "tablet" and has the same (original) meaning of flat inscription surface or writing pad. Yet Marinetti's "tactile tables" are not to be inscribed or carved

6 Parts of this discussion on Marinetti's "tactilism" have been published previously in Strauven 2005a and 2018.

 like the stone tablets of Moses. They are also not necessarily flat or smooth like the glass surface of smartphones and tablets. On the contrary, they are characterized by a mixture of textures to be explored by travelling fingertips.

Among the ten different applications of tactilism, Marinetti describes tactile tables for "hand travels," "different sexes," and "free-wordist improvisations," which are exercises for the new initiates who are not yet fully trained in tactile sensibility and are blindfold during the performance. Of specific interest for a history of tactile media are the "tactile shirts and clothes," precursors of today's wearables, and "tactile theatres," that prefigure Huxley's Feelies and today's virtual reality experiments, making use of moving and rotating "tactile ribbons" on which the spectators must rest their hands (Marinetti 2009, 267–68).

Marinetti stresses that tactilism has nothing to do with plastic art: the tactile tables are no painting, no sculpture. However, in an effort to provide evidence of the Futurist anticipation of Dadaist tactile creations, Marinetti cites the plastic art technique known as polymaterialism (*polimaterico*), which painter and sculptor Umberto Boccioni had been experimenting with since 1911.[7] In a revised version of the "Tactilism" manifesto (1924), besides citing Boccioni's pioneering in the field, Marinetti also refers to the research of Charles Henry, director of the Laboratoire de Physiologie des sensations de la Sorbonne. Unlike Dadaism, Futurism pretends thus to have "scientific" foundations.

Marinetti also questioned the "distinction between the five senses" and therefore its hierarchy. He was convinced that "many other senses" would be discovered and catalogued into the future (Marinetti 2009, 269). Likewise, Sergei M. Eisenstein proposed in 1929 an original reading of the fourth dimension, namely

7 From the moment Marinetti launched his ideas on tactilism, he got himself into a heated debate with Picabia, regarding the paternity of this new art form—a discussion that was documented in both the French and the American press. See Naumann 2003.

as exploration of new sensations, of new sensorial perceptions. This fourth dimension is indispensable to the expression of overtones. In Eisenstein's view, overtones are not merely audible or visible, but instead tangible, sensible, and physically perceptible. Therefore, he claimed, "For the musical overtone (a throb) it is not strictly fitting to say: 'I hear.' Nor for the visual overtone: 'I see.' For both, a new uniform must enter our vocabulary: 'I feel'" (Eisenstein 1977, 71). Eisenstein aimed at sensitizing the spectators to new sensorial perceptions; they had to learn how to feel the overtones, as they had to learn how to think dialectically, to be able to enter the "filmic fourth dimension." Whereas Eisenstein is clearly driven by synesthesia as new mode of perception (see also his later essay "Synchronization of the Senses," 1943), Marinetti's tactilism was in the first place an overt provocation in the face of the institutionalized museum culture. It was a reversal of the traditional hierarchy of the senses and the dominant ethos: "Please don't look, but touch!" In other words, it reopened the possibilities for tactile art.

To illustrate his concept of "hand travel," Marinetti made the tactile table *Sudan-Paris*, which consisted of a wooden board on which different types of material were attached, divided into three horizontal areas or sections: top (Sudan), middle (sea), and bottom (Paris). As one can read in the manifesto of "Tactilism":

> In its *Sudan* part this table contains tactile values that are crude, greasy, rough, sharp, burning (spongy material, sandpaper, wool, pig's bristle, and wire bristle). In the *Sea* part, the table contains tactile values that are slippery, metallic, cool (different grades of emery paper). In the *Paris* part, the table contains tactile values that are soft, very delicate, caressable, warm and cool at the same time (silk, velvet, and large and small feathers). (Marinetti 2009, 267)

The *Sudan-Paris* tactile table was used as a sample during Marinetti's public lectures on tactilism. He would let the work circulate among the audience in order to test his thesis on tactile values, according to which material qualities like softness or smoothness would not automatically imply positive tactile experiences, while sharp or rough surfaces would instead trigger pleasant feelings. Art historian Caro Verbeek has tested Marinetti's thesis with contemporary audiences. In 2010, she created, with the help of artist Edward Janssen, a replica of Marinetti's tactile board. Verbeek writes:

> I have used it in many lectures and let it be passed around audiences, just like Marinetti did, always curious about the reactions of the public. Unexpectedly, the rough and sharp parts at the top often seemed to evoke positive associations, in contrast to the smooth, elaborate textures at the bottom, which frequently made people giggle, squeak, and sometimes even shiver, especially when pausing at the feathers. (2012, 229)

In other words, it seems that to increase our sensory perception we need surfaces that are rougher, coarser. This is perhaps the tactile problem of today's media devices: while touching their very smooth screens without buttons, protrusions, or roughness, we do not *feel* anything.

Verbeek's essay is entitled "Prière de toucher!" It is a direct reference to Marcel Duchamp's 1947 provocation of the same name, a book whose cover presents a female breast made out of foam surrounded by black velvet, with a blue-bordered label on the back that offers the invitation: Please touch. Both Marinetti's *Sudan-Paris* and Duchamp's *Prière de toucher* are clear examples of irreverent intervention, telling us that art is not sacred, or "untouchable." The message is unequivocal: art should not be put on a pedestal but instead made accessible and be consumed. However, these two classic examples of the historical avant-garde are not just about the tactility of Art with capital A. Marinetti's tactile table was more an element of study than a true work of art to put on display in a museum. As seen above, it was used during his lectures as a test case. Ironically, when this tactile board is exhibited today, it is always protected by a glass plate, which prevents the visitor from directly touching it and which is of course a result of the institutionalization of Futurism itself.[8] As far as Duchamp's provocation is concerned, let us not forget that his object is a book, which is a medium that you literally take in your hand. Of all the media screens and display surfaces, the book cover is—or, at least, used to be, before the introduction of the touchscreen—the most touchable and most touched. Thus, Duchamp's provocation lies not so much in touching the book (or the object of art), but rather in touching the (polystyrene) breast. In sum, it is more an infraction of an erotic taboo than an infraction of a museum rule.

Here one could make a connection with the provocative street performance *Tapp und Tastkino* (*Tap and Touch Cinema*, 1968) by Valie Export, mentioned in Chapter 1. Verbeek proposes a comparison between Export's touch cinema and Duchamp's *Prière de toucher* to mark the fundamental difference between the two provocations: whereas Export compels the audience to touch her breasts in the banal yet concrete setting of the street, Duchamp's instigation remains purely conceptual because the naked breast on the catalogue cover is unmistakably fake. In this fakeness resides also, according to Verbeek, the fundamental difference with Marinetti's sensory education: "Duchamp was not seeking a pure tactile sensation or the obtaining of knowledge through the epidermis; the role of touch in *Prière de toucher* was conceptual" (Verbeek 2012, 232). Indeed, in Duchamp's case, there is no skin-to-skin contact. Another important difference to point out is that Export's naked screen stays hidden from sight, behind the little curtain of the cardboard box that is attached around her upper body, while Duchamp's fake breast is there for the eyes too. It basically remains a visual spectacle, inviting the sense of touch to join the experience.

8 This is how I have seen Marinetti's tactile table on display, protected by a glass plate, in Brussels at one of the Europalia 2003 exhibitions: *Futurismo 1909–1926*, Musée d'Ixelles, October 16, 2003–January 11, 2004.

 Another artist to mention in this discussion of "tactile tables" is Bruno Munari. Known for his idea of organizing hands-on laboratories for children in museums and schools in the late 1970s, Munari started his career as a Futurist artist. In 1926, at age of 19, he joined the group of Milanese Futurists (Marinetti, Paolo Buzzi, Enrico Prampolini, Farfa, Fillia, et al.). In this period, which marked the so-called Second Wave of Futurism (1920s–1930s), Munari made not only his first "useless machines," which I mentioned at the beginning of this chapter, but also some "tactile tables," following Marinetti's example. Made of wooden planks, Munari's creations combined materials such as sandpaper and cork to provide different visual and tactile sensations. Of particular interest is his 1938 *Tavola tattile* (Tactile table), on which Munari provided indications of the reading tempo, as if it were a musical score: slowly (*lento*), loudly (*forte*), with velocity (*veloce*), and as quickly as possible (*velocissimo*). Yet the reading of the table, which is a long and flat piece of organic wood (122 x 13 x 3 cm), should best be executed with closed eyes, so that the travelling hand can focus on the various textures, from left to right: felt, sandpaper, different types of cotton thread and cord wrapped around a thin stick, plastic, cloth, nails, fur, and iron. Thus, like Marinetti, Munari aimed at reversing the traditional hierarchy of the senses by saying, "Please don't look, but touch!"

(Non)interactive Tactile Art

The Futurist tactile tables can be considered early forms of "interactive tactile art." With this term, I refer to art that is interactive through touch, that is, those installations where the act of touching is necessary to make the artwork "visible" (or "readable," or "hearable"): in other words, the visitor *must* intervene not only to experience the artwork but also to bring it to life. A good case in point is Janet Cardiff's sound installation *To Touch* (1993). It shares the wooden materiality of the Futurist tables, but the visitor's tactile interaction provides an auditory output. The installation consists of an old carpenter's table, which is surrounded by small audio speakers mounted on the walls of a darkened gallery space. By running their hands over the rough wooden surface of the table, visitors activate photocells that, in turn, trigger specific sound bites, ranging from human dialogue and whispers to music and environmental sounds. Despite its rough and low-tech appearance, Cardiff's installation relies on electronic circuits.

The term "interactive tactile art" is intended also to cover artworks unrelated to new technology. As Peter Weibel illustrates in "It is Forbidden Not to Touch: Some Remarks on the (Forgotten Parts of the) History of Interactivity and Virtuality" (2007), there is a whole prehistory of non-computer-based art that relies on mechanical or manual interactivity. Weibel cites various examples of kinetic or programmed art, based on (intuitive) algorithms, as for instance Gianni Colombo's *Spazio elastico* (Elastic space, 1967). Here, the visitor is invited to walk in darkness through a cube-shape stereometric structure, made of white rubber bands attached to the walls and rendered luminescent by neon light. The elasticity of the space is only achieved thanks to the presence of (and the physical contact with) the human body in motion. Likewise, Erkki Huhtamo has drawn attention to the possible past(s) of computer-based interactive art. In "Twin-Touch-Test-Redux: Media Archaeological Approach to Art, Interactivity, and Tactility" (2007), he discusses Marinetti's manifesto "Tactilism" (1921), without however looking into the Futurist tactile tables. Instead his focus is on Duchamp's readymades and his collaboration with Frederick Kiesler for the 1943 Twin-Touch-Test experiment that invited visitors to caress a chicken wire fence between their hand palms. Among the many efforts to release the "tactiloclasmic tensions" in traditional museum culture, Huhtamo (2006) also mentions the nonprofit organization Experiments in Art and Technology (E.A.T.), launched in 1967, as a creative cooperation between artists and engineers.

It is not my purpose to offer here an exhaustive overview of non-computer-based and computer-based interactive art (Kwastek 2013; Stern 2013). Instead, I want to question the notion of "interactivity" in relation to actions of screen touching. If the term "tactile art" is reserved to designate those artworks that rely on the active intervention of the user, the term "touchable art" could be used to include those works of (visual) art that may be touched but do not undergo any (visible) change when being touched. In other words, there might be action from the side of the user, but no true interaction. Yet this is a rather problematic definition because it implies making a strict distinction between action and interaction, between feedback and lack thereof. For instance, when considering again the cactus artwork described in the Introduction, *Una storia* (2012), one could claim that it is an example of "touchable art" that is not truly interactive. Yet the two girls felt some pain (feedback) when touching it. One could also argue that the artist, Federica Barbieri, did not intend to make a touchable artwork and only the children turned it into a truly tactile experience. And what about the girl touching the panels of Bill Viola's *Going Forth by Day* (2002) at the Grand Palais? Was she not truly interacting with the video installation, even if she could not change its prerecorded narrative or unfolding?

I am particularly fascinated by children's interactions with noninteractive media art installations, by their "improper" engagement with non-touchscreens which they treat as touchable screens, in short, by their appropriation of the screen as a playground. Below are four examples to illustrate this point, four anecdotes from my private life, relating to my daughter between the ages of three and six, alone as well as in the company of other children. The examples are all "unique instances," embedded in a very specific historical and artistic context, but I take them to be symptomatic of a general trend of hands-on play and imagination among young children. The first two examples concern the "manual" (that is, by hand) touching of wall installations, while the last two are about floor screens touched by feet.[9]

9 The last two examples also feature in De Rosa and Strauven 2020, while the second anecdote was previously published in Strauven 2016.

The first instance took place at the Eye Filmmuseum in Amsterdam. When in 2012 I visited the new building located on the northern bank of the river IJ, there was a projection of soap bubbles on one of the walls in the basement. My then four-year-old daughter was immediately attracted by this rather minimalistic show. She jumped up to the wall and tried to catch the bubbles, or better, to make them burst (fig. 9). Since it was not an interactive installation, but just a prerecorded loop, nothing happened to the (projected) bubbles when she managed to actually touch them. Yet my daughter did not care. She went on jumping and chasing them, following—to say it with Walter Benjamin—"the great law that presides over the rules and rhythms of the entire world of play: the law of repetition" (2005, 120). Because for the child, "repetition is the soul of play . . . nothing gives [her] greater pleasure than to 'Do it again!'" (120). Two years later, we visited the Water Design event in Bologna, Italy, where my daughter got involved in a more complex interaction with a noninteractive shower installation. Designed by Diego Grandi for Zucchetti, the installation was entitled *Get Closer!* and consisted of several exhibits, among which an animation video that was projected on a huge wall and shown in a loop. My daughter and two other girls did indeed "get closer" and started to touch the animated bathroom items that appeared on the wall. The repetition, without any variation, did not stop the girls from touching the projection. Quite the opposite. Their interaction actually increased after each repetition, when they started to understand the little narrative and tried to choreograph their actions on time, so that they could take a "real" shower by standing, at the right moment, under the image of the water splash (fig. 10).

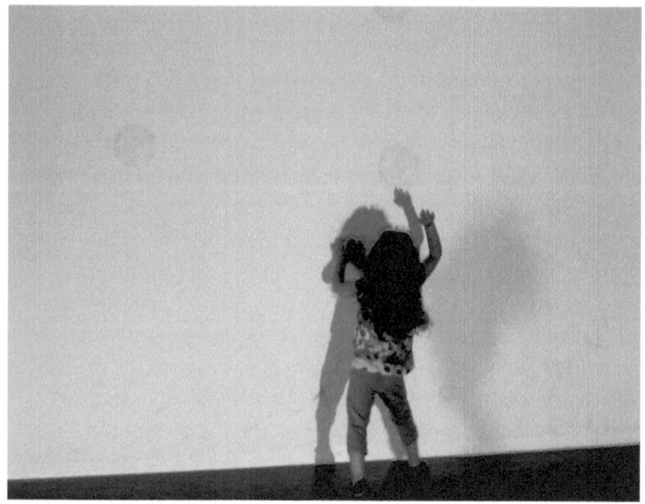

[Figure 9] Soap bubble projection, Eye Filmmuseum, Amsterdam. From author's personal archive, May 2012.

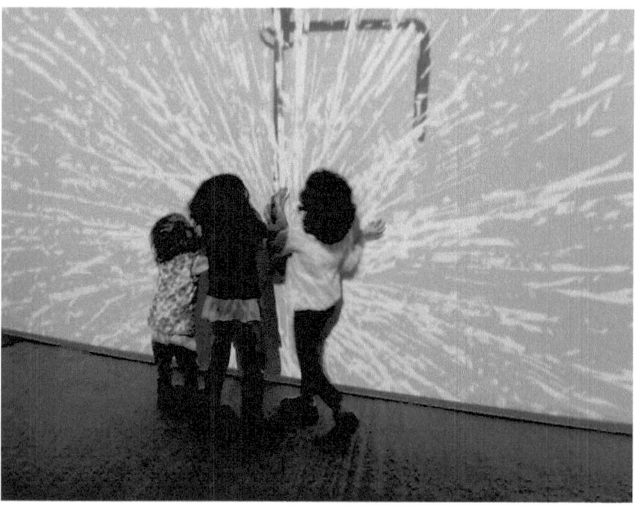

[Figure 10] *Get Closer!* by Diego Grandi, Water Design, Bologna. From author's personal archive, September 2014.

In February 2011, in a different museum context, my then three-year-old had a lot of fun by walking and jumping upon a floor projection. This took place at the Royal Belgian Institute of Natural Science in Brussels, where a noninteractive animation video was projected onto the floor, creating the pastoral setting of a green field with flowers, butterflies, snails, ducks, and birds. My daughter was soon joined by a little boy in her "feet-on" action of trampling the flowers and her attempts to catch the birds and make the ducks fly. The play quickly became an innocent, yet slightly competitive game. A similar principle was at stake in the fourth and last instance of noninteractive interaction that took place during the White Night of Bologna ArtCity in January 2015. In the inner court of Palazzo Bevilacqua, artists Marta Coletti and Larry Bird showed the second part of their installation *Spill Life* (2014–15), entitled *SPILL LIFE #2—Versus Natura* (2015).[10] At the well, located in the center of the old palazzo's court, visitors were invited to "spill" water into a receiving sink. When a certain level of water was reached it would trigger and put into motion the projection of a computer animation onto the ground. Like the floor screen of the Royal Belgian Institute of Natural Science, this stone carpet became a playground for my daughter who tried to catch the butterflies flying above the colorful flowers that continued to grow thanks to the water being poured. Even if the installation was truly interactive because of the water-spilling action, the animation video that my daughter was interacting with was again noninteractive.

Why are these children putting their hands and feet on projected images? Is it only because they expect that their touch will make something happen, like on a "real" touchscreen? Perhaps initially, yes, but when they realize that the installation is not interactive

10 The first installment took place at the Water Design event in Bologna in October 2014. The title of the installation is an obvious pun on "still life," which in Italian is called *natura morta* (dead nature). *Spill Life* is about the tension between nature and technology, between the (digitally) animated *natura morta* and the low-tech gesture of the human hand.

(and, surely, they realize it quite soon), why do they continue touching it? When observing my daughter and other children in such situations, I have often wondered whether they really believe they are interacting with the artwork. Is it not more likely that they like to *pretend* that they believe it? In other words, the screen of these media art installations becomes a play area where the act of touching is to be understood as a strategy of the pretend play, by which children are not just pretending that the work is responding to their touch, but they are also pretending that they believe this is really happening.

It is precisely this "childish" approach of tactile screen interaction that revealed to me a different way to look at the behavior of the rubes at the movie theater, in particular Michel-Ange's persistent touching of the screen in Godard's *Les Carabiniers* (1963). As discussed in Chapter 1, Godard's rube does not touch the screen only once, but continues touching it, caressing the projected image of the society lady's leg, as if he is not able to discern touching a human body from touching the screen. I would argue, however, that Michel-Ange is *pretending* that (he believes that) he touches the real body of a real woman. Like the children, he is fooling us, the film spectators, in making us believe that he believes.

The Art of Touchscreen Gestures

Opposed to these seemingly naïve but conceptually rather sophisticated actions of screen touching by children and rubes (where interaction is made possible even if the projected work is noninteractive), there are several contemporary media artists who turn the touchscreen interaction into a visual spectacle to be looked at from a safe distance, allowing thus no interaction from the side of the museumgoer or user. A telling example is the video installation *Touching Reality* (2012) by the Swiss artist Thomas Hirschhorn. In a five-minute video we watch an index finger of a female hand scrolling through images on a touchscreen device. The images are horrifying photos of mutilated, blood-covered bodies, on which the index finger, with the help of the thumb, zooms in by means of the pinching gesture (see Chapter 3). Despite the title *Touching Reality*, the index finger does not touch reality but merely glides over the material surface of a smartphone or electronic tablet; it touches a touchscreen without touching what is on display.[11] Moreover, the spectator remains excluded from the act of touching. In the art gallery, the touchscreen footage is projected on a huge wall or screen that prevents the spectator from engaging directly, tangibly, with the artwork. Like a well-disciplined museumgoer, she will contemplate from a safe distance this distant choreography of touchscreen gestures, performed by a female hand (as if it were some form of invisible labor).[12]

Here one can also make mention of art installations that fall under the denominator of "desktop cinema" and that display real-time actions executed by the artist on a computer desktop. Most often, these actions do not consist of touchscreen gestures, as in *Touching Reality*, but are instead undertaken by the clicking of a mouse. Thus, the choreography of gestures acquires a ghostly dimension because the source of the operation—that is, the hand—remains invisible. Examples of this new form of media art shot with special screen-capturing techniques are, for instance, Camille Henrot's *Grosse Fatigue* (Tiredness, 2013) and Kevin B. Lee's desktop documentary video-essays, such as

11 *Touching Reality* points to the contradiction inherent in many contemporary touchscreen-based devices that, despite their hands-on operability, create more detachment. Or, in the artist's own words, the new touchscreen gesture "seems to be a gesture of sensitivity but at the same time is a gesture of enormous distancing" (Hirschhorn 2012; my translation). See also Strauven 2016, 2018.

12 In discussion with Lisa Cartwright, during the Q&A of her keynote lecture "A Media Archaeology of the Clinical Camera-Body" at FilmForum 2018 in Gorizia, Italy, I became aware that the distancing effect of Hirschhorn's installation is indeed enhanced by the fact that the gesture is performed by a female hand, like the female hand of invisible labor in the medical context, where image analysis is often carried out by highly qualified yet invisible female assistants. See also Cartwright 1992.

Transformers: The Premake (2014). Besides integrating non-touchscreen gestures into computer-based videos, some artists also like to play with fake touchscreen gestures, imitating typical touchscreen actions, such as pointing and swiping, without using the interface of a touchscreen—not only in the exhibition setting but also during the production process. In *Belle Captive 1* (2013) by Victoria Fu, we see touchscreen gestures operating on a non-touchscreen: like in Hirschhorn's *Touching Reality* the gesture is performed by a huge index finger, but there is no physical contact with the surface upon which it is supposedly acting. It is like two layers that are not connected, but some images (pretend to) react to the touching gesture: for instance, a girl turns around when touched by the huge finger. In *Velvet Peel 1* (2015) by the same artist, fake touchscreen gestures are performed with the entire body instead of with the fingers: not only the head but also the butt are swiping (fig. 11).[13]

I would like to end this chapter with the multi-touch finger paintings by the American artist Evan Roth, who also turns the touchscreen experience into a visual spectacle. However, unlike Hirschhorn's *Touching Reality*, Roth's paintings are not so much about the (moving) gesture, but rather about its effects or traces, about what is left behind on the screen. The artist makes black ink prints of his own fingerprints on touchscreen devices, from the very simple gesture of "slide to unlock" to more complex multi-touching, such as typing with ten fingers on a keyboard or playing touchscreen games. A particularly striking example, called *Level Cleared* (2012), consists of 300 sheets of tracing paper that have the same size as the iPhone on which the game *Angry Birds* was played, hung along the wall, one by one, with the aid of a needle in each corner (fig. 12).

13 For a more in-depth discussion of these and other art installations, see De Rosa and Strauven 2020.

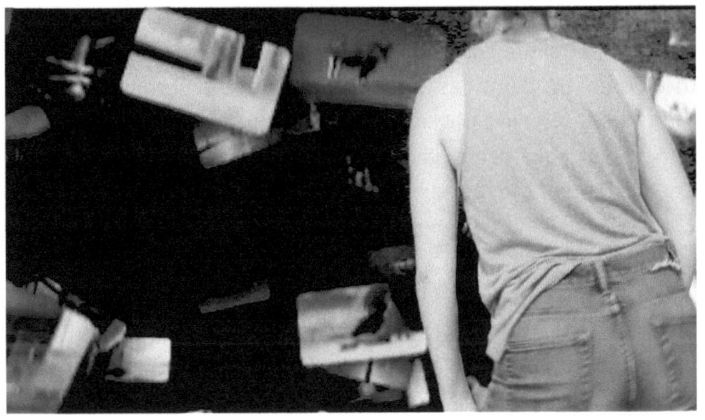

[Figure 11] *Velvet Peel 1* (Victoria Fu, 2015). Video installation with sound, 13 min. loop. Courtesy of the artist.

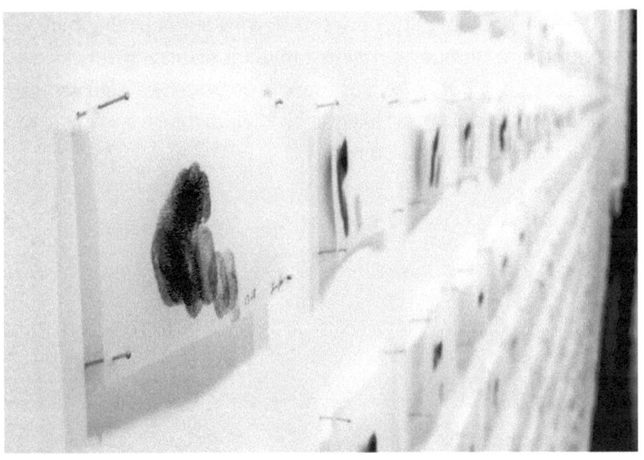

[Figure 12] *Level Cleared* (Evan Roth, 2012). Ink on tracing paper, 2230 cm x 260 cm. Photo by Vinciane Verguethen. Courtesy of XPO Gallery.

However remote this might seem from the notion of "tactile art," Roth's paintings make us aware of our actual touching of the screen. His paintings are nothing more (and nothing less) than traces of a real, physical skin-to-screen contact. The images underneath the fingers have disappeared; what remains is the visualization of the "hand travels" over the surface of the screen. Roth's work seems to reverse Duchamp's *Prière de toucher*: it addresses the eye by turning the traces of a tactile experience into a *Prière de regarder* (Please look). However, because of the presence of the needles that pierce the four corners of each paper screen, the installation foregrounds its tangibility. Even if the points of the needles are punctured into the wall, it somehow evokes a fakir's bed of nails as well as the cactus of Barbieri's *Una storia* (2012) with its spines that pierce the paper eyes.

Look, but do not touch? Or: touch, but do not look? It is exactly this tension, or ambiguity, between viewing and touching that is at work in contemporary art installations displaying touch-screen gestures. But as long as there is no "touch it!" sign, (adult) museum visitors will most likely keep their distance and observe the still dominant hands-off rule.

[3]

Sketching, Zapping, Pinching, Clicking, Thumbing

A corpus of tact: skimming, grazing, squeezing, thrusting, pressing, smoothing, scraping, rubbing, caressing, palpating, fingering, kneading, massaging, entwining, hugging, striking, pinching, biting, sucking, moistening, taking, releasing, licking, jerking off, looking, listening, smelling, tasting, ducking, fucking, rocking, balancing, carrying, weighing . . .
Jean-Luc Nancy

Hand Gestures, Hands-On Gestures

A wide variety of tactile screen gestures have already passed in review: pricking (cactus), ticking against the wall (bubbles), stomping on the ground (meadow), thumbing (flipbook), grabbing and tearing (early rube films), caressing with full palm (Michel-Ange), hugging (Joe), sword slashing (Don Quixote), breast tapping (Export), hand travelling (Marinetti), pinching (Hirschhorn), and butt and head swiping (Fu). This list shows that the notion of "screen gestures" is not limited to the hands, but can involve other specific body parts (such as the feet) or the full body. However, as noted in the Introduction, the concrete act of screen touching is usually executed by the hand and, in particular, by the index finger and the thumb. Because of the operability of the fingers during the process of screen touching, it is possible to talk about "digital gestures" (that is, gestures performed by digits) long before the introduction of the computer screen. In fact, as I will briefly discuss at the end of Chapter 4, the projection table of the camera obscura or the sheet of the magic lantern show were such surfaces for "digital gestures," to be understood as actions of direct contact.

On the connection between digit (as finger) and digital (as numerical), Mary Ann Doane observed that—besides the obvious gesture of counting to which fingers lend themselves—there is "the finger's preeminent status as the organ of touch, of contact, of sensation, of connection with the concrete" (2007, 142). Therefore, she adds, "the unconscious of the digital, that most abstract of logics/forms of representation, is touch" (142). In fact, "digitality" in its modern meaning and usage tends to repress this sense of touch, which I intend to bring to the fore again by putting the emphasis on the gesture as an action of direct contact.

The gesture is not just an action but rather the process of an action, which creates a contact between objects and humans, between screens and users. The gesture mediates/communicates. Defined by Agamben as the "exhibition of a mediality," or also the "communication of a communicability" (2000, 57–58), the gesture constitutes a morphological element of our body language.[1] Especially manual and digital gestures, but also facial ones, are expressive units in our interaction with other actants, both human and nonhuman. Impatient computer users might, for instance, express anger when an application is not responding, by increasing the pressure of the fingers on the keyboard or making furious grimaces at the screen.

About the interpretation of gestures, Vilém Flusser has observed that the "more information a gesture contains, the more difficult it apparently is for a receiver to read it" (2014, 8). In other words, an "empty" or information-low gesture communicates better than a complicated rich one. Flusser compares it with the deciphering of a code. A nice illustration of how gestures

1 It is beyond the scope of this book to look into sign language for the hearing impaired, which is a discussion à part.

convey "coded" information in very specific contexts is Bruno Munari's *Supplement to the Italian Dictionary* (first published in 1958). Leaving out the most vulgar and obscene gestures, Munari aimed at documenting and making comprehensible to foreigners visiting Italy the rich gesturality used by his compatriots. Re-issued with the title *Speak Italian: The Fine Art of the Gesture* in an Italian-English bilingual edition, the pocket-sized lexicon with its charming black-and-white hand illustrations features on its cover one of the most typical gestures of Italian communication, which derives from Neapolitan and is widely used in the entire nation: "Che vuoi?" ("What do you expect?").[2] Munari describes and explains the gesture as follows:

> The tips of all fingers of one hand are brought sharply together to form an upward-pointing cone. The hand can either be held motionless or be shaken more or less violently up and down, according to the degree of impatience expressed. (2015, 22)

Of particular interest, in light of this study on the touchscreen, are the Italian/Munarian gestures that use the hand as a kind of tablet or media surface. Most obvious are the hand signs meaning "to read" and "to write" that both evoke similarities with touchscreen actions, respectively swiping, whereby "the index finger of the right hand runs across the left hand as on a page" (86), and pen computing, whereby "the right hand pretends to write on the left hand, or vice versa" (84). Less obvious for non-native speakers is the gesture meaning "to insist," whereby "the

2 The gesture even has a Wikipedia entry, which gives a more literal translation: "What do you want?" The entry adds other Italian interpretations: "Ma che vuoi?" (But what do you want?), "Ma che dici?" or "Ma che stai dicendo?" (But what are you saying?), or simply "Che?" (What?). See https://en.wikipedia.org/wiki/Che_vuoi. According to *Italy Magazine*, who asked D&G male models to perform some of the typical Italian hand gestures, it is more appropriate to translate the "Che vuoi?" sign as "WTF." See https://www.italymagazine.com/learn-italian-hand-gestures-translating-dg-models-written-italian.

 index finger jabs rhythmically on the palm of the other hand" (106), as if on a nonresponsive smartphone screen. Yet the Italian gesture is not so much about a repetitive action by the speaker (or hand gesticulator) but rather aims at expressing annoyance about the interlocutor who does not know when to stop (and keeps on insisting).

In this chapter I do not intend to provide a comprehensive lexicon of hand gestures, which could consist of a cross-reading of Munari's gestural dictionary, Flusser's theory of gestures, and Jean-Luc Nancy's "corpus of tact," but instead I will focus on some typical media gestures that are executed by the hand and connected to the screen. The hand gestures I am interested in are, thus, all "hands-on": both in the sense of acting upon and of putting literally one's hands on something. More in particular, I will look at hand gestures related to (film) animation, TV zapping, and various hands-on operations of digital devices, ranging from the computer mouse to the smartphone's touchscreen. I will focus on these media gestures as concrete actions, or processes, and on the dexterity of our hands and digits while executing these actions.

A Praxeology of Media Gestures

Rooted in the work of French philosophers Louis Bourdeau and Alfred Espinas, praxeology as the theory of human action is to be considered as a science that incorporates different fields of science. Very generally, it departs from the notion that human actions are driven by purposeful behavior, as opposed to reflexes or involuntary bodily movements. Here I would like to make a connection with the notion of "thick description" as American anthropologist Clifford Geertz borrowed it from British philosopher Gilbert Ryle. In his canonical text of 1973, Geertz reflects upon Ryle's example of the difference between a twitch (as an involuntary muscle contraction of the eyelids) and a wink (as a conspiratorial signal). Geertz observes that the "two movements are, as movements, identical" (1973, 6). That is, "from an I-am-a-camera, 'phenomenalistic' observation" (6) of the movements alone, without context, one could not tell the difference. Yet when considering the two movements in their specific context, relying on concrete experiences, one knows that the difference is vast. The wink is an intentional action; it is a gesture, a gesture of communication. As Geertz puts it, "The winker is . . . indeed communicating in a quite precise and special way" (6).[3]

Apart from discussions of praxeology and reflexology, I suggest the need to address the technicity of gestures. Focusing on touch as a gesture, as a process or action of *touching*, this chapter will emphasize the bodily techniques involved, in particular those executed or practiced by the hand, from shadow casting to pencil drawing, from operating a TV remote control to clicking a computer mouse. It should be stressed that the dexterity of our hands and digits in their "encounter" or interaction with tactile devices is a historical given. Following French sociologist Marcel Mauss, bodily techniques are tied to their historical time and societal-educational context. In *Techniques du corps* (*Techniques of the Body*, originally published in 1934), Mauss looks at the specific techniques of swimming and walking, which both changed over time due to changes in technical instruction (such as new diving techniques) and fashion (as showcased by cinema).[4]

As a very simple gesture of communication, we can think here of the handshake, which due to the COVID-19 pandemic has

3 The full sentence reads: "The winker is communicating, and indeed communicating in a quite precise and special way: (1) deliberately, (2) to someone in particular, (3) to impart a particular message, (4) according to a socially established code, and (5) without cognizance of the rest of the company" (Geertz 1973, 6).

4 Insisting on the social nature of habits (from the Latin *habitus*), Mauss writes: "These 'habits' do not just vary with individuals and their imitations, they vary especially between societies, educations, proprieties and fashions, prestiges. In them we should see the techniques and work of collective and individual practical reason rather than, in the ordinary way, merely the soul and its repetitive faculties" (1973, 73).

 disappeared from the landscape of social interaction, tentatively replaced by elbow bumping. In this chapter, I will look at specific media techniques in which the body, as "man's first and most natural instrument" (Mauss 1973, 75), uses other technical objects, such as a pen, mouse, smartphone. For instance, techniques of writing (handwriting, typewriting, texting, thumbing, etc.) change over time and sometimes cause physiological changes in the hand and its digits. The use of the smartphone, on the other hand, gives shape to various techniques of the body: texting (as writing) vs. calling (as speaking), looking down (as reading) vs. holding close to one's ear (as listening). Its hands-free devices, such as ear buds with microphone, gave the user's body more freedom of movement, and in particular of gesticulation, which, at the beginning of the twenty-first century, blurred our distinction, at least at first sight ("from an I-am-a-camera, 'phenomenalistic' observation," to repeat Geertz's phrasing), between a crazy vagabond and a busy entrepreneur (Elsaesser 2003; Strauven 2013).

As pointed out by Benoît Turquety, in the French language the plural term *techniques* refers, as evidenced by Mauss's study, to technical objects and procedures, whereas *technologie* is the science that studies these techniques. In English the situation is quite different, with *technology* demarcating "the realm of the hardware-related, the machines, and their components" and *techniques* denoting "what concerns gestures, practices, and the conscious choices implied on the operators' side"; referring to Rick Altman's study on sound, the microphone is a matter of technology, while the practice of miking is "a set of techniques" (Turquety 2018, 242). In other words, the English term "technique" is more restricted than the French one, as it separates the gesture from the machine (or technical object). In what follows, I will adopt a broad notion of gesture, which comes close to the French notion of technique, as a concrete (bodily) action or procedure involving (technical) objects.

Performing/Animating Hands

In the previous chapter, I proposed reading the performance of the female hand of Hirschhorn's installation *Touching Reality* (2012) not only in terms of specific touchscreen gestures, such as swiping and pinching, but also as a choreography of cold detachment, or as a form of invisible labor, similar to that of the female technician in the medical context (see also Cartwright 1992). In a very limited way, the hand also animates the images on display: swiping makes images appear and disappear, while pinching magnifies and resizes them. Both are hands-on hand gestures that directly act upon the screen. As I will discuss below, the technique of pinching is a curious case of what Mauss calls "habit" (from the Latin *habitus*).

Concerning the "prehistory" and early history of cinema, some obvious hand performances are worth mentioning as techniques of both screen touching and image animation. In most cases the screen is not touched directly by the hand, but the hand's performance is directly responsible for what happens on the screen. For instance, the art of shadow play (shadowgraphy or ombromanie) relies on performing hands that cast shadows upon a screen; if the hands are not physically touching the screen, their shadows do. Likewise, the hand of the lantern-slide projectionist is instrumental in the techniques of projecting images on screen and creating special effects, such as dissolving views.

Moreover, as Lisa Cartwright discusses, projection was experienced as a source of pleasure, as "a process that was not simply in the service of making visible but which also entailed the pleasure of holding and manipulating the object at hand" (2011, 448). This physical relationship extended to the entire body, as the slides were stored in a wooden box that the itinerant projectionist strapped on his back, travelling from town to town, the box becoming "an extension of the body through its habitual wearing and carrying" (450).

 Besides the live shows of the slide-lantern projectionist, another popular form of "pre-cinematic" entertainment was the so-called chalk talk, equally live and hands-on, this time with the hand truly in action in front of the audience. The chalk talk consisted of a lecture that was accompanied by live, real-time, illustration on a chalkboard. Some performers excelled in rapidly transforming simple images into new images, like a magic trick, before the eyes of their audiences. These performances came to be known as "lightning sketches" or "lightning cartoons." The gesture of sketching, of drawing with chalk on a black surface, returns as a central motif in early animated films, made by professional chalk-talkers and cartoonists, such as James Stuart Blackton, Winsor McCay, and Georges Méliès. Most of these films combined a documentary dimension with the basic trick of stop motion. For instance, Blackton's *The Enchanted Drawing* (1900) first shows the cartoonist in medium full shot performing lightning sketches with charcoal on a white sheet, only to surprise the audience with the trick of grabbing his own drawings of a wine bottle and goblet and transforming them into real objects. Blackton's later *Humorous Phases of Funny Faces* (1906) further accentuates these hands-on gestures, featuring the hand variously drawing and erasing in close-up, without showing the full body of the cartoonist. Here, the lightning sketches truly "come to life," as they are put into motion, animated by means of the stop motion trick, whether or not in combination with the trick of reverse action.

Regarding this context of early animation, Edwin Carels has called attention to the pioneering role of the French caricaturist Émile Cohl (pseudonym of Émile Eugène Jean Louis Courtet), whose *Fantasmagorie* (*A Fantasy*, 1908) is "the first film where this documentary contextualisation is absent, and where the lively movement of the line drawings is more important than the figuration" (Carels 2012, 38). Carels adds: "For Émile Cohl, action was more important than representation, or as Panofsky would put it: animation is about space and time, not about the human figure" (38). Nevertheless, this first fully animated film also contains two instances of the animator's performing hand, first at the very beginning to draw the lines before they are coaxed into movement and then toward the end to glue together the "broken" stick figure after it has fallen out of a window (fig. 13).[5]

From the shadow play to the lightning sketch, the performing hand is clearly the hand of the creator, of the person creating the spectacle to be looked at, as opposed to the hand of the user, of the person putting his or her hands on the media device or artwork (as in the case of the Futurist tactile tables). More examples of cinematic hand scenarios could be mentioned here, from Claude Autant-Lara's *Faits Divers* (1923) to Robert Bresson's *Pickpocket* (1959), from Richard Serra's *Hand Catching Lead* (1968) to Bill Viola's *Four Hands* (2001). Or one could look more closely at the invisible hand at work over the course of the film production process, whether in animation or live action. For instance, as far as the editing process is concerned, Harun Farocki's *Schnittstelle* (*Interface*, 1995) demonstrates the operational differences between film editing and video editing in terms of fingertip activity, showing in close-up, on the one hand, fingers touching the filmstrip to feel the cut and the glue and, on the other, those pushing the buttons of the video editing console without physical contact with the video tape (fig. 14).

In the next sections, I propose to shift the focus from the maker's point of view to the user's act of screen touching. I will discuss hand gestures in relation to the TV set, the computer monitor, and cell phone screen, which oscillate between direct and indirect touch, always keeping in mind the concrete encounter between user and media object.

5 *Fantasmagorie* plays with some typical film genres of the early days, such as the chase film. Most remarkably, it starts at the movie theater where an animated film is shown and a woman wearing a very sumptuous and huge feathery hat gets a seat in the front row to the great annoyance of the gentleman behind her. Cohl anticipates here D. W. Griffith's *Those Awful Hats* (1909), which can be said to belong to the genre of "didactic" rube films.

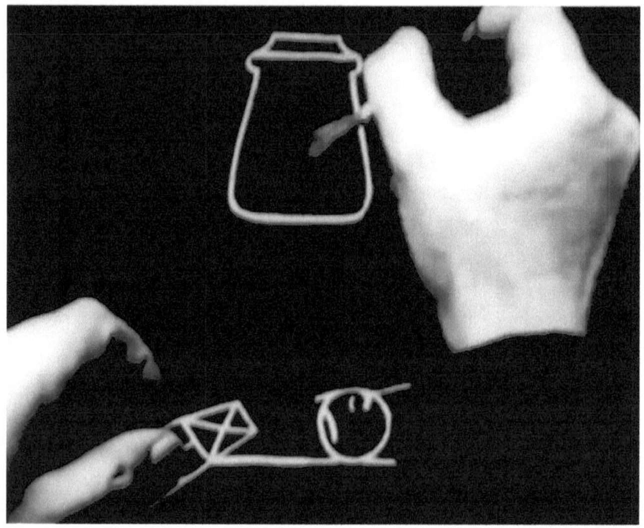

[Figure 13] *Fantasmagorie* (Émile Cohl, 1908).

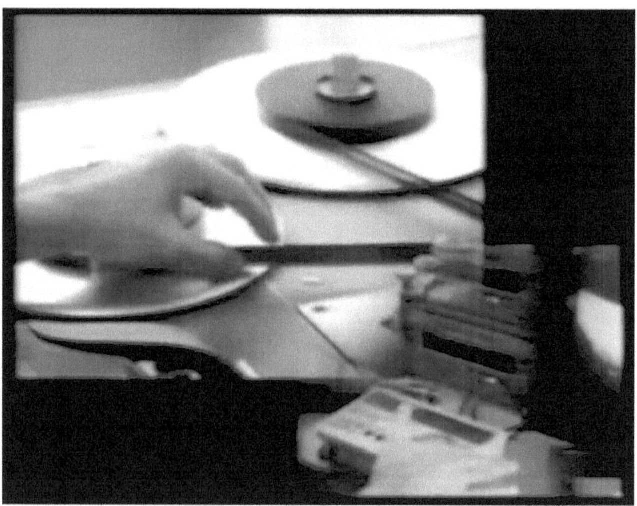

[Figure 14] *Schnittstelle* (Harun Farocki, 1995).

Hands-On TV Watching

On September 11, 1982, the French TV channel Antenne 2 broadcast the first episode of *Télétactica*, a curious series for children that was truly hands-on. Created by Albert Champeaux and Jean-Paul Blondeau, the program came with a kit of plastic geometric figures, the so-called *télétacs*, available in bookstores. Children could interact in each episode by placing the *télétacs*, at specific scripted moments, on the cartoon images on screen. The *télétacs* would stick to the TV screen thanks to its static electricity, literally put into effect as a McLuhanian medium of tactility. A typical challenge was, for instance, to get a little box up to a chalet at the top of a mountain. You simply had to wait for a dotted line figure to appear on screen, then select the corresponding *télétac* (in this case a big circle) and stick it on the dotted lines. In this way, the circle would turn into a hot air balloon that would bring the box to the chalet.[6]

Whereas *Télétactica* is an example of closeness and direct screen touching that for all its novelty was a dead-end in TV history, the remote control is a hands-on practice from a distance that has endured. As a technique, or televisual gesture, the practice of flipping through channels is connected not only to the technical object of the remote control but also to the phenomenon of TV advertisement.[7] According to the *Oxford English Dictionary*, the term "zapping," as a "practice of skipping advertisements when watching television programmes," emerged only in the early 1970s. To a certain degree, this new practice turned TV viewing

6 See the demonstration given by the INA Archive: https://www.youtube.com/watch?v=utZ3Ok6YbU4. I would like to thank Laetitia Gendre for bringing this "forgotten" piece of French TV history to my attention.

7 The history of the remote control can be traced back to the late nineteenth century to the figure of Nikola Tesla. Equally relevant are the histories of broadcasting and television advertisement, which started in the early 1940s in the United States. What is believed to be the first TV commercial was a 10-second spot that displayed a picture of a Bulova clock superimposed on a US map, accompanied by the voice-over, "America runs on Bulova time."

into a more tactile experience, although *away* from the screen. As Lorenz Engell similarly observes with reference to McLuhan's theory of touch,

> The small size of the television screen makes it a feature not of distance but of closeness; its coarse pixel structure leads to a scanning procedure in perception that has more to do with haptic than visual activities. The gaze itself becomes tactile. This idea is even more relevant if one takes into account the use of the remote control, in which the fingertip takes over the leading function from the gaze. (Engell 2013, 327)

Zapping can be a two-hand operation, with one palm holding the remote control and the index finger of the other hand pushing the buttons, or it can involve a single hand using the thumb as a controller. Engell points out how the single-hand use of the remote control brought about a change in the relationship between index finger and thumb, a tendency that will be pushed further by more recent media devices, such as the computer mouse and the touchscreen. He writes:

> In the use of the remote control, the old order of the thumb as counterweight and the index has already been partially subverted. Either you need two of your hands to operate it (in this case the index can keep its function) or you have to turn your hand around, take palm and fingers as solid ground for the remote control, and use the thumb both as deictic tool and means of causation. (334)

In other words, the will or intention, traditionally correlated with the use of the index finger, is conferred instead to the thumb when we zap using only one hand.

From Zaptitude to Zoomtitude

The original meaning of the verb "to zap," however, is not to operate a remote control but, according to the *Oxford English Dictionary*, "to kill, esp. with a gun; to deal a sudden blow to." Its etymology is onomatopoeic: *zap* imitates the sound of shooting. This echoic usage probably finds its origin in early comic strips, which were rather violent. In today's computer jargon, zapping means "to erase or change (an item in a program)" (*Oxford English Dictionary*). This is confirmed by *The Jargon File*, where the verb is associated with spicy food that can make non-hackers suffer, alongside more specific meanings of erasing, resetting, modifying, or correcting "with a debugger or binary patching tool" and "fry[ing] a chip with static electricity" (Raymond 2004). The connotation remains, thus, mainly destructive.

This original meaning of zapping as killing allows making a connection with TV watching as "killing time." As Thomas Elsaesser observed in the mid 1990s, reflecting on fifty years of television culture:

> The fact that Western Europe has been without a war, a famine, a plague or any other event that really went to the heart of everyday experience for precisely these 50 years of television . . . means that we have the luxury of building a culture and a cultural memory of the banal, the everyday, of what interests ordinary people, what amused them and what moved them, what they saw in the movies and on TV: a history of leisure and of "killing time," alongside the history of all the killing fields on television. (1994, 58–59)

Elsaesser's remark must be placed in a pre-9/11 world, when TV watching was more about cultivating idleness than about instilling panic (through breaking news and looped disaster footage). On the other hand, the tragic events of 9/11 were somehow anticipated by Belgian video artist Johan Grimonprez's *dial H-I-S-T-O-R-Y* (1997). This controversial video artwork looks at hijacking through the mode of zapping, which Grimonprez considers a form of "iconoclastic pleasure" (Bal-Blanc and Margerin 1998). But the viewer no longer needs to do any channel surfing because it is already done by the TV channels themselves: "No need to zap though, the poetry is right there on CNN." Hence

 Grimonprez suggests watching this TV poetry *on mute* and "tun[ing] the stereo to some inflight groove" (Obrist 2011, 268).

With the advent of channels such as CNN and MTV in the 1980s, something profound has happened. Grimonprez talks about an epistemological shift. The practice of TV zapping has led to a new attitude, which he proposes to call "zaptitude." In a 1999 interview, the artist explains:

> A zapping mode splices blood with ketchup, like CNN: images of war cut with strawberry ice-cream. It would rather point at an epistemological shift in how a "zaptitude" has transformed the way we look at reality. A jumpy fast-forward vision has replaced our conventional models of perception and experience. Sometimes I don't even know anymore if we're still in the middle of the commercial break or whether the film has already started. Soon we'll be mistaking reality for a commercial break. (Obrist 2011, 271)

dial H-I-S-T-O-R-Y portrays mostly airports, airplanes, and people (both hijackers and victims), but we also see images of buildings collapsing and being hit by planes. It is a destructive process. But it is also, importantly, a process of de-contextualization (and re-contextualization). Grimonprez explains how the "theme of hijacking planes can be read as a metaphor for the hijacking of images out of their context" (Bal-Blanc and Margerin 1998). Zapping, thus, destroys and de-contextualizes. More generally, one could say that the televisual mode of zapping has the effect of fragmenting both our reality and our imagination.

At the beginning of the twenty-first century, we might wonder if we are still in the episteme of "zaptitude." Rather than confronting channel surfing (TV) with net surfing (computer), I propose to look at the practice of zooming and describe what can be considered as a shift to "zoomtitude." By zooming I mean *digital* zooming, which ranges from high professional filmmaking to daily life practices by means of simple tools, such as the zoom levers of nonprofessional digital cameras, the magnifying tool in software photo-editing programs, the zooming in (+) and out (-) tool of Google Maps, etc. Zooming has become a very common practice, especially when engaging with pictures on the small screens of our mobile devices. Today's digital *flâneur* uses the zoom option to get closer to (or farther away from) a specific location, turning a visual map into a tactile field. The gesture of pinching, whereby one touches the screen with two fingers, either away from each other to zoom in or toward each other to zoom out, operates as a visual form of tactility. Zooming by pinching allows digging into the image, into its countless digital layers. One touches the screen to *see* better, to get closer and penetrate the image.

Symptomatic of today's "zoomtitude" is the phenomenon of the so-called cosmic zoom in contemporary cinema. For instance, the opening and end credits of *Burn After Reading* (Coen Brothers, 2008) take us from an earth view to the CIA Headquarters in Langley, Virginia, and back again. Another famous example is the opening zoom of *Moulin Rouge!* (Baz Luhrman, 2001), which brings the film spectator to the heart of Paris and to the entrance of the cabaret. This second example is taken from Jennifer Barker, who borrows the term "cosmic zoom" from Garrett Stewart to discuss how it visually renders the "phenomenological process of syn-aesthetic experience" (Barker 2009a, 313). According to Stewart, the cosmic zoom is "a technique of digital rhetoric capable of drastic shifts in scale—as when plummeting from satellite-range to a facial close-up, or lifting back out again" (2007, 283). The cosmic zoom is a digital (or "postfilmic") zoom. Unlike the optical zoom, it does not flatten the image; on the contrary, it allows for a true travelling through countless layers, thanks to new laws of parallax. Unlike the optical zoom, the digital zoom makes it possible to look behind the object we zoom into and opens up new perspectives that broaden our vision.[8]

8 As such, the cosmic zoom is closer to the filmic dolly shot or crane shot because we can change direction and physically move through space.

 As Barker observes, the cosmic zoom bears resemblance to synesthesia because it operates between the sense of vision and the sense of touch:

> We do not *see* the spaces of the "past" as much as *feel* them rush by as we plunge through them. As an effect and event, the cosmic zoom is not only somewhere between the conventional zoom and the travelling, tracking, or dolly shot; it is also somewhere between optical and kinetic movement, and more generally between vision and touch. (2009a, 312–13)

Yet the film spectator does not actually touch the layers through which the cosmic zoom moves. The viewer can see or even feel a delving into the digital depth of the image, but that does not mean that the operation is under the control of the viewer's hands. Zooming in and out by pinching a touchscreen, however, is truly hands-on.

To Pinch Is to Seize with Love

Pinching is a multi-touch gesture, primarily intended to be carried out by the index finger and thumb jointly, but other fingers can also be involved or take over. The gesture is directly linked to capacitive touchscreen technology, popularized by the introduction of Apple's iPhone in 2007. Before the wide adoption of the smartphone, the competitive touchscreen technology was the resistive screen, implemented and promoted by Blackberry and Nokia. The resistive screen is composed of two layers of conductive material that, when you touch the screen, come into contact with one another enabling the device to determine the location of the touch. The advantage of this type of screen is that you can operate it with normal winter gloves on (which in Finland, Nokia's home country, was an asset not to be underestimated). The capacitive screen, on the other hand, opened up the possibilities for multi-touch gestures for the ungloved hand, as it requires "the intimacy of the bare finger as a working principle" (Kaerlein 2012, 184).[9]

As Alexandra Schneider observes, Steve Jobs cleverly decided to introduce a new vocabulary for the innovative Apple gestures when launching the iPhone in January 2007. The expression "pinching" was a real find, even if it finally did not catch on with the general public. In Apple language, to pinch means to touch the screen with a soft and gentle gesture whereby two fingers either move toward each other (*pinch-in*) to zoom out or pull away from each other (*pinch-out*) to zoom in. The delicateness Jobs envisioned for these digital movements counters, of course, the "habit" of pinching as a painful gesture. Schneider writes: "The idea of being 'pinched' does not necessarily evoke the sense of a tender touch, and the etymology of the corresponding French verb *pincer* (from which the English word derives) confirms this intuition" (2012, 54). One could indeed say that we are pinching the skin of our mobile device, that we literally squeeze it between our fingers, because of its capacitive (or skin-based) technology. However, as Schneider points out, the French verb *pincer* originally also meant *saisir d'amour*, referring to "a state of being touched (or moved) by a feeling of love" (54). So, interestingly enough, Jobs's twenty-first-century neologism goes back to a centuries-old expression (from the twelfth century, to be exact).

Even if it does not fully reflect our personal experiences of daily screen interaction, I would like to emphasize the (possible) origins of these terms, with "zapping" falling into the category of violent gestures and "pinching" in contrast belonging to the register of love. Pinching intended as a tender touch, as a soft caressing of the touchscreen, evokes the language-game that my daughter invented at the age of three when she "robbed" me of my iPad and named it her "aaienpet." As narrated in the Introduction, this

9 In COVID-19 times, I experienced that latex gloves, though not to the same degree as special capacitive touchscreen gloves, allow for some simple gestures such as sliding-to-unlock the iPhone.

phonetic interpretation of the "i" of iPad works only in Dutch: it sounds like the verb *aaien* (pronunciation: /ˈaːi̯ə(n)/), which means "caressing." Thus, the term "aaienpet" could be freely translated as "tablet to caress," a not far-fetched interpretation since it is confirmed by the activity of caressing itself. It is a good example of how language is woven into an action, as implied by Wittgenstein's notion of "language-game" (*Sprachspiel*). According to Wittgenstein, the meaning of words depends on the language-game in which they are used; so, the same word, for instance "to pinch" or "I," can change meaning when becoming part of a specific activity. As the philosopher states, "the term '*language-game*' is meant to bring into prominence the fact that the *speaking* of language is part of an activity, or of a form of life" (Wittgenstein 1986, §23).

The glass surface of Apple's iPhone and its successors and competitors is, however, too smooth to be fully tactile. Or better: it still relies too much on the eye, for we cannot operate our smartphones without looking at them, as we could instead in the "good old days" of the first cellular phones with a 12-button keypad. As I will discuss further below in this chapter, the eye dependency of touchscreen gestures has led to the looking-down attitude of today's *phubbers* (neologism from phone + snubbing). The antisocial trend of phone snubbing is generally seen as a disturbing form of addiction that could, however, also be read as a love affair with a technical, touch-based object, as a state of being touched ("pinched") by a feeling of love.[10]

At the extreme other end of the spectrum is the solution of Google Glass: a touchless wearable. Google Glass reintroduces the screen in the shape of (reading) glasses. It is a screen that is placed between the user and the world, to be looked through and

10 This double reading of the user's relationship with her smartphone is emblematic of the "irreducible ambivalence" of technology in general and of the twenty-first-century technological process in particular (Stiegler 2012). For technology is "both enhancing human capabilities and delegating them with detrimental or 'toxic' effects" (Kaerlein 2012, 188).

looked at, but not to be touched. Yet it is only partly a hands-free device: besides the round power button located on the inner right side of the device, which must be pressed to turn the Glass on or off, there is also a touchpad on the outer right side, near your temple. In fact, alongside voice control, Google Glass introduces a whole range of new head and hand gestures. In 2011, Google filed a patent on "hand gestures to signify what is important," to be connected to and recognized by its wearable head-mounted display (Gomez et al. 2013). For instance, the "field of view" hand-gesture, which consists of two L shapes formed by index finger and thumb of both hands, serves to "frame" something and take a snapshot. Coming back to the register of love, there is also the popular hand heart that Google Glass users can use in front of any object or image to "like" it (fig. 15a–b).

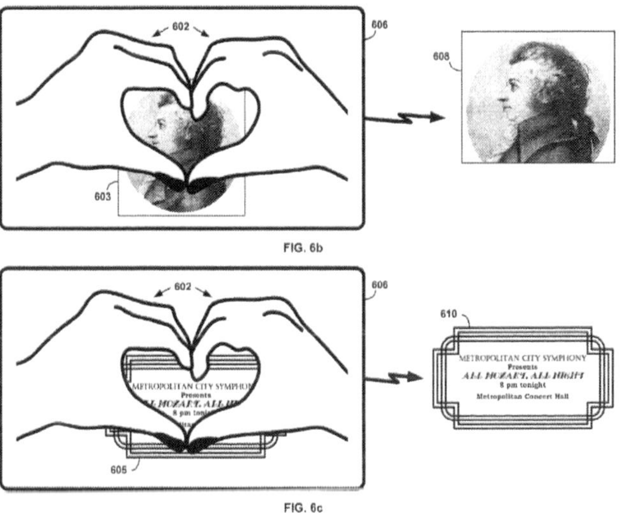

[Figure 15a–b] "Hand gestures to signify what is important." Google patent, October 15, 2013. https://patents.google.com/patent/US8558759B1/.

 The very first claim of the Google patent, filed on July 8, 2011, and registered under the number US 8,558,759 on October 15, 2013, reads as follows:

> In a wearable head-mounted display (HMD), a computer-implemented method comprising: making a determination that video data from a video camera of the wearable HMD includes a hand gesture forming an area bounded by two hands in a shape of a symbolic heart; determining that the two hands are associated with the wearable HMD via analysis of the video data including the hand gesture; generating an image from the video data, wherein the image includes the area bounded by the two hands; matching the shape of the symbolic heart with a predetermined action associated with the image; and executing the predetermined action on a processor of the wearable HMD. (Gomez et al. 2013)

Especially widespread and well-liked among the youngest generations of media users who do not wear smart glasses, the hand heart has become a true media gesture, or even screen gesture, usually performed in the air, that is, between users and screens. It has become an interface for framing not only objects in front of you but also yourself. Or one could call it a double-hand screen, which enables you to display pictures, including your own portrait, as you "curl the index fingers on both hands with the thumbs pointing down and join them to make a heart shape" (Meltzer 2011). It is a sign of approval, a sign of love, that can also be made by two users together.

The Clicking Hand Cursor

In the mid 1960s, Jean Baudrillard observed that the hand was "no longer the prehensile organ that focuses effort" but instead "nothing more than the abstract *sign* of manipulability" (2005, 55). The idea of an effortless hand gesture brings to mind again Hirschhorn's *Touching Reality* (2012), where the index finger of a female hand glides, impassively, over the images of the bloody bodies mutilated by war. Here the hand seems to be reduced to the level of a sign, a sign of detachment, of lack of engagement. It is not abstract insofar as it can be identified as a female hand; however, it could be anyone's hand, travelling over any kind of images. Hirschhorn observes that this "Apple gesture" does not distinguish, for instance, between war pictures and holiday pictures; it remains the very same gesture, super cold ("hyper froid") and uncommitted ("non-engagé") (2012).

In 1964, around the same time that Baudrillard made the above observation, Douglas Engelbart invented the computer mouse as a device for selecting text on the computer screen.[11] The cursor or mouse pointer, called a "bug" by Engelbart's team, was originally a "stick arrow, about the height of a single character, pointing straight up" (Reimer 2005). The diagonally oriented arrow-shaped cursor appeared with the Xerox Alto computer in 1973. The hand cursor icon, which turned the hand literally into an "abstract sign of manipulability," made its appearance in the early Macintosh design of the 1980s. We need to distinguish between the open-hand cursor, designed by Susan Kare for the original 1984 Macintosh, and the pointing-finger cursor, introduced in 1987 with the release of HyperCard (fig. 16a). The former was designed to grab and pan, while the latter designated the ability to navigate stacks and later to click hyperlinks. Of course, as we know, it is not the hand cursor itself but the hand on the mouse that clicks. Nevertheless, the hand cursor has become the sign of this screen interaction or operability. In the late 1990s, before the launch of Mac OS 9, the computer mouse's operations were connected to a gloved-hand cursor, the so-called Mickey Mouse hand pointer, characterized by three black vertical lines on its back (fig. 16b). In 2012, with the release of Mac OS X 10.7.3, this gloved-hand cursor was restyled for high-density displays (fig. 16c). The glove

11 Besides the mouse, Engelbart's team tested also the light pen and the joystick as possible "display-selection," "cursor-controlling," or "bug-positioning" devices (English et al. 1967). For a more extensive history of the computer mouse, see for instance Atkinson 2007.

 appears, for instance, when the arrow-shaped cursor hovers over buttons or clickable hyperlinks when browsing online.

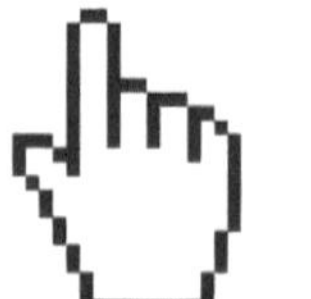
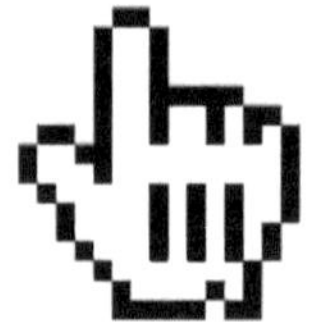
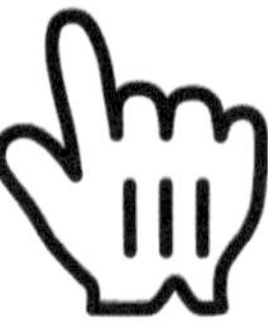

[Figure 16a–c] Evolution of Apple's hand pointer from the 1987 to 2012 until the release of Mac OS X 10.7.3. https://osxdaily.com/2012/02/07/high-dpi-cursors-found-in-os-x-10-7-3/.

As discussed on *User Experience Stack Exchange*, an Internet forum for UX researchers and experts, Mickey's hand had already been used as a "pointer" since the 1930s, notably as a clock hand to indicate the time on the Mickey Mouse watch. It is also well known that Mickey and Minnie made their first appearance on the silver screen without gloves, in the short cartoon *Steamboat Willie* (1928). Mickey was given white gloves as a way of contrasting his naturally black hands with his black body. Arguably, Apple's gloved-hand cursor is a trace of America's racist heritage: it is a normalized white hand, which is also clearly right-handed. As Philippa Jones observes,

> The icon is evidently a right hand. This is deduced from the fact that we are viewing it from the front with the palm behind and invisible. . . . So the hand's usability credentials rest on the depiction of a right hand with its index finger on the point of clicking a mouse. (2011, 238)

Pointing and clicking are the two actions undertaken by the cursor, two actions that the hand cannot fulfill directly upon the screen, but which it commands via the mouse; in other words, these are indirect hands-on gestures, performed by a hand sign or arrow.

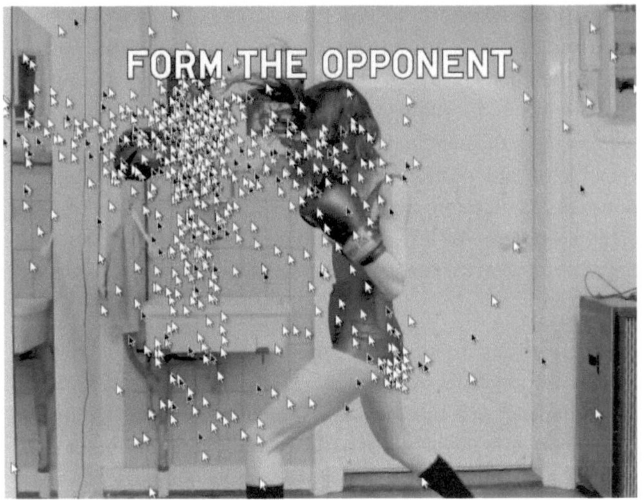

[Figure 17] Interactive music video for the song "Kilo." Source: Moniker 2013.

The cursor is a concrete indication that we are dealing with a non-touchscreen, that is, a cursor-based or pointer-based screen. In the near future, the cursor will probably become a relic of the pre-touchscreen area. To mark the impending end of the cursor, design studio Moniker created a crowd-sourced music video in 2013 for a song called "Kilo" by Dutch band Light Light. On their website, one can read the following statement:

> We celebrate the 50th anniversary of the computer pointer. For decades this ubiquitous, yet inconspicuous arrow has formed the essential interface connecting user and computer. With the rise of multi-touch interfaces, we are slowly seeing these disconnected phantom limbs disappear. Reason enough to gather our pointers together and have some fun. (Moniker 2013)

After starting the clip on donottouch.org, the user is invited to stay (and click) with the cursor in the green zone, which starts as a dot against a black background, then grows to take different forms, and finally becomes the green screen of a computer. A zoom out brings us into a room, presumably the design studio, where the band is playing, and the user is challenged, among other things, to form the (invisible) opponent in front of a boxing woman (fig. 17). The result is an ever-changing music video, for it records the actions of the cursor and accumulates a multitude of arrows as they continue to appear with each new viewing. The screen is covered by a swarm of cursors, akin to bugs (to use Engelbart's term for the pointer), that go with the rhythm of the song "Kilo."

Another curious creation with a mouse cursor was made in July 2012 by a first-grader for her mother. The creation was a foldable "paper laptop" with birthday wishes on the screen and a movable cutout cursor in the shape of a black arrow. Here the cursor is a sign of hands-on operability that needs to be manually moved over the paper screen. In other words, there is a conflation between direct touch (the finger) and indirect touch (the cursor), in that the latter is moved by the former. Interestingly enough, this creation made by a post-Millennial girl points toward the obsolescence of the mouse, which remains absent in the media *bricolage*.[12] Or, to put it differently, the non-touchscreen is simply conceived as a touchscreen.

Thumbelina's Gesturality

Whereas today's children are commonly referred to as post-Millennials, their predecessors belong to the so-called Generation Y. Born between the early 1980s and the early 2000s, they are called Millennials. French philosopher Michel Serres has coined the name "Thumbelina," or in French "Petite Poucette,"[13]

12 For a further discussion of this and other paper laptops made by post-Millennials, see Schneider and Strauven (forthcoming).

13 "Petite Poucette" is the feminine form of "Petit Poucet" (Little Thumb, or Tom Thumb) of Charles Perrault's fairy tale. It is also the French translation of the Danish fairy tale *Tommelise* (Thumbelina) by Hans Christian Andersen.

to indicate today's young adult, who no longer has the same body as her parents and who interacts with the world via (mobile) screens. The Millennials live in a different space and think differently because, as Serres observes, they write differently, very rapidly and with two thumbs:

> He or she writes differently. While observing them, with admiration, send an SMS more quickly than I could ever do with my clumsy fingers, I have named them, with as much tenderness as a grandfather can express, Thumbelina (*Petite Poucette*) and Tom Thumb (*Petit Poucet*). These are their real names, much nicer than the old pseudo-scientific French word, *dactylos* (typists). (2015, 7)

In other words, it is not so much the touchscreen experience as the writing of text messages with the thumb ("au pouce") that prompted the notion of "Petite Poucette" or "Thumbelina." While having some problems with Serres's fairy tale's naïve reading of our control society, I am nevertheless charmed by his tenderness as a grandfather and his unconditional faith in the new generation of media users, condemned by so many others precisely because of their too-invasive media usage. Serres is asking for our understanding for the new youth, who need to reinvent everything, to learn everything anew, because the world has changed so drastically over the last decennia.

When interviewed by *Le Journal du dimanche*, on the occasion of publishing his provocative essay, Serres told an anecdote about one of his grandsons, who came to visit him on his motorbike. The grandson had a mechanical breakdown. So he dismantled the gear of his bike, but there was a little piece he did not know where to put back. He asked his grandfather for his mobile phone and, in no time, found the solution to his problem. For Serres (2012), this was a telling example of how the new generation lives "in" the computer, whereas the old generation still lives "with" the computer.

 In the same interview, Serres explains that Petite Poucette was born in the early 1980s, with the arrival of new technologies such as the personal computer. So she is about thirty years old now. Yet the big changes came about a decade later, in the 1990s, with the growing network of mobile telecommunications and the popularization of the short message service (SMS) protocol, which is at the origin of the practice of thumbing. Limited to 160 characters per message and dependent on a 12-button keypad (from 1 to 9, plus 0, *, and #), the original SMS protocol was rather cumbersome. For instance, the input of the word "feet" required the following steps:

> First, the "3" key must be pressed three times to enter the "f" character. A short pause is then necessary before the "3" key can be used to input the first "e" (rather than change the already typed "f" character). The pause allows the phone to recognise that a new character is to be inputted. A further pause is then needed before the "3" key can be pressed again to input the second "e." Finally, the "8" key is pressed once to input the "t." (Taylor and Vincent 2005, 78)

It should be remembered that SMS was not designed for use on mobile phones but instead conceived as a one-way communication system for call centers to send short messages such as voice mail notifications to subscribers (when their phone was off, for instance, or when they were out of reach). The GSM group who started offering this service in the early 1990s could never have foreseen the immense success that this "unsexy" protocol was to have, especially among young people, as a point-to-point application (Taylor and Vincent 2005, 79). And youngsters started to develop a new language, the SMS shorthand, with its text-based emoticons, and became very dexterous in adopting the rather complex multi-tap writing method—a gesture which, apparently, started to cause physiological changes of the thumb at the beginning of the twenty-first century (Cloosterman 2002).[14]

Most interestingly, in media-archaeological terms, is the repurposing of an existing media device to recreate the features of older media. That is, through the use and appropriation of the SMS protocol, adolescents turned the telephone (transmission of the *spoken* word) back into a telegraph (transmission of the *written* word). Or, more simply, the telephone became a handheld writing machine. Consequently, the gesture of telephoning became a gesture of writing, a gesture of no longer holding the phone with one hand pressed against one's ear but of holding it with two hands and typing with both thumbs on the 12-button keypad. In his theory of gestures, Flusser opposes the gesture of writing on the machine to that of writing with a (fountain) pen:

> Writing on the machine is a gesture in which particular keys are chosen in accordance with the specific criteria of orthography, grammar, semantics, information theory, communication theory, and more, with the intention of producing a text. It may be that even more refined articulations of thought will develop through the use of word processing. (2014, 21)

The Czech-born philosopher refers here to writing on a typewriter or computer keyboard, hypothesizing a possible change in our mental operations, in the way we formulate ideas and thoughts. The SMS shorthand can be considered as the beginning of such a transformation, which has continued and intensified with the advent and wide adoption of the smartphone. At first it looked like the iPhone, when introduced in 2007, announced another trend—away from the gesture of writing. On the one hand, the cell phone became a screen, that is, a surface to look at as well as to touch; on the other, it was very quickly adopted

14 The new argot of SMS was characterized by the omission of subject pronouns and the use of abbreviations such as CUL8R ("see you later"), acronyms such as LOL ("lots of laughter"), and text-based emoticons such as :-), :-(, :-o, 8-), ;-), not to forget the mathematical kisses (xxx).

as an image-capturing device, a pocket-sized camera, that you always carry with you. However, as a multi-purpose device, the smartphone again brought the gesture of writing to the fore, at the expense of making regular phone calls. Why do we still call it a "phone"? Especially among the youngest generation of media users we see that chatting via text is more popular than chatting via speech (even if the phenomenon of voice messages may be changing the picture). Chatting via text means also and especially posting smileys, emoijs, GIFs, and memes. These are all new "gestures of technology" modeled, according to Flusser, on the "gesture of searching" (2014, 147). This new gestural paradigm resides, quite literally, in the hands of the new generation of media users, who are reinventing how to live and how to learn. To paraphrase Serres, it is via hands-on gestures of thumbing that Millennials and post-Millennials access the world, that they use search engines online, that they app and post on social media. Their thumbs, as well as index fingers when necessary, no longer touch physical buttons but icons on a touchscreen. Yet their gestures in texting, as well as their conventions for abbreviation, remain quite close to those of the early SMS users.

As mentioned above, the touchscreen gestures of thumbing, pointing, swiping, and pinching are often accompanied by a posture of looking down, which in the long term might lead to further physiological changes of both the neck and the spine.[15] Despite her gestural dexterity, Thumbelina cannot operate her smartphone without looking at it, with the exception of some (mainly audio-based) gestures, such as making phone calls, recording voice messages, and listening to sound tracks with ear buds. The looking-down attitude has become emblematic of the so-called

15 In reference to Bernard Stiegler and his writings about pharmacology, Gerald Moore observes how, according to the French philosopher, "technical objects bring about a function-shift in our physiological organs, transforming our field of experience. Just as the experiential coordinates of the drunk revolve around inebriation, those of one who lives through their smartphone will be mediated by the habituation of their eyes and hand to the touchscreen" (Moore 2018, 196).

phubbers, who are constantly looking at their phone, constantly checking their social media platforms, and therefore constantly ignoring their offline surroundings and interlocutors.

The typical present-day habit of walking around while looking down at your mobile device, possibly colliding with other users, was already envisioned, quite brilliantly, in a 1947 French documentary film directed by J. K. Raymond-Millet, *La Télévision, oeil de demain* (Television, tomorrow's eye). Inspired by René Barjavel's *Cinéma Total: Essai sur les formes futures du cinéma* (Total cinema: Essay on the future forms of cinema, 1944), the film imagines various future TV applications, including a portable pocket-sized screenic device and 3D television.[16] The latter recalls Albert Robida's *téléphonoscope*, as it brings live holographic images into the bedroom and invites the male TV viewer to reach out and touch a bohemian girl who is dancing on his bed. The film depicts an angry wife who taps her husband on the fingers and scolds: "I forbid you to caress the images!" Especially uncanny is the footage with the portable TV because it captures so well, in anachronistic black-and-white images, how today's users depend on their smartphones to provide a constant feed of moving images. Their gaze is glued to the small screen, held at breast level, causing their upper body to bend down.[17]

In the last decade, many cartoons and videos ridiculing the asocial behavior of social media users have made their appearance online.[18] Apposite for my history of hand gestures is Dan Piraro's satirical depiction of the afterlife, which shows future heaven dwellers looking down and staring at their empty hands. Whereas previously the cursor stood for the hand, now the hand stands for the smartphone. An empty hand is a hand without smartphone.

16 On Barjavel's prophetic essay, see Leotta 2018.

17 I would like to thank Laura Schuster for pointing out this McLuhanesque prophesy with her Facebook post of June 30, 2020. The documentary can be watched in its entirety at: https://www.youtube.com/watch?v=ieRQJ67laOI.

18 For a selection of those phubbing parodies, see Strauven 2016.

Without wanting to pass judgment on the many phubbers, who, incidentally, do not belong exclusively to the generations of Millennials and post-Millennials, my goal is here to draw attention to the specific gestures of interaction with mobile screens. Thumbelina's hands-on operation is not limited to thumbing but also involves the actions of sliding, swiping, and scrolling. These are new ways of accessing the world that young children quite intuitively acquire and master as elements of a new tactile language. Instead of blaming the new media for changing or damaging children's cognitive learning processes, I believe there is a heuristic potential in Serres's turn toward youth and the unconditional trust in this new generation of media users. Most importantly, Serres's essay denotes a reversal in the learning process: that is, today's children are media users (and even media producers) before they start learning about media in a more traditional way of (passive) knowledge transfer. And that is how, I would argue, they are actively making media history.

To conclude this discussion, I want to recall a YouTube clip that went viral in the fall of 2011. Entitled "A Magazine Is an iPad That Does Not Work," the clip shows a one-year old girl applying typical touchscreen gestures, such as scrolling and pinching, to an electronic tablet and a paper magazine.[19] The magazine images, obviously, did not respond to her gestures. Whereas the father, who edited and posted the video clip on YouTube, referred this hands-on interaction in terms of an "OS upgrade," many posts that commented on the clip doubted the true digital intuition of the baby, pointing out for instance that she did not know how to read the iPad properly (since she held it upside down). This is not a matter of "coding" the baby's brain, but, as I see it, a very simple and typical play of trial-and-error. As opposed to pretend play, this is a play of exploration, of trying out the effects of one's actions, similar to the gesture of dropping objects on the floor or knocking over a block tower; the play's logic is that the child

19 https://www.youtube.com/watch?v=aXV-yaFmQNk.

repeats these actions over and over again to find out whether they will lead to the same chain of reactions (among which also the reaction of the assisting adults). Undoubtedly, the iPad gave the little girl the idea of checking out, repeatedly, whether her finger also worked on other touchable surfaces, the magazine pages as well as her chubby leg. Through this play of trial-and-error, the one-year-old is learning hands-on what the difference is between a touchscreen and a non-touchscreen, between a clickable icon and non-clickable icon, between capacitive glass and human skin, by employing new "gestures of technology."

PART TWO:

SCREEN AS TOUCHABLE OBJECT

[4]

Hands-On Screenology

And immediately I thought of making of this lady a screen before the truth: and I pretended to it so often in so short a time that my secret was believed known by most of the people who speculated about me.
Dante Alighieri

Between Surface and Interface

From the perspective of cinema and media studies, the screen is most commonly considered a surface for projection or display. As such it also disappears as an object. It makes itself invisible in order to make visible what is projected or displayed: ranging from the moving images of a filmstrip to the data flow of algorithms translated into graphs, texts, and pictures. In this chapter I will propose to think of the screen as an interface, as something that literally stands in between, as a medium (singular of media). As suggested in the Introduction, my working definition of media approximates the idea of channels, not so much for their auxiliary quality (media as means) but more for their intermediate position (media as middles, as things that are, physically, located in the middle or in between). In the thirteenth century, Italian poet Dante Alighieri used the notion of a "screen lady" to indicate a beautiful woman seated between him and his true love Beatrice. Intercepting the line of their gazes, the screen lady concealed the truth, making others believe that Dante was instead in love with her. As pointed out by Giorgio Avezzù, Dante's screen lady is both a surface, that is, a screen of "illusory, deceptive representation," and an interface, that is, a screen of protection and separation, of "setting the beloved woman apart" (Avezzù 2016, 33). For the audience, she is the image on display, but in fact she only covers—or functions as the interface of—the image of Beatrice. In a similar way, Seung-hoon Jeong has proposed the terms "interface" and "interfaciality" to designate the "contact surface between image and spectator" (2012, 230). In Jeong's analysis of rube cinema, this contact surface is a touchable interface, allowing for tactile experience.

Chapter 4 will study the screen as an object that continually oscillates between surface and interface, by making evident that the notion of in-between-ness characterizes the original meaning(s) and usage(s) of the screen. The tension between surface and interface emerges throughout history and persists until today due to the omnipresence of interactive screens, those screens that are both surfaces to be touched and interfaces (or portals) to the world. Or as Francesco Casetti puts it, screens are no longer surfaces on which reality is simply represented but have become "transit points," that is, places where "free-floating images stop for a moment, make themselves available to users, allow themselves to be manipulated, and then take off again along new routes" (2014, 103–04). Whereas Casetti talks about this transformed screen in terms of display, Simone Arcagni suggests that today's screens, in particular the mobile or portable screens, are in fact all computers, because they are interactive screens, connected to the Internet, with their own storage capacity, programs, and apps (Arcagni 2012, 76). So, it seems that the screen and the computer are colliding. The question, however, remains: Is the interactive screen by definition a computer screen? Or can we think of an interactive screen in a pre-computer age?

In "Towards an Archaeology of the Computer Screen" (1998), Lev Manovich sees the interactive computer screen as the fourth (and, for the time being, final) stage in the screen's development.

In his linear overview, Manovich traces the following steps: 1) the classical screen of painting and photography which offers a fixed image; 2) the dynamic screen of cinema which adds to the classical screen the property to display an image that changes in time, that is, a moving image; 3) the "real-time" screen of television which shows an image that changes (or moves) in real time; and 4) the interactive screen in which changes in the image happen not only in real time but also as a result of user action and intervention, as by changing computer data. In Manovich's genealogy, the characteristics of the various stages are accumulative. Or as Manovich puts it, "In my genealogy, the computer screen represents an interactive type, a subtype of the real-time type, which is a subtype of the dynamic type, which is a subtype of the classical type" (1998, 34).

Importantly, the starting point for Manovich is the definition of screen as a flat surface. In Manovich's words the classical screen is "a flat, rectangular surface," which is "intended for frontal viewing" (1998, 28). All the elements of such a definition—flat, rectangular, surface, frontal, and viewing—can be questioned when looking into the screen's etymology and various historical usages. Taking inspiration from Erkki Huhtamo's "screenology" (or screen archaeology) in its departure from the history of the word "screen," I will trace six different etymological lineages, which I propose to analyze in tactile terms. My hands-on screenology will discuss all kinds of screens that are not flat or rectangular: from the fire screen to the decorative lady's fan, from the gate to the closet, from the shield to the mirror, from the skin to the skirt, from the wall to the sheet and the sieve. The "from . . . to . . ." construction might seem to imply a teleological progression, but the various lineages are bifurcations of multiple etymological roots that go back and forth in time and often overlap. In other words, it is a media-archaeological mapping of the screen as a written instance or discursive unit.

At the center of the discussion is the materiality of the screen, which is also the focus of Giuliana Bruno's *Surface: Matters of*

 Aesthetics, Materiality, and Media (2014). Bruno's main areas of interest are clothing, architectural walls, canvases, and other art and projection surfaces. For Bruno, "surface matters" because it is where artistic expression takes shape. She proposes to "think about the surface as a place of connection, as a meeting place, beginning with the fact that our primary form of habitation is our skin" (Oppenheimer 2014).

We could say that the screen is a material phenomenon because its surface is. The surface is a thing, to rephrase Charles Acland, who bluntly notes:

> Screens are things: they are the products of industry and labour; they take up space; they are made of solid substance; they change people's bodily orientation; and they send light into our eyes and, with the audio component of most screens, soundwaves into our ears. There is nothing immaterial about any of this. (2009, 149)

This is indeed the paradox of today's society of screens. On the one hand, the screen is omnipresent (from urban screens to portable devices), and, on the other, the screen tends to disappear, to become invisible. Huhtamo's plea for establishing a "screenology" is grounded in the need to make the screen visible again. He states:

> As they become part of the practices of everyday life, screens have a tendency to become invisible; they mediate perceptions and interactions, effacing their own identities in the process. We don't stare at the screen; we gaze at what it transmits. But there is more: screens also hide the history of their own becoming, turning into a kind of ever-present non-presence, an anomalous object. (Huhtamo 2012, 145)

Despite their ubiquitous presence, screens are elusive and difficult to grasp. As surfaces of moving images, continuous flow of text and data, they have the appearance of elasticity, transparency, and immateriality (or even virtuality). Some near-future visions predict that screens will become more and more "immaterial" or elusive, that they will eventually disappear or at least end up merging with, or disguising as, windows. Drawing on a series of "design fiction" videos, entitled *A Day Made of Glass,* Arcagni discusses this tendency of the screen "to camouflage, to transparency, to blending in and disappearing as hard object, bounded by frames" (2012, 79; my translation). In fact, these five-minute videos are advertisements for Corning Gorilla Glass, showing the daily life of a family in the near future. Thanks to specialty glass, all possible surfaces can become interactive screens, including the bedroom window, bathroom mirror, kitchen worktop, fridge door, car dashboard, and even a thin piece of bendable plastic.

Instead of a return (or flash-forward?) to the Age of Windows, which, according to the 1936 film adaptation of H. G. Wells's science fiction novel *The Shape of Things to Come* (1933), "lasted four centuries," it seems that we are rather moving toward an Age of Surfaces.[1] The future of the screen is not limited to windows (or glass), for every surface can become, or be used as, a screen. Yet this is nothing new. When looking into the past of the screen, we see a similar tendency: all types of material surfaces could function as screens, from silver shields to bamboo fans, from wooden cabinets to silk dresses.

Screen's Etymological Lineages

Etymological study of the word "screen" is a true Foucauldian exercise, as it reveals how the meaning of the term changes over time and how it is connected, through time, to different discourses and practices, particularly, for our purposes, sensorial or tactile practices. The word "screen" not only carries multiple meanings, which have accumulated over time, but also has multiple origins. Or rather its etymological origins are uncertain.

1 In *A Day Made of Glass*, the family father is reading another H. G. Wells's classic, *The Time Machine* (1895), on his filter thin glass book. About the Age of Windows, see also Friedberg 2006.

The exercise consists in tracing different possible screen lineages without trying to find the "pure" origin. It is by definition a contaminated history, where different Germanic and Romance languages intersect.

Another curious point is that early cinema turns out to be a fertile terrain to illustrate this alternative history of the screen. This might be an indication that early cinema belonged indeed to another, much older screen culture. In particular, the film oeuvre of Georges Méliès is a rich source for what I propose to call the "early touchscreen," which is not necessarily a display or projection screen.[2] As will emerge from the discussion, it includes all forms of touchable surfaces, such as folding partitions, pictorial and advertising canvases, umbrellas, and fans. All of these surfaces can be traced back to the (albeit uncertain) etymological origins of the word "screen."

From Fire Screen to Lady's Fan

According to the *Oxford English Dictionary*, the English word "screen" probably derives from the Old French *escran* in its Old North French variant *escren*. The first documented occurrence of *escran* dates from 1318, in the meaning of a screen against heat ("paravent contre le feu"). The connotation is that of a barrier, of an object that is placed in between, to protect and to prevent one from being "touched" by the fire's sparks. Huhtamo's screenology starts with the fire screen, which he calls a "floor-standing piece of furniture" (2004, 5). One could make here a connection with the TV set, not only as a decorative piece of furniture in the living room but also as a technological fireplace around which the family gathers.[3]

2 I coined the term "early touchscreen," as an analogy with "early cinema," for Strauven 2012. However, the editor of the journal advised me to change it to "early touchable screen." The six lineages proposed in this chapter are an extension of this previously published text.

3 Dutch media artist Jan Dibbets made a video recording of a fire burning in a hearth, entitled *TV as a Fireplace*, which was broadcast on German TV during

In the Victorian era, when cinema emerged, fire screens in the form of a huge fan were popular. They were commonly made of brass or bronze and were foldable, that is, able to be closed when not in use. They were adjustable and therefore touchable (when cooled down!). Two Star Films by Georges Méliès can be cited here to illustrate this concept of the fan-form fire screen. In *L'Homme-orchestre* (*One Man Band*, 1900), an enormous fan appears toward the end, creating a barrier that first hits and then prevents Méliès from leaving the scene. However, Méliès finds a way to disappear via a stage trapdoor, after which he reappears at the other side of the fan, jumps over it, and literally goes up in smoke (fig. 18). The fan is an obstructing screen that can be connected to the original French meaning of "paravent contre le feu" because of the presence of smoke (and the saying, "no smoke without fire"). In *Le Merveilleux éventail vivant* (*The Wonderful Living Fan*, 1904), Méliès stages another huge fan. Unlike the screen of *L'Homme-orchestre*, the magical fan has individual panels and is foldable (like the Victorian fire screens). The fan is brought onstage in a huge box. While being unboxed, it opens "magically" in front of the royal representative who visits the fan merchant. The latter, played by Méliès, emphatically touches some of the panels before producing living women (fig. 19). Cognitively, the magician's touch before the execution of the magic trick is to prove to the audience that what they see is indeed just a fan. Magically, touch is linked here to the power to animate the inanimate, to turn the individual panels into living women, which also brings in the issue of gender: the result is a series of women on show and within reach for the male characters (and, indirectly, male viewers).[4]

the last evenings of the year 1969. Uneventfully hypnotizing, burning fires in fireplaces became popular screensavers and are nowadays among the "most looped videos 'of all time' on infinitelooper.com" (Poulaki 2015, 92).

4 This triple reading (cognitive, magical, and socio-sexual) corresponds to the three variations of tactility in the Renaissance *paragone* debate. See Johnson 2002.

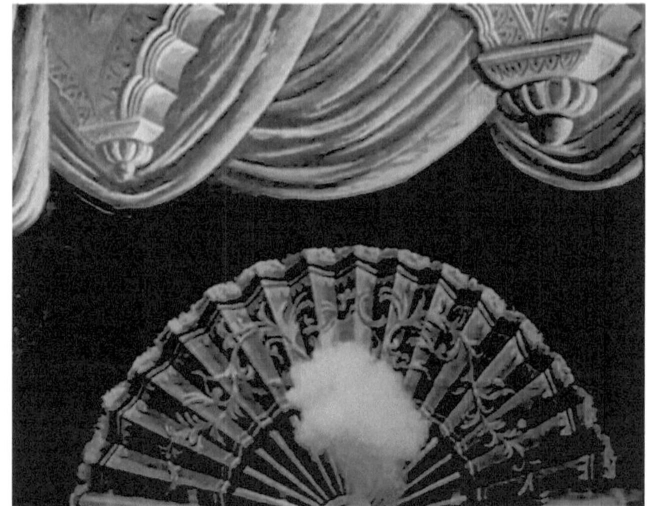

[Figure 18] *L'Homme-orchestre* (Georges Méliès, 1900).

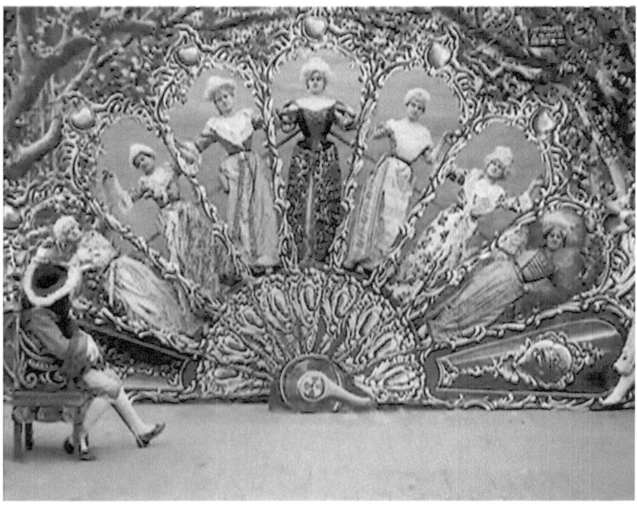

[Figure 19] *Le Merveilleux éventail vivant* (Georges Méliès, 1904).

In other words, the magic fan is a screen of *display* rather than of *protection*; there is no smoke this time, the connection with the fire screen is purely formal (because of the fan form and its huge size).

This not-so-portable and not-so-woman-friendly device brought on stage by Méliès is in striking contrast with the oriental hand-screen, which was a typical fashion accessory for Victorian ladies. Inherited from Japanese culture, the folding fan permitted women to partially hide from sight in addition to circulating air. As Bruno points out, the fan also had a more imaginary function, allowing women to travel to remote places thanks to the vistas depicted on the panels. Bruno calls it the "ladies' own private cinema" (before the invention of cinema, that is) that they could literally hold in their hands:

> As one opened it, the depicted panorama—often painted as a succession of views—unfolded. Its motion told the story of a moving site. The fan . . . was the everyday version of a *veduta* in motion—a mobilized view painting. A prepanoramic device, the fan was the ladies' own private cinema. (2002, 134)

Likewise, Huhtamo has suggested that "from a media archaeological perspective such fans could indeed be considered a mobile and portable information channel" (2004, 63), similar to today's mobile media devices. He also insists on the similarity between the handheld fan and another Victorian device, "the 'moving panorama hand-screen' that contained a small 'stage opening,' across which a long strip of images was wound from one roller to another" (63).

These hand-screens, both the fashion accessory and entertainment device, were obviously touchable screens, to be operated manually. The quick opening and closing of the foldable fan with one hand certainly required some dexterity but could also be deployed as a communicative gesture in a (society) play of hide-and-seek or flirtation. It is not historically proven that there existed a true, codified fan-gesture language among ladies in the eighteenth and nineteenth centuries, even if this notion circulated as a male fantasy and was eventually used as marketing strategy. As Hugh Davies observes,

> Not only were these decodes of women's secret fan languages authored by men, but by men fan makers, no less: individuals with a vested interest in promoting their wares with invented histories and applications. (2019, 316)

Davies cites as a case in point the French fan house Duvelleroy, founded in 1827 in Paris by Jean-Pierre Duvelleroy. The London branch, which opened in 1861, produced leaflets entitled *Le Language de l'éventail* (*The Language of the Fan*), with codes such as "Open and shut" (meaning "You are cruel") and "Touching tip with finger" (meaning "I wish to speak to you").[5] Even if the coded language was "plainly devised as a commercial ruse to sell more fans" (Davies 2019, 316), it is remarkable how this nineteenth-century gestural vocabulary was conceived as a collaboration between hand and screen, with the fan functioning as both surface and interface.

The screen as barrier against heat existed also in the form of a portable hand-screen to shield the face from the burning fireplace. Littré's *Dictionnaire de la Langue Française* of 1889 lists such a device after the traditional fire screen and, notably, uses the notion of fan in its description: "sorte d'éventail qu'on tient à la main pour le même objet," which translates as "a kind of fan that you hold in your hand for the same purpose," that is, to protect yourself from the heat of the fire. A mention of such a portable face screen can be found in Charles Dickens's novel *Bleak House* (1853), more particularly in the second chapter where Lady Dedlock sits "on a sofa near the fire, shading her face with a hand-screen" (9); the novel also contains a drawing by H. K.

5 A photograph of this little guide can be found at https://mosaic.gr/duvelleroy/. The House of Develleroy continues to design and manufacture fans to this day.

Brown depicting such a scene, when Mr. Guppy pays a visit to Lady Dedlock in Chapter XXIX (323) (fig. 20).

Unlike the previously discussed fashion fans, the handheld fire screens were not unfolding or adjustable; they came as a fixed screen on a fixed handle. This model goes back to the earliest origins of the fan: already known in Egyptian times, when it even made its appearance as hieroglyph, and subsequently in Greek antiquity, as evidenced by vase decoration, the fixed fan marks also the beginning of fan history in China. Here the oldest screen artifacts, made of woven bamboo, go back to the second century before Christ, whereas the Japanese folding fan appeared much later, around the sixth to eighth centuries AD.

What is most relevant in media-archaeological terms is the resemblance of the fixed fan with the phénakisticope (better known as *phenakistiscope* or the later misspelling *phenakistoscope*), the optical toy designed in the early 1830s by Joseph Plateau to illustrate his theory of the persistence of vision (see also Chapter 5). The toy consists of a spinning cardboard disk with a series of images, representing successive moments of an action, drawn along its circumference. In the original mode, the disk is mounted on a stick and requires a two-handed operation: one hand holding the stick and the other rotating the disk. The user has to stand in front of a mirror, with the images directed toward the mirror. To properly see the animated view reflected in the mirror, one must partially hide one's face behind the spinning screen-disk while looking through its cutout slits. In other words, the phenakistiscope functioned also as a concealing barrier, precisely like the lady's fan (fig. 21).

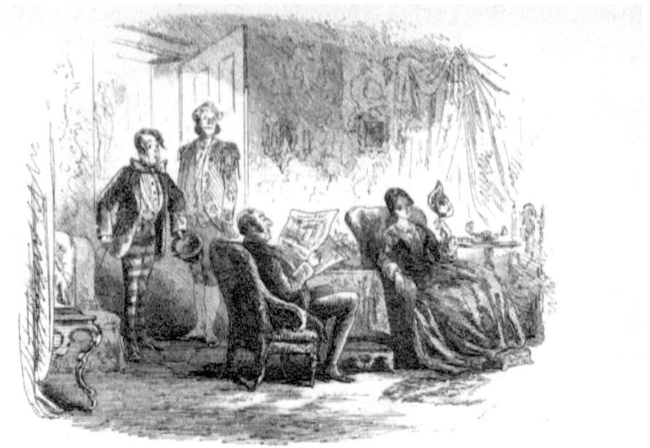

[Figure 20] Lady Dedlock holding a fire hand-screen in the scene "The Young Man of the name of Guppy." Illustration by H. K. Brown. Source: Dickens 1853.

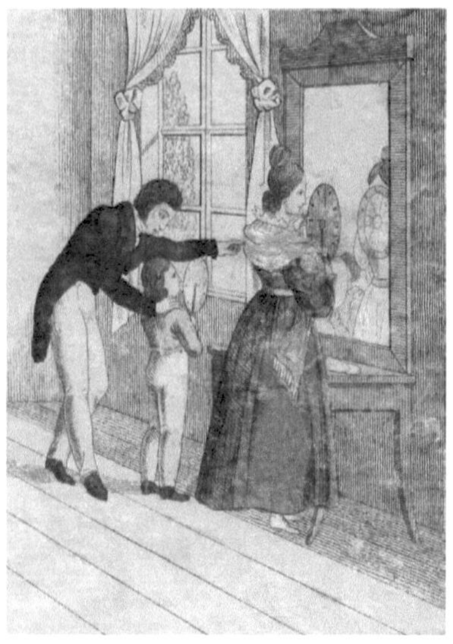

[Figure 21] A woman looking through the slits of a phenakisticope in front of a mirror. Detail of an illustration by E. Schule on the box label for Magic Disk (ca. 1833). https://en.wikipedia.org/wiki/Phenakistiscope.

Bruno mentions the phenakistiscope in her discussion of ladies' fans, but not to stress the difference between the Chinese-style fixed fan and the Japanese-style folding fan. Charles Baudelaire, on the other hand, draws a direct connection to the handheld fire screen in describing the two-disk version of the phenakistiscope, which is a bit more difficult to operate but does not require a mirror. In "Morale du joujou" ("The Philosophy of Toys," 1853), one reads:

> Images are depicted round the edge of a circular disc made of card. This card, as well as a second circular disc, perforated at equal intervals by twenty little windows, is attached to a pivot at the end of a handle, which you hold as you would a hand-screen in front of the fire. (Baudelaire 2018, 18)

What all these different fans seem to share is the potentiality of a visual barrier, of hiding from onlookers. Dissimulation is also the function of the folding partition, which in French is called *paravent* and which was originally designed to protect oneself from currents of air (the French *vent* meaning "wind") inside the home. From a functional and protective "wind screen," the *paravent* became a "dressing screen," another hide-and-seek screen, made of fabric, which often displayed exotic vistas similar to those of the lady's fan. It can be concluded that in this first screen lineage a shift in meaning is taking place, from the screen that protects (against heat, against draft) to the screen that hides (or protects from sight). It remains, however, a screen that separates, that is placed in between. Its form is not necessarily rectangular (or flat), and in its portable version, it is clearly a "touch(able) screen." Because of its decorative function, it is also a visual screen or display screen.

From Gate to Cabinet

Whereas the English word "screen" probably stems from the Old French *escran*, the French *écran* derives in its turn—according to the *Larousse Dictionnaire étymologique*—from the Middle High

 German *schrank*, meaning "gate, railing," or from the Frankish *skrank*, meaning "barrier." Here we can think of lattice partitions in architectural spaces, like the sixteenth century iron screen of the Royal Chapel (Capilla Real) in Granada, Spain. This masterpiece by Bartolomé of Jaen stands in between two spaces, as it separates the crossing with the royal mausoleums from the rest of the nave. It is a screen both of separation and of display, its upper section representing the Passion and Resurrection of Christ in a horizontal stripe of gilded forged iron.

Another possible track places "screen" in a direct lineage with the modern German *Schrank*, allowing for a connection between the screen and the closet, more specifically the baroque *Wunderschrank* or cabinet of (touchable) curiosities. The *Wunderschrank* is a *Wunderkammer* in miniature, an (almost) portable closet-screen. In Chapter 2, I have referred to Barbara Stafford's work and her suggestion to think of the *Wunderkammer* collector in terms of a "user," or even better "performer," who must activate the objects and explore hidden relations among them. This comes close to the notion of a (proto)interactive screen. Moreover, as Frances Terpak has shown, the *Wunderschrank* principle is recycled in mid-nineteenth-century political cartoons, for instance by the Viennese caricaturist Cajetan (pseudonym of Anton Elfinger). His *Grosses noch nie gesehenes Kunst-Cabinet* (Large never-before-seen *Kunstkabinett*) satirizes the political chaos of the 1850s by means of a "circus barker dressed as a seventeenth-century musketeer [who] points to posters of the curiosities on display in his sideshow" (Terpak 2001, 156). In teleological terms, we can see in the figure of the musketeer-barker an anticipation of early cinema's lecturer and in the use of the stick a very early form of pointer (or computer cursor).

The motif of the poster-cabinet returns in Méliès's *Les Affiches en goguette* (*The Hilarious Posters*, 1906). Here, individually framed posters come to life, turning a two-dimensional publicity board into a three-dimensional cabinet with living curiosities (ranging from a cook and a liquor seller to several coquettes). *Les Affiches en goguette* also connects back to the original meaning of the Middle High German *schrank*—that is, "gate, railing"—when, toward the end of the film, the once-again two-dimensional billboard falls on top of a group of gendarmes and tears open, revealing a metal gateway. The latter blocks the police from the poster characters in a much more efficient way. Thus, Méliès combines the two aspects of the second screen lineage: the original meaning of *schrank/skrank* as barrier and its second possible meaning as closet. The first usage imposes a separation between two worlds (or two people), implying avoidance of direct touch, whereas the latter is a form of visual organization that relies on touch.

More generally, the closet lineage comprises the tension between hiding and displaying, between closed-ness (closed wardrobes, storage room, locked away items) and openness (showing off, exposing, "coming out of the closet"). Here one could look into the history of the department stores and their visual order of fashion items, the use of display cases (inherited from the natural history museums), and the shop window as an anticipation of the cinema screen, as argued by Anne Friedberg:

> The shop window was the proscenium for visual intoxication, the site of seduction for consumer desire. . . . From the middle of the nineteenth century, as if in a historical relay of looks, the shop window succeeded the mirror as a site of identity construction, and then—gradually—the shop window was displaced and incorporated by the cinema screen. (1993, 65–66)

In addition to the window-screen genealogy drawn by Friedberg, I would like to insist on the action of "window dressing," by which the window becomes a screen/closet where items have to be placed and organized and where the hands-on operation of the window dresser is key, as for instance thematized in *Trouble in Store* (1953), a film by John Paddy Carstairs that stars Norman

 Wisdom as a department store clerk. Trying to get a promotion as a window dresser, Wisdom ends up being on display in the shop window and—to the great amusement of the people on the street—misplaces several pieces of porcelain tableware before finally breaking it all. In other words, it is a scene of hands-on window dressing put on display as if it were a cinema screen, an open closet for all to look at.

From Military Shield to Mirror

In addition to *schrank/skrank*, the *Larousse Dictionnaire étymologique* indicates another possible root for the French *écran*: the Dutch *scherm*, or the Middle Dutch *screm*. The Dutch word "scherm" presumably derives in its turn—and here we are really going in circles—from the Old German *skirm*, meaning a "shield made of [animal] skin." A trace of the Old German *skirm* is still visible in the English expression *skirm*ish (which in Dutch is *scherm*utseling). Thus, the screen is a shield that not only protects from the heat of a fireplace (or from various weather conditions) but also acts as a means of defense against the enemy. This is a good example of how military influences pervade—not only technologically but also etymologically—different levels of our media history.[6]

As opposed to the many cardboard flats and paper screens that appear in Méliès's films and that are more often than not torn open, the military shield is obviously supposed to be impenetrable. This is quite literally thematized by Méliès in *Le Royaume des fées* (*Fairyland: A Kingdom of Fairies*, 1903), in which the Genius of Invulnerability grants Prince Bel Azor the gift of impenetrable armor ("bouclier impénétrable"). This magical shield, made of silver, makes the Prince's entire body invulnerable. Right after receiving the shield and while holding it in his left hand, the

6 On the role of the military in cinema and media history, see for instance Kittler 1999, Virilio 1989, Elsaesser 2017, and Grieveson and Masson 2018.

Prince briefly pats its shiny surface as if it needed some encouragement for the battle to come.

The first battle shields were made of animal skin or wood. But already in the Hellenistic period silver was used, which made the shield not only more solid or impenetrable but also reflective like a mirror. Here a connection can be made with cinema's silver screen, a term that appeared in the early 1920s in reference to the projection screen being covered with metallic paint to make it more reflective, "thus giving the appearance of a brighter picture" (Christie 2016, 75). This material practice in fact laid the basis for psychoanalytic film theory and the Lacanian idea of the screen as mirror (Baudry 1974–75).

In Jean Cocteau's *Le sang d'un poète* (*The Blood of a Poet*, 1930) a mirror transforms from (reflecting) surface to (penetrable) interface. This happens in the first part of the movie, when the poet (Enrique Rivero) sketches on a piece of paper an androgynous portrait whose mouth comes to life. The mouth transfers to his palm, continuing to move. The poet then rubs it onto an armless female statue. She tells him to enter the large mirror on the wall. He follows her order and falls through the mirror (which, by a substitution trick, has turned into a pool of water), descending deep into a void. Both the piece of paper and the palm of the poet's hand can be considered as screens for display, where the inanimate becomes animated, while the mirror evokes Lewis Carroll's *Through the Looking-Glass* (1872) as well as Narcissus's reflection in a pool: it is a mirror that is "less reflecting than attracting" (Jeong 2012, 236).

In the early days of the "cinema of attractions" two practices of screen projection coexisted. On the one hand, there was the principle of rear projection, which belonged to the phantasmagoria tradition and consisted of placing the projector behind the screen (as depicted in the Porter's 1902 rube film *Uncle Josh at the Moving Picture Show*). In such a *dispositif*, the screen did not reflect the light but instead absorbed it. And, more relevant for my argument about the tension between interface and surface, the principle of rear projection put the screen in the middle; the screen thus created a separation, or in-between-ness. It was a physical barrier between two worlds, between the image projection and the image consumption. In the case of front projection, spectator and projector are on the same side of the screen. The screen is no longer a screen of division, but "merely" a surface on which the images are projected (as implemented at the Salon Indien of the Grand Café for the first public screening of the Lumière brothers' Cinématographe). This screen practice, which is inherited from the magic lantern tradition, will become the dominant practice with the phenomenon of the reflective "silver screen."

In sum, the third lineage suggests, on the basis of its silver materiality, a shift in meaning from shield (screen to protect) to mirror (screen to reflect). The latter undermines the original meaning of screen as physical barrier, but it continues to create a separation. It repels advances, on account of its reflective capacity, unless it turns into water and can be trespassed.

From Skin to Skirt

The Dutch dictionary *Van Dale Groot woordenboek van de Nederlandse taal* provides the Latin and Greek roots of the Dutch word "scherm": *corium*, *korion*, both meaning "skin." In prehistoric times, animal skins were used not only to make battle shields, but also to cover human bodies and protect against cold weather. Clothing as second skin marks the beginning of textile technology with the invention of the needle as one of the earliest artifacts of humankind. Second Skin is also the name of an e-textile platform specializing in garments made of stretch electronic fabrics that adapt to the shape of the body (Freire et al. 2017). The human skin is a screen of separation, constituting a boundary between inside and outside. According to Derrick De Kerckhove, the skin as means of protection that "needs the projection of layers of clothing" makes very little sense in media-theoretical (that is,

McLuhanian) terms: "The skin as a communicating, not a protecting device makes perfect sense" (De Kerckhove 1997, 86–87).

Both membrane and organ, the human skin stands for touch. It is indeed a very physical and literal touchscreen, as demonstrated by Valie Export in her 1968 expanded cinema performance *Tap and Touch Cinema* (see Chapter 1). Conversely, we can think of the human body as a defense screen in wartime, the "human shield" as used by terrorists, etc. In filmic terms, both the French and Italian word for film strip incorporate the idea of "skin": *pellicule, pellicola* (deriving from the Latin *pellicula*: "little skin"). At the movie theater, the human skin becomes a screen as well: the light projected onto the silver screen is reflected back onto our faces; our naked skin becomes a projection screen. Or as Acland puts it: "Our faces are the surfaces on which . . . projections . . . settle" (2012, 167). Another connection can be made with today's media facades, which are the new skins of buildings; Arcagni (2012, 54) talks about these screen-based architectures in terms of "media surfaces" (*superfici mediali*) or "media skins" (*pelli mediali*).

As evidenced by Export's feminist intervention, the link between skin and screen brings the gender issue to the fore. An eloquent example is Dante's expression of the "screen lady" mentioned at the beginning of this chapter. Casetti briefly refers to Dante's notion in terms of human masking, for the poet used somebody (that is, the body of a woman) to "mask the interests of another person" (Casetti 2015, 157). As already pointed out, Dante's screen lady is both a screen of protection against the true love being discovered and a screen of projection of the false love that appears real to others (Avezzù 2016, 31–34). Especially remarkable is Dante's intuition of the concept of "interface," conceiving of the screen as a thing (or person) in between two other things (or persons). And at the same time, the screen lady comes close to the idea of reducing the woman to a screen, to a screen to contemplate (and to touch).

Early cinema exhibits plenty of this latter type of screen ladies. Particularly in Méliès's oeuvre, the female body is constantly covered and uncovered by means of screens, cloths, curtains, and so on, to eventually be turned into a screen itself—that is, a screen *for* and *on* display (as already evidenced by the above discussion of *The Wonderful Living Fan*). Moreover, female bodies are treated by Méliès as concrete barriers in the execution of magic and filmic tricks. For instance, in *L'Illusionniste double et la tête vivante* (*The Triple Conjurer and the Living Head*, 1900), a duplicated Méliès entertains himself by crawling underneath a small table on which a living female head is placed; her body is an invisible, traversable barrier, an illusionary black screen against the black backdrop. Then Méliès makes the table disappear and she appears full body. At her two flanks, the two Mélièses try to kiss her on the cheek. The Méliès on her right then moves his hands along her (clearly superimposed) body, without really touching her, after which she vanishes, fading into the black backdrop.

Inherited from the stage (and his own experience as conjurer at Théâtre Robert-Houdin), the vanishing lady is a recurring motif in Méliès's films, in which the magic trick is often substituted by film tricks (such as superimposition, stop motion, etc.). The earliest example is *Escamotage d'une dame chez Robert-Houdin* (*The Vanishing Lady*, 1896), where magician Méliès guides his female assistant (Jeanne d'Alcy, his future wife) to a chair placed on top of a newspaper. Jeanne, who holds a nice feather fan, is covered by a tablecloth. When Méliès removes the cloth, Jeanne's body has disappeared (while the paper screen on the ground remains intact). Méliès then conjures a skeleton and covers it with the cloth to reproduce Jeanne onstage.

Another remarkable play with different types of screens and the female body can be found in *Le Parapluie fantastique* (*Ten Ladies in One Umbrella*, 1903). The film starts with Méliès playing around with his magic hat, which he transforms into a ball and then into a piece of black cloth. Together with his walking stick the cloth takes the form of an umbrella. More than just a simple magic hat, the umbrella functions as a masking device, shielding from our eyes not only the magic trick but also and especially the filmic trick of substitution. For Méliès conjures up ten ladies out of the black rain shade. After the multiple umbrella-trick, the ten ladies transform from neoclassical muses into contemporary suffragettes dressed in black; their change of outfit happens in an almost imperceptible cut. And then, as Caroline Evans has observed, they "exit off screen like a row of fashion mannequins" (2011, 116). As with *The Wonderful Living Fan*, a series of women become a "visual spectacle" for the (male) spectator. Yet instead of using the folding fan, Méliès plays here with yet another screen, to which both the French *écran* and the English *screen* are etymologically connected via their Old German root *skirm*: the umbrella. In modern German, umbrella and screen are still directly connected: *Regenschirm* (umbrella) and *Bildschirm* (image screen).

American Mutoscope and Biograph made the idea of the female body as screen even more explicit in *Kiss Me* (1904), where Rose Sydell appears framed as a living billboard among three other life-sized vaudeville posters on the street. Instead of stepping out of the frame, as happened in an earlier American Mutoscope and Biograph film, *A Midnight Fantasy* (1899), the woman seems immobilized; she only very slightly moves her head to wink at a male passerby. The whiteness of her nude shoulders contrasts with her black dress and the black background of the poster, thereby annulling any sense of depth. Like in many of Méliès's films, the female body is treated here as a flat image, as a statue reduced to a two-dimensional screen for visual pleasure.

Around 1900 the female body also literally became a projection screen with the emergence of modern dance, thanks to the inventiveness of the American dancer Loïe Fuller. By putting both the shimmering quality of silk and the technology of electricity to her advantage, Fuller turned her costumes into surfaces for the interception of multi-colored light beams. Her famous Serpentine Dance was imitated all over the world, most famously in early cinema by Annabelle Moore for the Edison Company (Gunning

2003; Guido 2006). In Méliès's *La Danse du Feu* (*The Pillar of Fire*, 1899), Jeanne d'Alcy appears from within the fire and performs a skirt dance à la Fuller. As in the other filmic recordings of the Serpentine Dance, the multi-colored projection effect is obtained by hand-tinting. Thus, paradoxically, whereas on stage Fuller's silk costumes clearly belong to the episteme of the projection screen, on film they become canvases to be painted or dyed. In both cases the skin of the dancer is sometimes covered (or colored) as well, creating a direct continuity between the two screens—that is, the naked skin and the so-called second skin or clothing. Here a connection can be made with Robert Whitman's expanded cinema *Prune Flat* (1965), in which, as discussed briefly in Chapter 1, the (naked and dressed) skins of live actors are used as projection screens in front of a film screen.

From Veil to Wall

Michel Serres's *The Five Senses* (originally published in French in 1985) opens with a chapter dedicated to touch, in which the philosopher discusses a series of paintings by French Post-Impressionist Pierre Bonnard, paintings that "display skins in full bloom" (Serres 2008, 37). Serres describes the visual spectacle of female models in tactile terms. In particular, *Le Peignoir* (*The Dressing Gown*, ca. 1892), a long vertical painting in Japanese style, gives rise to such an interpretation. Here, in the midst of foliage, the rich and colorful texture of the gown covers the woman's skin almost entirely, leaving only a small part of her face exposed in profile. Serres observes:

> Pierre Bonnard is not so much appealing to sight as to touch, the feeling beneath the fingers of films and fine layers, foliage, material, canvas, surface, defoliation, undressing, refined unveilings, thin caressing curtains. His immensely tactful and tactile art does not turn the skin into a vulgar object to be seen, but rather into the feeling subject, a subject always active beneath the surface. (30)

The section of the chapter is entitled "Canvas, Veil, Skin" (in French "Toile, Voile, Peau") and explores the various layers at stake in Bonnard's depictions of veiling and unveiling, dressing and undressing, of the female body. Serres talks about the painter's canvas as a screen or "patterned curtain" (32), which offers itself as a skin—a skin to be touched. Serres also refers to Veronica, who caressed the crucified Christ's face and wiped it with her veil, on which it left an imprint (like on canvas, or on film). The veil, even if not etymologically connected to the screen-as-skin, belongs in Serres's philosophy to the same lineage of the "second skin," or the idea of covering the naked skin. He writes: "We never live naked . . . nor ever really clothed, never veiled or unveiled" (38).

That the notion of dressing and undressing, or of clothing as "second skin," can also be applied to the walls inside a house is a direction indicated by Bruno, first in *Atlas of Emotion* (2002) and subsequently in *Surface* (2014), where she suggests thinking of fashion as a form of architecture. Here she follows the nineteenth-century German art and architecture historian Gottfried Semper who showed that "walls have an origin in textiles, as hanging cloth or woven mats." Bruno adds:

> In speaking of dressing walls, Semper fashioned a textural theory of space, activating the vital connection between surface and ornament. And let us not forget that in establishing a relationship between ornament and mobility, he termed the wall a *Wand*, that is, a partition or screen, and set it in relation to *Gewand*, meaning garment or clothing. (2014, 48)

This opens a different etymological lineage, which does not start from the English "screen," but from the German term for wall: *Wand*. Indeed, the wall as a dividing screen between two rooms, or as the back of a film studio, can be clothed as well—that is, covered by other more or less touchable screens. Revealing is Bruno's own discussion of the panoramic wallpaper that became fashionable in the late eighteenth century. She calls this element of home design not only a "prefilmic screen" but also "the 'in-between' of interior and exterior" (Bruno 2002, 169). As she writes, "Panoramic wallpaper reframed the inside as an outside" (166). And, as I would like to emphasize, it brought the remote, the inaccessible, or the exotic in close proximity with the inhabitant—literally within the reach of her hands.

In "Haptical Cinema" (1995), Antonia Lant discusses early cinema's spatiality in terms of layered flatness, which comes into full play thanks to the use of painted and movable décor pieces, transparent curtains, and bas-relief-like superimpositions. The painted flats and fake walls, which are so typical of early cinema, somehow recall the domestic tradition of wallpaper and folding screens, although their direct lineage is theatrical. Generally, these flat décor pieces are very noticeable due to their visible instability. Often actors touched them unintentionally. Yet in Méliès's *Le Cauchemar* (*The Nightmare*, 1896), it becomes a deliberate act. When the main character (played by Méliès) wakes up from his nightmare, he wants to be sure he is indeed awake, and therefore he touches the wall in the back as a reality check. This cognitive touch ironically shows how unstable the "real" world is because the touched wall/screen is visibly swaying.

The wall as architectural divider between inside and outside can also function as a very basic screen for projection, as exploited by early cinema in many dream scenes—see for instance Porter's *Life of an American Fireman* (1903) and *Dream of a Rarebit Fiend* (1906). Here the wall is naked, uncovered. It is a screen-less screen. In Athanasius Kircher's description of the Laterna Magica in the Amsterdam edition of *Ars Magna Lucis et Umbrae* (1671), the bare wall proved indeed to be sufficient as a surface for projecting images. The German Jesuit used the Latin word "paries" to indicate the wall of a room on which he projected colored images (Kircher 1671, 769). Likewise, in *La Lanterne magique* (*The Magic Lantern*, 1903), Méliès projects directly onto the wall.[7] This screen-less screen remains untouched as long as

7 The result of Méliès's magic lantern projection is technologically (or rather magically) advanced: the device not only operates without slides, it also

the (live) projection goes on. Once the show is over, the character of Pierrot approaches the wall, as if to check where the images have gone, just like the little girl at the end of the screening of Scorsese's *Hugo* (2011) (see Chapter 1).

The first documented uses of the French *écran* in the meaning of a projection surface go back to the 1820s. *Larousse Dictionnaire étymologique* gives the definition of a projection board upon which an image is projected: "tableau sur lequel on projette une image." Littré's *Dictionnaire de la Langue Française* (1889) gives a similar definition without, however, using the verb "to project." Instead, Littré refers to the casting of shadows, which seems to evoke the tradition of *ombres chinoises* (or hand shadow play); yet the term is attributed to the field of physics and defined as follows: "Tableau blanc sur lequel on fait tomber l'image d'un objet."[8] Here we can think of the technique of geometric or orthographic projection, which is a means of representing three-dimensional objects in two dimensions by tracing the contours of their (imaginary) shadows (fig. 22).

In the early 1880s, the French term was already in use to indicate projection screens designed for home entertainment, in particular for Émile Reynaud's projection-praxinoscope (1880) (fig. 23). In 1882, *La Nature* published an article by Gaston Tissandier that describes Reynaud's home-viewing apparatus and mentions twice the term "écran." From the illustration it can be deduced that the screen is a piece of fabric (or paper?), pinned to the wall and provided with an ornamental frame.

produces *moving* images that somehow seem to be "live" or "candid" (as if filmed by a hidden camera). Together with the two characters Polichinelle and Pierrot, we first "spy" on a couple dressed in Louis XV-style who are kissing one another, then on a couple of eccentrics making funny faces and, eventually, on Polichinelle and Pierrot themselves.

8 Literal translation: "White board on which one drops the image of an object."

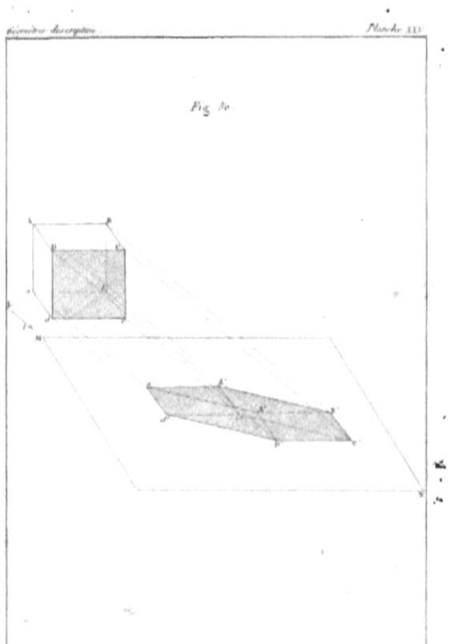

[Figure 22] Geometric projection. Source: Monge 1827.

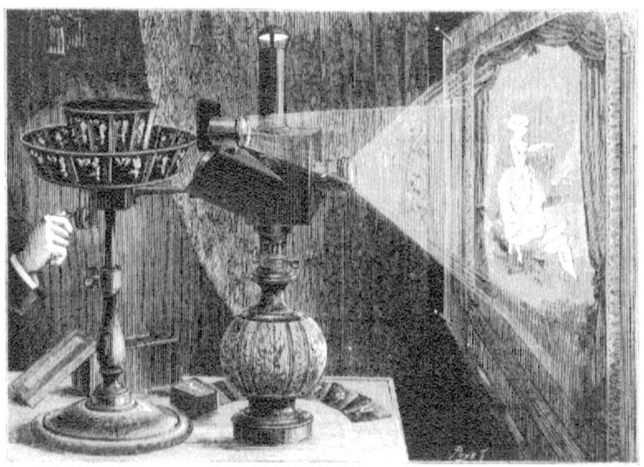

[Figure 23] Reynaud's projection-praxinoscope. Source: Tissandier 1882.

In *Le Lexique français du cinéma: Des origines à 1930* (The French glossary of cinema: From the origins to 1930), Jean Giraud confirms that *écran* is used in the language of the physicist, next to which he mentions also the "montreur" and the "illusionniste"—as if those *métiers* were indeed interchangeable at the end of the nineteenth century because of their specific use of the screen as a projection board (and no longer as a barrier, according to its original meaning). Giraud (1958, 108) gives the place and date of the first official usage of *écran* as film screen, which, not surprisingly, coincides with the (official, French) birth of cinema: Grand Café, December 1895. In fact, on the Lumière program sheet for the first public screening of the Cinématographe at the Salon Indien of the Grand Café one reads:

> This apparatus, invented by Messrs. Auguste and Louis Lumière, makes it possible to capture, by means of a series of instantaneous photographs, all the movements which, during a given time, succeeded one another in front of the lens, and then to reproduce these movements by projecting their images, life size, on a screen in front of a whole audience. (Quoted in Caradec and Masson 1975, 149; my translation)

According to Stephen Heath, who partially quotes these lines in an early psychoanalytical essay, the choice for the term "screen" is "fixed from the start, with neither challenge nor fluctuation" (1977, 31). However, when consulting Webster's *American Dictionary of the English Language* from 1900, the cinematographic usage of the word is not even mentioned. The first meaning of the English "screen" in the early days of cinema was still that of protective shield. Another (new) connotation was that of filter or sieve, which was linked to the coal industry. Going to the screenings in 1900 meant going to a coal factory to pick up bits of coal that were screened out by the sieves (Webster 1900, 992).

As William Paul (2005) points out, two other terms competed with the term "screen" in early writings on cinema published in the United States: "curtain" and "sheet." Whereas the first is a clear reference to the theatrical curtain and was often used in connection with moving picture shows at vaudeville theaters (as in Porter's *Uncle Josh at the Moving Picture Show*), the latter evokes the whiteness of the screen awaiting images for display. This association of the screen as a white, immaculate sheet evokes the work of the Japanese photographer Hiroshi Sugimoto, particularly his Theaters series from the late 1970s in which he photographed old American movie palaces and drive-ins during the projection of a film. The exposure time of Sugimoto's pictures is the duration of the entire film, and the effect is a luminescent screen, a screen touched only by light—an untouchable surface.

The screen as sieve, on the other hand, connects back to the original meaning of screen as fire screen, which is also to a certain extent a filter: the fire screen protects us from being touched by the fire sparks while letting the heat and light pass through. In particular, the working of the color TV screen could be said to be similar to that of a sieve, for it filters electrons and light bundles, which are subdivided into red, green, and blue (RGB). Instead of a surface-screen that stops the light projected on it, it is an interface-screen that transmits light and stands in between the user and the source of light or information. Without entering into technical details, the concept of the sieve applies also to digital displays.[9] Indeed it is the film screen that seems to be the exception to the rule here. For it suggests the transparency of a window (Friedberg 2006), rather than the opacity of a filter (Manovich 1998). On various levels, the film screen is an anomalous screen: it projects instead of protects, it makes visible instead of hides, it brings close instead of separates.

9 On the historical development of electronic displays, see for instance Castellano 1992.

Nevertheless, cinema's projection screens can also be thought of as sieves or filters.[10] The first movie screens as well as the "pre-cinematic" screens (for magic lantern shows, etc.) were usually made of calico, a plain-woven textile made of unbleached, not fully processed, cotton that is full of little holes. With rear projection the light was literally filtered through these holes to create an inverted, mirrored image on the other side of the screen. Even more telling are the modern projection screens for the Digital Dolby multi-channel audio system, which are purposely designed as perforated screens to ensure continuity of the central channel, that is, to let sound through (from behind the screen) to reach the audience.

Thus, the sixth and last etymological lineage—from sheet to sieve—brings about an important shift in meaning, from protecting to separating, which is confirmed by the double meaning of the verb "to screen" documented in 1900 by Webster's dictionary: on the one hand, screening as the action of protecting by cutting off from danger or by hiding, sheltering, concealing (e.g., "Our houses and garments *screen* us from cold; an umbrella *screens* us from rain and the sun's rays"); and on the other hand, screening as filtering, as "pass[ing] through a screen" (intended as sieve). More specifically, the second meaning of "to screen" is defined as "to separate the coarse part of any thing from the fine, or the worthless from the valuable" (Webster 1900, 992). It is precisely this very material and tangible filtering process that I would like to keep in mind when talking about the "abstract" data flows on our digital devices (see Chapter 6).

10 One could also mention here the pinscreen invented in the 1930s by Alexandre Alexeieff, which is however not a projection screen but an animation screen (i.e., a tool for making animated films). The screen, filled with thousands of pins that can slide back and forth through the holes, is lit from the side so that each pin casts its own shadow. The result is a very textured, tactile image.

Some Notes on the Electronic Touchscreen

As an add-on to the screen-sieve genealogy, the history of the electronic touchscreen is directly related to radar technology. Most often, the invention of the touchscreen is associated with the name of E. A. Johnson who worked at the Royal Radar Establishment and who published in 1965 a short article entitled "Touch Display: A Novel Input/Output Device for Computers." While the use of the touchscreen for air traffic control is described in 1968, the first touchscreens for general use were developed in the early 1970s at the University of Illinois, and implemented on university terminals. In those same years, Alan Kay developed the concept of the Dynabook, a notebook with a touchscreen-based display, designed as a "personal computer for children of all ages" (Kay 1972; see also Chapter 5). Gradually, touchscreens were then successfully applied in sales kiosks, public information services, and museums (as already discussed in Chapter 2). These early touchscreens, which were screens in the public sphere (precursors to today's ATM machines and the like), did not have a good reputation: they were imprecise, slow, and poorly designed. Therefore, in the late 1980s and early 1990s, research focused on so-called high-precision touchscreens.

From today's perspective, it is difficult to imagine that in the early 1990s the touchscreen was looked upon as old-fashioned. "If you thought touch screens were a thing of the past," American computer scientist Ben Shneiderman wrote back in those days, "this essay will bring you up to date on improvements to this input device's user interface. I suspect we will be seeing touch screens used for more applications than ever before" (1991, 93). The article ends with some wonderful "predictions" or possible future applications:

> The most exciting breakthroughs will probably be in innovative applications, like controlling 3D artificial realities (let your fingers do the walking), selecting irregular shaped objects (for example, pointing at human body parts and

> getting lab results), or selecting moving objects (for example, pointing at fish swimming in a pool to find out more about the species, or pointing at a rotating globe to select countries). (Shneiderman 1991, 107)

In 1983, Shneiderman founded the Human–Computer Interaction Lab (HCIL) at the University of Maryland. In the early 1990s, this lab conducted many touchscreen experiments, which were all documented in video reports. There is, for instance, the appealing demonstration of the PlayPen II (aka Penplay II), a finger-painting program very similar to today's "coloring for kids" apps for electronic tablets. Developed by Andrew Sears, this touch-painting program allowed users to draw directly on the computer screen, by finger, using different types of brushes and colors. The HCIL also carried out a typing experiment involving different-sized touchscreen keyboards, which resulted in an average speed of 15 words per minute in the case of novices and 25 words per minute in the case of experienced users.

It is important to keep in mind that in those years, the touchscreen was thought of as an alternative of the computer mouse, that is, as an "input device," a "selection device," a "pointing device," or a "computer interaction tool." Because the first-generation touchscreens had the reputation of not being very precise, the main goal of the touchscreen experiments conducted by the HCIL was to improve the accuracy of selection. They designed new selection strategies, such as "land-on" and "take-off" (following air traffic terminology). The latter technique positions a cursor slightly above the user's finger, allowing one to drag the cursor to the desired region and select it by lifting the finger from the screen, if the region is indeed "selectable" (Sears and Shneiderman 1991).

Nearly two decades later, in 2009, researchers at the MIT Media Lab presented their SixthSense project, which consisted of a "wearable gestural interface that augments the physical world around us with digital information and lets us use natural hand gestures to interact with that information" (Mistry 2010). The main idea behind the project, run by Belgian professor Pattie Maes, is that smartphones are still cumbersome in terms of accessing data. Relying on the principle of projection, SixthSense proposed to improve accessibility by enabling any surface to function as a screen, even, or especially, the hand. The promotional video for the project shows for instance how the hand becomes a phone display with buttons to be pushed in order to dial a number. Here the skin becomes literally a (technological) screen. It becomes a surface onto which data are projected, a surface similar to the (classical) film screen but with the possibility of interaction and manipulation due to tactile technology. SixthSense gives us a nice illustration of how touchscreen technology "touches" our own skin. And, by doing so, it brings us back to one of the possible etymological origins of the word "screen."

As discussed in Chapter 3, the success of the iPhone, which was first launched in 2007, has led to the standardization of the capacitive screen for smartphones. This type of touchscreen can be considered in epidermic terms. The capacitive screen consists of a glass panel covered with a thin, transparent coat of metallic oxide. The latter is an electrical conductor, as is the human body. The contact between these two conductors creates a distortion in the electrostatic field underneath the glass panel and "electric particles with opposing charges interact with those on the screen" (Kaerlein 2012, 179–80). The distortion is measurable as a change in capacitance which can be interpreted "either by circuits located in the four corners of the screen (so-called *surface capacitance* technology) or—in the case of the *projected capacitance* screen—directly at the impact point by an underlying matrix of conductive wires" (180). It is the latter type that is installed in today's smartphones because it is the most accurate in determining the exact location of the touch and in following the finger's movements on the screen's surface. As already mentioned in Chapter 3, the capacitive touchscreen requires the naked finger; or better, it requires a skin-to-metal-oxide contact.

Thus, the (coverless) screen can be considered as the (naked) skin of the technological device—not only metaphorically, but also very literally.

On the other hand, touchscreen technology designers have started to explore new tactile surfaces as an answer to the felt need of physical buttons, which would for instance facilitate typing even in semi-darkness. Tactus Technology, founded in 2008, has developed an interface that enables "real" tangible buttons to emerge from the surface of the touchscreen and then, after use, disappear again. A prototype of this "magical" membrane was presented at the 2013 International Consumer Electronics Show (CES). The morphing touchscreen is not only "touchable" but also "tactile": a touchscreen with three-dimensional buttons, not just to be touched, but also to be felt. The industry is of course thinking in practical terms in introducing a tactile keyboard and tactile buttons. But this very same technology could maybe, in the near future, also lead to a more artistic implementation, enabling not only functional buttons to arise, but also various textures to appear and to be explored by naked fingertips, following the lessons of Futurist tactilism (see Chapter 2).

Post-Scriptum: Early Media Screens

While the electronic touchscreen is a relatively new phenomenon of the last five to six decades, the practice of screen touching, as this book aims to demonstrate, is nothing new at all. Of course, this largely depends on the definition of the screen (are we referring to the fire screen, the lady's fan, the military shield, or our skin?), or even better on which etymological lineage we decide to follow or not. Yet to conclude this chapter, I would like to insist that the screen in the strictest sense of "media screen" was already tangible (and touchable, and touched) centuries ago.

For instance, the camera obscura in observatories or watchtowers was designed to project live images on a concave horizontal screen, as on a table, literally within a hand's reach for those surrounding the screen and touchable either by (index) finger or by stick. Another example is the *dispositif* for solar microscope projections, popular in the eighteenth century. Unlike the (individual) tabletop microscope, the solar microscope allowed more people to take part in the viewing because it projected the enlarged microscopic images onto the wall (using the sun as light source). German naturalist Martin Frobenius Ledermüller also conceived of a "portable paper screen on which an artist could trace the projected image" (Terpak 2001, 215). Such a screen, to be placed between the projector and the wall, was truly touchable (and touched). Furthermore, one could mention the mirror anamorphosis, which consists of a plane surface with distorted image on which a conical mirror is placed in order to reveal the non-deformed image: both the painted surface and the mirror cylinder are, again, touchable (and touched) screens. Likewise, the more obvious examples of "pre-cinematic" projection screens, such as the simple cloth of magic lantern shows and the elegantly framed screen of Reynaud's projection-praxinoscope, were screens allowing for "digital" operation and interaction. Jonathan Crary has drawn attention to the presence of stock characters, such as the dwarf-rube, touching and "pulling open a curtain" in advertisements for magic lanterns in the late 1880s and early 1890s (2001, 274). Other illustrations reveal the lack of distance between the magic lantern screen and some spectators, often the youngest among the audience, who reach out their hand.

In other words, there exists a centuries-long lineage of screen-based educational and entertainment forms, in both the private and public spheres, where the screen is not only the projection surface, but also a physical, tangible element of the auditorium space. Because of early cinema's use of rear projection, I would tentatively conclude that the first film screens, as well as those of the phantasmagoria shows, are closer to today's "post-cinematic" notion of *interface* than to the cinematic notion of *surface*. However, this does not automatically turn the "early touchscreen" into a distant predecessor of contemporary touchscreens. On the contrary, the early (nonelectronic) touchscreen rather belongs to a long "pre-cinematic" tradition of protective and dividing shields, which goes back to the uncertain and multiple etymological roots of the word "screen."

[5]

Manually Operated Optical Toys

[Some children] do not make use of their toys, but save them up, range them in order, make libraries and museums of them. Only rarely do they show them to their little friends, all the while imploring them not to touch. *I would instinctively be on my guard against these* men-children.
Charles Baudelaire

Mischievousness

In 1910, French cartoonist and animator Émile Cohl made a couple of flipbooks with photographic images of his son André, among which was *Gaminerie* (Mischievousness). For the occasion, the "naughty" little boy makes a mocking gesture by putting the tip of his thumb to his nose and moving his open hand back and forth (fig. 24). This fool nose gesture, which would perfectly fit in Bruno Munari's gestural dictionary discussed in Chapter 3, needs to be activated by the thumb of the user who holds the flipbook. In the German language the flipbook is called *Daumenkino* ("thumb cinema"), a term that must have appeared only after the emergence of cinema, or rather after the first use of the term *Kino* (as abbreviation of *Kinematograph*) at the beginning of the twentieth century.[1]

1 See *Etymologisches Wörterbuch des Deutchen* on DWDS: dwds.de/wb/Kino. *Daumenkino* refers in particular to a flipbook with *photographic* images. Such a booklet of serial photography was first presented to the public by German film pioneer Max Skladanowsky in 1894.

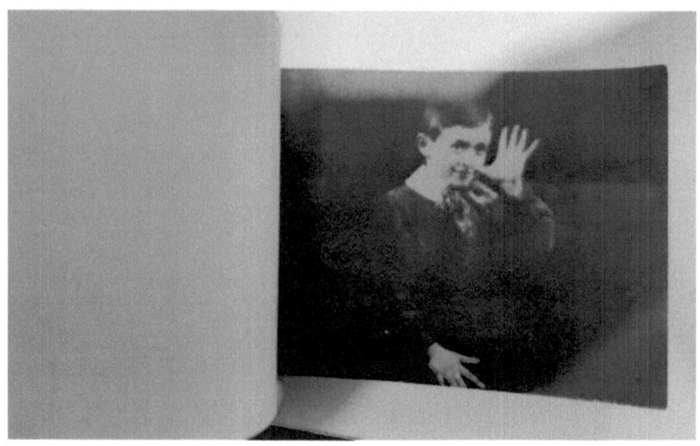

[Figure 24] *Gaminerie* (Émile Cohl, 1910). Source: La Cinémathèque canadienne 1967.

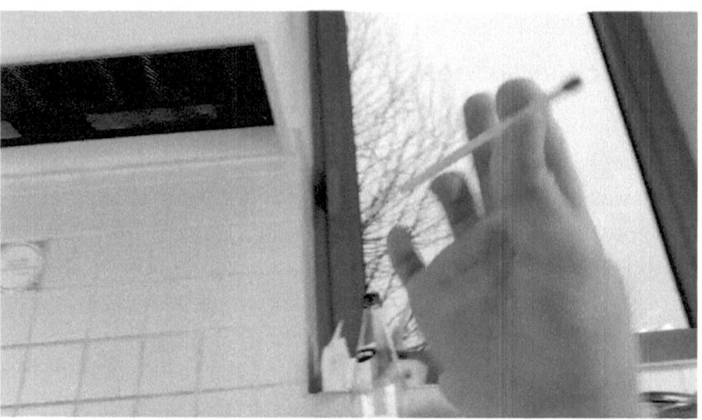

[Figure 25] Kitchen vlog. From author's personal archive, December 2017.

The flipbook is a portable mini-cinema that you can put in your pocket like a mobile media device. To operate it, you use different hands-on actions, such as holding (by pinching), opening (by pulling apart), and browsing (by thumbing). These operations are needed for the disclosure of a temporal moment, in this case of the little boy's mocking gesture.

In 2017, during the Christmas break, a seven-year-old brother and his younger sister got up very early and "stole" their mother's iPhone. Unbeknownst to their parents, who were still asleep, they made a vlog together. In the three-minute video they put their hands on all kinds of kitchenware, showing each piece to the selfie camera, until they hit upon a box of matches. The boy challenges his sister to demonstrate to their intended YouTube audience how to light a match by striking it to the side of the matchbox. Before doing this, the "naughty" little girl holds the match high in the air, between thumb and index finger, in a gesture of demonstration (fig. 25). Thanks to the girl's reluctance to turn her doing-as-if-acting or pretend playing into real action, the game ends well. As with Cohl's *Gaminerie*, there is a double hands-on operation at stake: the playing with matches and the filming with a smartphone. This expensive gadget for adults has become one of the most coveted toys among young children today, especially if it is forbidden (to touch).

Playing and touching are interrelated. Only a few forms of "purely" verbal games (based for instance on the alphabet) can be played without involving any tactile dimension or hands-on operation. Even a mental sport like chess requires the involvement of the hand to move the chess pieces around. Most playground games involve not only manual but also pedestrian contact (among the players, or simply between the player and the ground). And, as I will elaborate further below, a toy stops being a toy when it is no longer touched. Hands-off playing would turn children into contemplative viewers of their own rooms, of their "libraries and museums" of toys, as Charles Baudelaire put it in his essay "Morale du joujou" ("The Philosophy of Toys," 1853).

 Chapter 2 discussed how the gradual institutionalization of the museum caused a shift from hands-on to hands-off ethos. However, the practice of touching artworks and artifacts on display persisted until the mid 1820s. Precisely in this period several optical toys were devised that required a manual, hands-on operation. As Jonathan Crary argues in *Techniques of the Observer* (originally published in 1990), this period coincides with the shift from the Cartesian conception of monocular vision to a new conception of embodied vision. Crary draws in particular on the invention of the stereoscope, which he sees as "a crucial indication of the remapping and subsumption of the tactile within the optical" (1992, 62). Subsequently, in *Suspensions of Perception* (originally published in 1999), Crary also stresses how the nineteenth-century observer's brain was psychophysically educated in terms of perception. The "effects" of early-nineteenth-century optical toys such as the phenakistiscope and zoetrope, which accustomed the observer to images in motion, "were primarily a kinematics and only secondarily a semantics" (Crary 2001, 271). Perception, in Crary's thesis, is an active process; we do not passively receive images but instead actively grasp them in our "*making* of perception" (2001, 155).

This chapter focuses on such early-nineteenth-century optical devices designed for home entertainment—in particular the thaumatrope, phenakistiscope, zoetrope, praxinoscope, flipbook, and stereoscope—and only marginally takes into consideration public peep-show machines, such as Edison's Kinetoscope, that Erkki Huhtamo included in his archaeology of arcade gaming (Huhtamo 2005; see also Strauven 2011). Concentrating analysis on the role of the hand and the image surface as touchable screen, I want to question the "pre-cinematic" dimension of the optical toys and reconsider or revaluate them instead as *tactile* media. I will continue to put "pre-cinematic" along with similar teleological expressions between scare quotes, as I consider them problematic because of their implied idea of progress toward perfection. For sure, the early-nineteenth-century optical toys are not just some minor precursor to the big visual screen of Hollywood. What I am interested in is the way that these toys ensured a continuation of the hands-on practice that for more than a century pervaded the semi-private sphere of the early museums. The hands-on practice then moved from the private sphere (optical toys as home entertainment) to the public sphere with the advent of the hand-cranked viewing machines at the end of the nineteenth century, when cinema emerged as a new form of (visual) spectacle.

As Meredith Bak argues in *Playful Visions: Optical Toys and the Emergence of Children's Media Culture* (2020), it is crucial to think of these nineteenth-century devices as the "new media" of their era, and like all new media they were the cause of some fear or distrust, if not media panic. The continuity that Bak brings to light with her extensive study is indeed the preoccupation of adults about the media use of children:

> From the image of the child's retina characterized as an "exposure" or "impression," to optical play as a "productive" way for children to spend leisure time, these toys and the practices they participated in reveal adult worries over children's time, attention, development, and influences as a longer historical phenomenon. (2020, 11)

Nonetheless, the nineteenth-century optical toys were used not only as educational devices at home but also as pedagogical tools at school, an aspect that I will discuss in the second part of this chapter and that allows for a further connection with today's electronic devices.

For a historical overview of theoretical reflections on toys and uses of the hand in play in philosophical and pedagogical contexts, I will address some key writings and ideas by Henri Focillon, Walter Benjamin, Charles Baudelaire, John Dewey, Bruno Munari, Maria Montessori, and Alan Kay. Other toys will also be taken into consideration to question their tactile dimension in relation to ownership as well as design. The main point is to demonstrate a continuous thread of engagement with the tactile dimensions of play in theory and to review theoretical concepts that may provide a handle on the contemporary forms of tactility in media use.

From Handheld to "Handled" Optical Devices

Early-nineteenth-century optical toys were devices to be operated manually, to be set in motion by one hand or by the coordination of two hands. They were also called "philosophical toys," referring to their double aim of play and education, of entertainment and enlightenment. They were mostly marketed to children, as numerous advertisement plates from the epoch demonstrate. These were toys to play with, but also to learn from, hands-on, for they were supposed to illustrate scientific principles, in particular principles of human perception.

In his aptly titled article "Hand and Eye," Tom Gunning underlines the role of the hand:

> Operated by hand and intended to produce a visual effect, these toys were both manual and perceptual. They not only united amusement with education, but also employed a mechanical device to manipulate human perception by coordinating the hand and the eye. (2012, 496–97)

Further on in the essay, Gunning writes:

> I am interested in these devices primarily as visual media and their role in the creation of this new phenomenon I call the technological image. That phrase encompasses not only images produced by technological means (such as mechanically produced tapestries or prints, or the chromolithographs that set off the age of mechanical reproduction), but images that owe their existence to a device and are optically *produced* by it rather than simply reproduced. (499–500)

Unlike Gunning, I would say that these optical toys are significant not so much as visual media, but rather as *tactile* media. Yet I agree with Gunning's fundamental idea that the images are *produced* instead of reproduced. The idea of (image) production appropriately evokes the idea of manipulation or action—manual action.

Disk-Based Devices: Thaumatrope and Phenakistiscope

Let us first consider the thaumatrope, the simplest form of optical device, despite its sophisticated name, which derives from the Greek *thauma*, "wonder," and *tropos*, "rotation, turning." It consists of a small cardboard disk and two pieces of string attached at opposite sides of its contour. The "user" must take the ends of the two strings between thumb and index finger, making them turn gently to get a quick rotation of the disk. On each side of the disk is depicted an image. By rotating the disk, the two images are blended into one. The faster the rotation, the better the illusion. It is important to stress here that we need both hands to operate the toy, plus the ability of our fingers.

The thaumatrope was invented in the mid 1820s. As Gunning recounts, its invention was the result of a bet between Charles Babbage (who invented the Difference Engine in those very same years) and the astronomer John Herschel. The bet was to show the two sides of a coin, heads and tails, at the same time (without the use of the mirror). Herschel solved the problem by turning the money so quickly that the two sides seemed to appear simultaneously: he achieved a (visual) combination of front and back by means of a mobile (and manual, I add) operation. Then, William Henry Fitton, a friend of Babbage and Herschel, built a device to better illustrate this finding: a cardboard disk with two pieces of sewing thread and two drawings: a bird on front side of the disk and a cage on the back. By rotating the disk, the bird appeared to be in the cage (Gunning 2012, 500–01).

 In the meantime, John Ayrton Paris—a medical doctor from Edinburgh—created the same device, naming it a "thaumatrope" and commercializing it as a "toy." Paris gave a chapter-length description of its workings in *Philosophy in Sport Made Science in Earnest: Being an Attempt to Illustrate the First Principles of Natural Philosophy by the Aid of Popular Toys and Sports*, stressing the Greek origins of the term and translating it as "'a *Wonder-turner*,' or toy which performs wonders by turning round" (1827, 363) (fig. 26). The toy was clearly meant to teach young people about the nature of the universe and the principles of perception, such as the persistence of vision. This nineteenth-century theory aimed at explaining the fusion between two consecutive images through the persistence of images on the retina. This now-disputed theory was for a long time seen as the basis for cinema, that is, for understanding how motion is perceived in cinema. This also explains why the optical toys have been inscribed, unproblematically, into the "prehistory" of cinema. However, despite the rapid movement of the device, the thaumatrope is not creating the illusion of motion. It creates the illusion of fusion, of melting two separate images into one.

As Edwin Carels points out, the thaumatrope's illusion consists of a "two-phased animation," by which a maximal effect is achieved in the most minimal way, as two images are sufficient to trigger a "flicker fusion" in the eye of the observer (2015, 35). Here, one may recall that in the early days of the World Wide Web, in the mid 1990s, the first GIF loops were made as two-phased animations, often in the form of "under construction" signs and banners. However, the frame rate was too low to trigger a true "flicker fusion," which the thaumatrope achieves precisely through a manual operation.

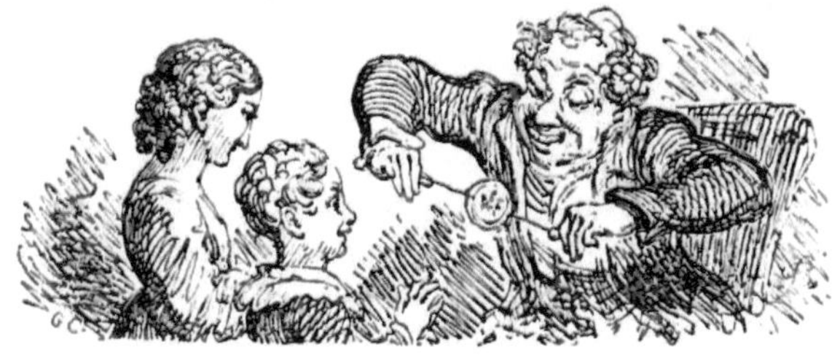

[Figure 26] Two-handed operation of the thaumatrope. Source: Paris 1827.

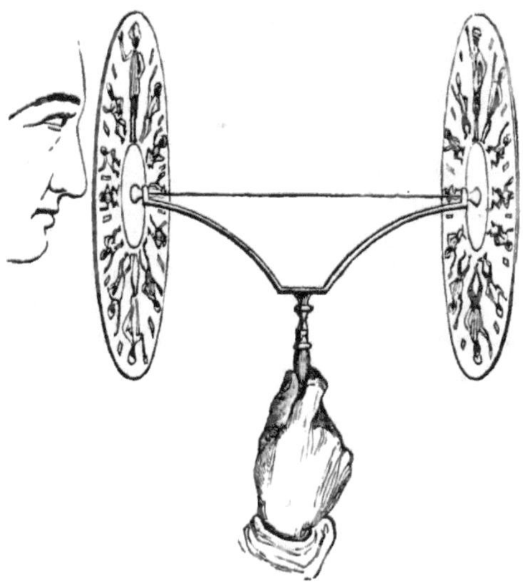

[Figure 27] Double-disk model of the phenakistiscope. Source: Paris 1827.

The same principle is at stake in the phenakistiscope. Invented in 1832, simultaneously by the Austrian Simon Stampfer, who called his device a "stroboscopic disk," and the Belgian scientist Joseph Plateau, who used the French term "phénakisticope," the device is closely connected to Plateau's perception theory, described three years earlier, in 1829, in the doctoral thesis presented at the University of Ghent.[2] The English term "phenakistiscope" is a Greek neologism composed of two verbs: *phenakizein*, "to deceive," and, *skopein*, "to look." Unlike the term "thaumatrope" (which underlines the action of rotation), there is no direct reference to a manual operation. But like the thaumatrope, the phenakistiscope is disk based and needs to be rotated, this time not as a coin flip but as a wheel spinning around its own central axis.

In the original 1832 model, the disk is mounted on a stick. As already described in Chapter 4, it requires a two-handed operation: one hand holding the stick and the other rotating the disk. While facing a mirror, the user rotates the disk and looks through its cutout slits. The images on the back of the disk are reflected via the mirror and trigger the "deceptive" view, that is, a series of separate images (the successive moments of action) merging into a single image (the action itself, in motion). Different from the thaumatrope, the phenakistiscope creates the illusion of movement; thanks to the interval between the cutout slits, the images do not melt together. Whereas the original phenakistiscope required two hands, other models would provide the device on a stand, allowing for a one-handed operation. Still other models would come with a crank to turn the disk, or with an attached mirror. The original handheld phenakistiscope also existed in a variant with two disks that could be operated without the need of a mirror and looked at from both sides, as explained by Paris in his essay on the thaumatrope, "enabl[ing] two persons to witness the deception at the same time" (1827, 384) (fig. 27).

2 Plateau's thesis was entitled *Dissertation sur quelques propriétés des impressions produites par la lumière sur l'organe de la vue* (Dissertation on some properties of the impressions produced by light on the organ of sight).

Like the thaumatrope, the phenakistiscope differs from the successive optical toys because of the simplicity of format and the conflation, so to say, of hardware and software (each disk is concurrently viewing apparatus and view). The drum-based devices, for their part, introduced a system of changeable and combinatory strips, which required some basic preparation before the actual operation could take place.

Drum-Based Devices: Zoetrope and Praxinoscope

The zoetrope (deriving from the Greek *zoe*, "life," and *tropos*, "rotation, turning") is also known as the "Wheel of Life." William Georges Horner is generally considered as the device's inventor for having described or theorized its workings in 1834. However, the toy itself appeared on the market only in the mid 1860s, consisting of a cylinder open at the top and with vertical cutout slits in its circumference. Along the inside wall of the drum are placed strips with separate consecutive images. It is actually possible to create original combinations, combining strips of different series and thus obtaining interesting metamorphoses. Once the drum is ready for use, more people can take part in the viewing process and discover the little animation from various positions around the drum, looking through the cutout slits.

Nicolas Dulac and André Gaudreault, in their essay on optical toys, have drawn attention to the creative (and "pre-cinematic") editing process allowed by the zoetrope. They write:

> The use of a flexible strip opened up new possibilities for presenting the figures. The zoetrope made it possible to exhibit images from two distinct strips at the same time. This was far from a negligible innovation, especially if we consider how this kind of manipulation bears a strange similarity to editing. (Dulac and Gaudreault 2006, 235–36)

Then they quote from an 1870s catalogue distributed by the London Stereoscopic and Photographic Company: "Very effective and humorous Combinations can frequently be made by overlapping one strip of Figures with the half of another strip. Amongst some of the most effective of these combinations, the following numbers will give very amusing results: 4 & 5, 7 & 10, 3 & 13 [etc.]" (Dulac and Gaudreault 2006, 236).

But Dulac and Gaudreault also suggest—in a somewhat teleological way—that the zoetrope's separation between apparatus (hardware) and strip (software) is symptomatic of "the movement towards a 'viewer mode of attraction' as opposed to what we might describe as a 'player mode of attraction'" (2006, 233). As they claim, "With the apparatus on one side and the strip of images on the other, the user of the zoetrope thus felt the presence of the apparatus a little less during the viewing" (233). I would argue that besides the potential creative input of the user *before* the viewing process, hands-on experience remains vital also *during* the viewing process. The most basic model of the zoetrope is set in motion manually, simply by grasping and spinning the drum around its axis, with one or both hands. But what is more, you can interrupt the movement, or even reverse it.

The praxinoscope, on the other hand, is equipped with a crank in its original design, patented in 1877 by Émile Reynaud. The praxinoscope (deriving from *praxis*, "action," and, *skopein*, "to look") gets rid of the viewing slits of the zoetrope and incorporates a dodecagonal prism of mirrors in the middle of the apparatus. This prism reflects each of the twelve images of the strip placed inside the drum individually. Here, similarly to the zoetrope, software and hardware are separated. As Crary observes, Reynaud "grasped" this fundamental relationship and "only produced viewing and projection devices for which he would supply the visual 'software'" (2001, 260).

Reynaud's praxinoscope produced, during gyration, a perfect illusion of moving picture, clear and bright, without blur. As in the case of the zoetrope, more people could participate in the viewing process. In the following years Reynaud invented the praxinoscope-theater (1879) and projection-praxinoscope (1880) for the purpose of home entertainment (see also Chapter 4). The praxinoscope-theater is an ingenious wooden box with a praxinoscope placed inside. The box is provided with two viewing apertures: one in the lid of the box and another in the inclined panel positioned between the (opened) lid and the praxinoscope drum. The aperture in the inclined panel is covered with a reflecting piece of glass that serves to mirror the drawing of a fixed (interchangeable) backdrop at the opposite side, inside the lid. By looking through the aperture in the lid, the observer perceives a moving figure not only *surrounded* by a theater-style proscenium arch drawn on the inclined panel but also *superimposed* on the backdrop reflected from within lid. The moving figure actually appears in the front of the stage. For this three-dimensional optical illusion to be effective, it is imperative that the praxinoscope figures are drawn on a black strip.[3] The three-dimensional effect can only be viewed from a privileged position, that is, from one side of the box, through the viewing aperture. This fixed position also offers an enhanced illusion of motion due to the contrast with the immobile surroundings and background. Yet the "banal" illusion of motion remains perceivable from all sides of the drum, admitting therefore more spectators to join the spectacle, like in the case of the original praxinoscope.

Likewise, the projection-praxinoscope is accessible to multiple viewers at a time. Relying on the magic lantern principle, this model of the praxinoscope replaces the candle with an oil lamp on which two optical systems are mounted: one for the projection of the fixed background and another for the projection of the moving images (still "limited" to the number of twelve). Both layers are projected onto a flat surface, that is, a projection screen, creating a spectacle viewable for a non-active audience. Yet the operation of the projection-praxinoscope, similarly to

3 Crary describes this effect in terms of "spatial dislocation": "The synthesis of moving figure and stagelike background produces an effect that seems three-dimensional, but it is rather a sense of spatial dislocation that results from the overlapping of disparate two-dimensional systems" (2001, 263).

 the early cinema projectors, is hands-on. The "user" remains in close, physical contact with the apparatus, by manually turning the crank: this also allowed for some manipulation of the image projected, as was also the case for the earlier optical toys.

The Flipbook or Folioscope

Invented by the French Pierre-Hubert Desvignes in the early 1860s, the flipbook was first patented by John Barnes Linnett in 1868 under the name "kineograph." Also known as folioscope, the flipbook initially consisted of a little booklet with hand-drawn pictures on each page, representing sequential stages of a movement or action. As already described at the beginning of this chapter, the usage is very simple: with one hand you hold the booklet, with the other you quickly browse, by means of your thumb, all the pages from beginning to end (or vice versa). The flipbook has a linear sequence and therefore breaks with the circularity of the previously discussed optical devices. Even the zoetrope and the praxinoscope, despite their horizontal strips, have a circular (or looping) structure. Another remarkable difference is the prominent role assigned to the thumb.

Flipbooks with serial photographic images appeared in the mid 1890s, likely for the first time in 1894 when German film pioneer and inventor of the Bioscop film projector, Max Skladanowsky, exhibited his first booklet with "Lebende Photographien." Also in the mid 1890s, American inventor Herman Casler designed the Mutoscope, which is a large, coin-operated version of the flipbook. In the Mutoscope the cards are mounted in a circle, in the manner of a Rolodex. One reel contained about 850 cards, corresponding to a minute of viewing time. Unlike Edison's Kinetoscope, the Mutoscope is not motor driven but manually operated by means of a crank. This feature allowed the user to adjust the speed of vision and even arrest it, as Huhtamo explains:

> Viewers could freely adjust the cranking speed, and interrupt the session at any point to observe a particularly interesting

> frame (perhaps a half-naked lady). The only limitation was that the movement could not be reversed. Of course, this was an economic rather than a technical imperative. For just one coin, the user could not be allowed to spend too much time with the device; the profit had to be maximized. (2005, 9)

Huhtamo also recalls that some of the first cinemas, the so-called nickelodeons, opened in the back rooms of existing penny arcades, which compelled the cinemagoer to walk through many "proto-interactive" Mutoscopes in preparation of the (not-so-interactive) cinematic spectacle. Such a combination of arcade and cinema confirms the coexistence of two paradigms or, as Huhtamo puts it, the tension between "two modes of consuming moving images—the hand-cranked peepshows and the screen projection" (2005, 13). Whereas the hands-on operation of the Mutoscope ensured a physical contact with the device, cinema's projection imposed distance and a hands-off ethos. However, during the early years of cinema history, a film projection was not merely "contemplative." Indeed, early cinema was potentially "interactive," with live music and sing-alongs, smoking, public talking, and freely walking in and out. In the same way that the camera was operated manually during filming, so too the projector was hand-cranked during exhibition, which made it possible to slow down or speed up the action, depending on the reaction of the audience (or the mood of the projectionist). In short, as with early museum culture, a proto-interactive ethos prevailed. This dimension would gradually disappear, however, with the institutionalization of cinema.

The flipbook, like the other optical toys, is traditionally considered to be "pre-cinematic." Its invention in the 1860s "prepared" the invention of the Mutoscope, which is another "imperfect" form of cinema, which eventually led to the "birth" of cinema as projection. The nineteenth-century optical toys are generally inscribed in the "prehistory" of cinema for their illustration (or application) of the persistence-of-vision theory. The focus is on their visual dimension: these toys are *optical* toys, toys that create a spectacle for the eyes. In this (still dominant) view, the role of the hand is not taken into consideration. However, if there is a continuity between the optical toys and the early cinema, it is precisely this manual operation. Thus, I would say that the nineteenth-century optical toys are indeed "pre-cinematic," precisely like early cinema is "pre-cinematic" (that is, cinema before institutionalized cinema with its hands-off ethos and prohibition against rubes touching the screen). In other words, they are "pre-cinematic" not in the meaning of announcing cinema, but simply in the meaning of coming before cinema. The link with cinema does, of course, exist and lies in the toy's movement (*kinema*), but this movement is not only visual (perceptual illusion) but also manual (hands-on operability).

The Stereoscope

In general, British scientist Charles Wheatstone is considered the inventor of the stereoscope, which is another interesting term that derives from the Greek *stereos*, "solid," and *skopein*, "to look." In 1838, Wheatstone described the principle of stereopsis in the first part of his essay "Contributions to the Physiology of Vision," entitled "On Some Remarkable, and Hitherto Unobserved, Phenomena of Binocular Vision." In 1832–33, the scientist already designed a mirror stereoscope to view geometric drawings, which he patented in 1838.[4] A decade later, Scottish scientist David Brewster, who had invented the kaleidoscope in 1817, developed the lenticular stereoscope to view stereoscopic photographs. Brewster also designed a camera to produce such pictures. Noteworthy is the specific use that Brewster prospected for his binocular camera, as can be deduced from the title of one of his essays: "Account of a Binocular Camera, and of a Method of Obtaining Drawings of Full Length and Colossal Statues, and

4 The working of the device was quite simple: in the middle, two mirrors were positioned to reflect the slightly different drawings that were placed on the two opposite sides of the stereoscope.

of Living Bodies, Which Can Be Exhibited as Solids by the Stereoscope" (1851). This is stereoscopy, or rather stereography, as an instrument for making sculptures, as the writing of solid art.

When discussing nineteenth-century stereoscopy, one needs to make a distinction between the writing device (the stereoscopic camera) and the viewing device (the stereoscopic viewer). It is only the latter that is usually included in the series of nineteenth-century optical toys. The stereoscopic viewer existed in various models: from the portable handheld viewers to the salon stereoscopes. During the second half of the nineteenth century, the stereoscope became the television of the epoch. "No home without a stereoscope," as the London Stereoscopic Company's slogan said. Thus, stereoscopy established itself as a form of home entertainment, as happened with the other philosophical toys (Weynants 2003).

Still, the question remains if we can consider the stereoscope as a *toy* for the same reasons as the thaumatrope, phenakistiscope, zoetrope, and flipbook. First of all, the manual operation is limited to the preparation phase, which consists in selecting and placing a pair of stereoscopic pictures in the device. When looking at the pictures you do not need to operate the device, you just hold it in your hand and sit still. In other words, it is a handheld toy, not a "handled" one. The Brewster stereoscope is best taken with two hands, whereas the American model invented by Oliver Wendell Holmes (ca. 1860) can easily be held with one hand, thanks to the stick on which it is mounted. Unlike the other optical toys discussed above, the stereoscope does not require the hand to animate the images, that is, the hand does not put them in motion.[5] Nevertheless, there is a direct, physical contact with the device. In the case of the Holmes model, which is an early head-mounted display, there is even skin contact because the hood touches the face to ensure a darkened viewing condition. It

5 The View-Master stereoscope (patented in 1939) will rely on the hand once again for rotating cardboard disks with stereoscopic images.

 is a truly embodied viewing experience, but most importantly, it is a two-eyed viewing experience.

According to Crary, it is precisely binocularity, that is, the discovery of binocular vision, that lays the ground for modern vision. Crary is mostly concerned with new theories of human vision and the mechanics of the eye. Yet there is a strong dimension of tangibility in his analysis of the stereoscope, as David Trotter also observes. Crary writes, for instance, that the purpose of stereoscopic images, for the one who produced or watched them, was "not simply likeness, but immediate, apparent *tangibility*" (1992, 122–24). Trotter quotes this passage and adds:

> The [stereoscopic] illusion is a product of the assertiveness with which objects in the foreground occupy space: the feeling that one could reach out and touch them, or be touched by them. . . . Of the two effects it generated, of tableau and of tangibility, the less memorable, the less disturbing, in 1850, or in 1900, or in 1910, must surely have been the former. (2004, 41–42)

In other words, the most durable effect must have been the tangible dimension (or illusion) of the stereoscopic images. Furthermore, Trotter cites Holmes, who, in 1859, wrote the following: "By means of these two different views of an object, the mind, as it were, *feels round it*, and gets an idea of its solidity. We clasp an object with our eyes, as with our arms, or with our hands, or with our thumb and finger, and then we know it to be something more than a surface" (Holmes 1859, as quoted in Trotter 2004, 42). It is precisely because of this dual nature—device of physical contact (*to grab with your hands*) and device of tactile three-dimensional vision (*to grasp with the eyes*)—that the stereoscope became a pedagogical tool toward the end of the nineteenth century within the American school context, as will be discussed below.

The Philosophy of Toys

If I have highlighted in my description of optical toys the importance of the hand, it is because I want to underline how the "pre-cinematic" observer plays with and interacts with the toy or, as Gunning's "Hand and Eye" also suggests, how the eye depends on the hand. Whereas Chapter 3 was concerned with the technicity of gestures, following a Maussian line of thought, here I want to look more closely at the relationship between the hand and the toy as an example of *technogenesis*, or coevolution of humans and technics. Thanks to skillful hands, the human being is a technical animal. And according to anthropologist André Leroi-Gourhan (1964), thanks to vertical walking, the hand is linked to the face, that is, to the talking instance: gesture and word are fundamentally intertwined, making therefore rather futile the opposition between *Homo faber* (with lithic tools) and *Homo sapiens* (with verbal tools). As observed by Bernard Stiegler, Leroi-Gourhan's thinking is "grounded in an interpretation of the technical phenomenon, which for him is the principle characteristic of the human, through which peoples distinguish themselves more essentially than through their racial and cultural characters in the spiritualist sense of the term" (Stiegler 1998, 45). Such a thesis, as Stiegler points out, leads the anthropologist to focus on the technical intelligence of *Homo faber*, causing him to fail to bring "light to the question of the emergence of the so-called 'nontechnical' intelligence" (161).

Within the context of the emerging technical media at the turn of last century (and the appearance of wireless telegraphy operators and typists), one could say that the optical toy was an early tool of technical intelligence, allowing children to develop manual skills that helped to train their brains and prepare them for modern life. As Bak emphasizes, these educational toys were "part of a wider pedagogical paradigm that stressed the ability to interpret, analyze, and scrutinize visual material" (2020, 2). For young users of nineteenth-century optical toys were seen to be "destined to become professionals who balance ledgers, oversee factory floors, perform surgeries, tend to needlework, coordinate the colors of household goods, and interpret dynamic traffic patterns" (2–3).

Optical toys were not without reason called "philosophical toys." The eye communicates with the brain, that is, the eye fools the brain, via the hand. Or to put it differently, it is the brain of the user that ought to make sense of all the illusions that the hand puts into motion. In "Slots of Fun, Slots of Trouble," Huhtamo comments on the importance of the "keyboard tradition" as a form of technical intelligence, starting off with a citation of sociologist David Sudnow who in the early 1980s made a comparison between playing the piano and mastering an Atari home video game console. Sudnow observed:

> Pushing the hand to its anatomical limit, [the piano] forces the development of strength and independence of movement for fourth and fifth fingers, for no other tool or task so deeply needed. This piano invites hands to fully live up to the huge amount of brain matter with which they participate, more there for them than any other body part. (Quoted in Huhtamo 2005, 3)

The nineteenth-century optical toys, obviously, did not require such sophisticated finger skills, but the comparison nonetheless stands; the hand of the playing child had to be active in order to make the device rotate and the images reach the "brain matter." And as such it trained the child's technical intelligence.

In 1934, French art historian Henri Focillon published a beautiful essay on the skillful hand, entitled "Éloge de la main" ("In Praise of Hands"), in which he developed three central ideas: the hand as agency, the principle of tactile vision, and the hand–object bonding. Firstly, Focillon advances the notion that the hand renders the act of touching active, for it is the hand that "wrenches the sense of touch away from its merely receptive passivity and organizes it for experiment and action" (1989, 184). The hand puts the act of touching it into action. Although Focillon does not mention the optical toys, this observation is particularly relevant for the manual operation of the early-nineteenth-century devices. It also evokes Lorenz Engell's definition of the remote control as a device of will, as discussed in Chapter 3. Whereas the German media philosopher argues that "technologies of the will or intention, such as the remote control or the computer mouse, are linked so closely to touch and to the tactile, and precisely to our use of the index finger" (Engell 2013, 324), Focillon writes:

> The hand means action: it grasps, it creates, at times it would seem even to think. In repose, the hand is not a soulless tool lying on the table or hanging beside the body. Habit, instinct and the will to action all are stored in it, and no long practice is needed to learn what gesture it is about to make. (1989, 158)

Whereas Engell discusses the relationship between two specific fingers, namely the index finger and the thumb, Focillon talks about the hand in general. Secondly, besides its role as action, the hand also completes our deficient visual perception in terms of spatial sense and density; the hand seizes, quite literally, the fullness (weight, volume, and mass) of things. In the art historian's words: "The hand's action defines the cavity of space and the fullness of the objects that occupy it" (Focillon 1989, 162). We cannot measure space by merely looking around, but instead we need to move in it with our body. Thirdly, Focillon describes the appropriation of objects (or tools) and the friendship that develops between the hand and those objects. He writes:

> Between hand and implement begins an association [in French: *amitié*] that will endure forever. One communicates to the other its living warmth, and continually affects it. The new implement is never "finished." A harmony must be established between it and the fingers that hold it, an accord born of gradual possession, of delicate and complicated

> gestures, of reciprocal habits and even of a certain wear and tear. Now the inert instrument comes alive. (165)

In other words, the tool (or optical toy or media device, I would like to add) takes the form of the hand, or rather it sets itself to the shape of the hand. In "Morale du joujou," Baudelaire similarly suggests that the toy comes to life in the hands of the playing child, and he even advances the idea that the toy is the "child's earliest initiation into art" (2018, 15). Yet for Baudelaire this is mainly a matter of imagination ("inside the *camera obscura* of the childish brain," 13) and therefore less connected to hands-on actions than it is in Focillon's essay.

Conversely, Focillon's notion of intimate relationship between hand and tool is akin to the concept of "fit" that Heidi Rae Cooley develops in relation to modern "mobile screenic devices" (MSDs). Whereas Focillon in the 1930s talks about tools (*outils*), Cooley's article "It's All About the Fit" looks into the first generation of handheld screen-based devices, such as PDAs, flip phones, and digital compact cameras and camcorders, and the way they mold to the hand. The notion of fit comes from biomechanics and industrial design, which Cooley describes in terms of "interpenetration." She writes:

> When hand and MSD articulate, the surfaces of the palm and the MSD mold each to the other, they interpenetrate. Thenar (thumb) and hypothenar (pinky) muscles cup the rounded edges of the MSD, which in turn sidles into the cradle of semi-flexed digits. The experience is tactilely pleasing, as hand and MSD fold into each other. (Cooley 2004, 137)

The notion of design as the "skin of culture," as advanced by Derrick De Kerckhove, can be considered as an early intuition of Cooley's fit. Claiming that "design is more than an afterthought, bolted onto industrial production to facilitate marketing," De Kerckhove invites us to think of the enveloping effect of technology in both sensory and cognitive terms:

> In a very large sense, design plays a metaphorical role, translating functional benefits into sensory and cognitive modalities. . . . Being the visible, audible or textural outer shape of cultural artifacts, design emerges as what can be called the "skin of culture." (1997, 154)

Yet design also clearly has its marketing reasons, "glamorizing [technology's] products" (De Kerckhove 1997, 153), seducing the eye and stimulating our purchasing drive. As a nicely designed mechanical object, the optical toy belongs to the history of (purchasable) gadgets; it is a novelty, a must-have. The lineage of gadgets points indeed toward the idea of possession: the optical toy, like today's smartphones and tablets, is an object that you can buy, and therefore own. Its sense of ownership is directly linked to (the right to) touch.

Here one could make a comparison with the collector of the *Wunderkammer*, the owner of unique items, as discussed in Chapter 2, as well as with Walter Benjamin, who was a fervent collector of books, especially rare manuscripts and illustrated books for children. In his 1931 essay "Ich packe meine Bibliothek aus: Eine Rede über das Sammeln" ("Unpacking My Library: A Talk about Book Collecting"), Benjamin describes the personal and intimate relationship that binds a collector to his collection. He speaks of the "predominantly irrational" need of possession. Interestingly enough, he reads this need in tactical terms: "Property and possession belong to the tactical sphere. Collectors are people with a tactical instinct" (Benjamin 1978, 63). Later in the essay, Benjamin reinforces his argument: "For a collector . . . ownership is the most intimate relationship that one can have to objects. Not that they come alive in him; it is he who lives in them" (67). Thus, when a bibliophile acquires an old book, it is not so much the object that is reborn, but rather the person who buys it. It is the bibliophile who is reborn through the book. Here Benjamin makes a comparison with the capacity of children to renew existence (or to rebuild their lives):

> For children can accomplish the renewal of existence in a hundred unfailing ways. Among children, collecting is only one process of renewal; other processes are the painting of objects, the cutting out of figures, the application of decals—the whole range of childlike modes of acquisition, from touching things to giving them names. (61)

In this essay on book collecting, Benjamin also speaks of his passion for children's books, on which he had already published an essay five years before: "Aussicht ins Kinderbuch" ("A Glimpse into the World of Children's Books," 1926). This earlier essay talks, among other things, about the phenomenon of "pull-out books" and books with little windows and doorways to be opened manually. In this respect, Benjamin alludes to the coordination between mind and hand, as discussed above in relation to the optical toy: "Just as children's books opened up a wide field for thought and the imagination, they did the same for the active hand" (2008, 231). He mentions *Le Livre-joujou*, one of the first examples of an interactive book, published in Paris in 1831 by Janet Library. Contemporary with optical toys like the thaumatrope and the phenakistiscope, *Le Livre-joujou* was designed as a book to animate with your hands (and not just your mind), as a true tactile media device.[6]

Baudelaire's "Morale du joujou," published two decades later, returns to the relationship between possession and touch, this time in terms of toys in general. The 1853 essay has, in fact, a double moral. First, a toy does not have to be expensive or

6 Benjamin addressed the issue of tactility in many of his writings, most notably in his Artwork essay where the tactile approach of technical media is discussed in opposition to the auratic distance of traditional works of art. Nicolas Pethes (2000) proposes to read Benjamin's famous essay in the light of "industrial psychotechnics," a field of training for factory workers that around 1900 aimed at improving tactile skills in the name of industrial productivity, thus leading to alienation instead of closeness. For this critical reading, he compares Benjamin's ideas with David Katz's *Der Aufbau der Tastwelt* (*The World of Touch*, 1925).

beautiful to attract the child's interest, an idea that Baudelaire corroborates with the passage where a poor child plays with a living rat to the envy of a rich child.[7] Second, a toys needs to be touched, to be played with; otherwise it has no *raison d'être* as toy. Toward the end of the essay, Baudelaire expresses his contempt for those parents who do not let their children play with their toys, deeming them too beautiful or too fragile. These are parents who consider toys "as objects for mute adoration," as if they were artworks to be contemplated (Baudelaire 2018, 19). Some children, called by Baudelaire "men-children" (*enfants-hommes*), act the same and do not let their friends touch their playful possessions. When a toy is no longer touched, it simply stops being a toy. It might become an object of contemplation, or of neglect, hidden away, no longer acted upon, no longer "animated." Playing means touching, manually and mentally.

Furthermore, Baudelaire describes the increasing phenomenon of what he calls the "scientific toy," by which he means the "philosophical toy." Here he mentions the stereoscope (as a device that "creates a flat image in the round") and the phenakistiscope (see Chapter 4). Baudelaire declares to have no value judgment on them. Yet their main defect is that they are too expensive and therefore not available to children of the lower social classes. But, as Baudelaire admits, "they can continue to amuse for a long time, and they develop in the mind of a child the taste for marvellous and unexpected effects" (2018, 17–18).

Object Lesson as Early Model of Hands-On Teaching

In the last decades of the nineteenth century, the optical toy made its appearance as not only an educational toy at home but

7 This passage of the essay was later published as a "little poem in prose," entitled "Le Joujou du pauvre" ("The Poor Child's Toy"), included in the posthumously published collection *Le Spleen de Paris* (*Paris Spleen*, 1869).

 also a pedagogical tool at school. As Bak explains, it became part of the new educational approach of the object lesson:

> Contrasted with earlier pedagogical models that foregrounded written literacy and memorization, the object lesson mandated learning through the senses, offering pupils exposure to and experience with real things in nature. The visual and tactile attributes of optical devices like the stereoscope echoed the logic of the object lesson, which privileged sensory perception over reading comprehension as a learning method. (2012, 147)

Most interesting in this late-nineteenth-century pedagogical debate is the discourse on the senses, that is, the need to address the various senses, not only sight (through reading) but also touch (through physical contact with objects).

According to Bak's findings about the American school context, the stereoscope was an ideal teaching tool for various reasons. First, it was a scientific instrument that could demonstrate the phenomenon of binocular vision. Second, it could be used as a visual support for teaching other subjects, offering realistic views (i.e., photo-realistic views with depth of field) that traditional schoolbooks could not provide. Third, looking at these hyper-realistic views resulted in sensorial experiences similar to visiting remote locations, allowing virtual travel to places where only the richest could go. Fourth, it did so in a very disciplined way because the stereoscope required a most attentive and repetitive look from an immobile body. Last and most important for my purpose, the stereoscope was an ideal teaching tool for the object lesson because you could hold it in your hand.

"Object lesson" is the English term for a practical lesson (or demonstration) where the "object" is at the center of attention. The approach of the object lesson derives from the educational philosophy of Johann Heinrich Pestalozzi, according to whom teaching must start with the observation of objects through which students can recognize (or learn) new concepts. Known as *Anschauungspädagogik*, the approach led to a more active, concept-oriented autonomy of the pupils. Pestalozzi was a Swiss pedagogue and reformer in the second half of the eighteenth century (and early nineteenth century). His formation took place in contact with the Enlightenment, albeit in a diluted form, under the influence of Jean-Jacques Rousseau and his ideas expressed in *Émile ou de l'éducation* (*Emile, or On Education*, 1762), in particular the need to return to nature, to rediscover the senses, and to avoid abstract intellectualism. Nonetheless, Pestalozzi disagreed with Rousseau on one important aspect: namely, the idea that men are born good. Pestalozzi believed the opposite and considered it the task of education to make them good, to bring them to perfection.

In her study, Bak refers to Pestalozzi, more particularly when she discusses the Scottish educational theorist Alexander Bain, who in the 1870s aimed to give an unequivocal definition of the object lesson method, as the term was used very broadly, often with very diverging interpretations. Bain distinguished three modes in which the term "object lesson" was used:

> The first . . . followed in the tradition of the Swiss educator Pestalozzi, who favored bringing concrete examples of things into the classroom. Secondly, the object lesson . . . was a kind of sensory training whereby children learned to refine their observational powers, classifying and discriminating between the things they perceived. Third, the object lesson involved language acquisition and the association between written words and the things they described. By sensorily experiencing an object—seeing it or touching it—children could come to recognize its written equivalent. (Bak 2012, 156)

In short, object lessons proposed an early model or method of hands-on teaching, whereby children put their hands on concrete objects and learning takes the shape of sensorial training, involving more than just the two dominant senses of sight and hearing.

At the end of the nineteenth century, American philosopher John Dewey published his first writings on education. Well-known for his educational pragmatism and pedagogical activism, Dewey was remarkably negative about object lessons. He considered the method artificial, for the objects were isolated, removed from their "natural" setting. It should be remembered here that, initially, object lessons centered on objects from nature; the use of the stereoscope and other optical devices is an extension of this didactic method.

According to Dewey, the problem of artificial isolation also applies to the sensory activity, which becomes an end in itself. In *The School and Society* (1907), he argued:

> No number of object-lessons . . . can afford even the shadow of a substitute for acquaintance with the plants and animals of the farm and garden, acquired through actual living among them and caring for them. No training of sense-organs in school, introduced for the sake of training, can begin to compete with the alertness and fullness of sense-life that comes through daily intimacy and interest in familiar occupations. (Dewey 1907, 24–25)

And, later, in *Democracy and Education* (1916), he critically observed:

> "Object lessons" tended to isolate the mere sense-activity and make it an end in itself. The more isolated the object, the more isolated the sensory quality, the more distinct the sense-impression as a unit of knowledge. The theory worked not only in the direction of this mechanical isolation, which tended to reduce instruction to a kind of physical gymnastic of the sense-organs. (Dewey 1916, 314)

Instead of isolating the objects, Dewey proposed to let pupils interact with them in their "real" context, that is, in the context of real life. For Dewey, the school was a place to practice life. Hence, the school was to be conceived as a laboratory, where children would be apprentices who learned a *métier* (or craft).

As Svenk Brinkmann and Lene Tanggaard point out, the tradition of pragmatic philosophy to which Dewey belonged postulated that ideas are not fixed or predetermined, like Plato's ideas or "forms"; ideas are instead tools that we create to face the world. And that is how, in Dewey's view, school should be conceived: not as the transmission of fixed ideas, but as the construction and transformation of ideas (that is, ideas as tools) to face life and interact with society. In other words, knowledge does not derive from a passive observation of reality (which constitutes the still dominant "epistemology of the eye" of frontal or verbal pedagogy); instead, it should be made, specifically "made by hand" (following Dewey's "epistemology of the hand"). In this context, "hands-on" means both manual and in the field, that is, no abstract exercises with artificially isolated objects, but real activities, such as building houses, cultivating vegetable gardens, and making clothing. As Brinkmann and Tanggaard conclude, it is a "process that necessarily involves creativity," whereby one should think not of abstract, romantic genius but rather of concrete "creativity of action—a creativity of the hand" (2010, 256).

Tactile (Media) Pedagogy

As briefly alluded to in Chapter 2, Italian designer Bruno Munari organized in the late 1970s a series of hands-on laboratories, or so-called tactile workshops, in museums and elementary schools in Italy. These workshops were a typical expression (or implementation) of his experimental educational philosophy. Throughout his career, Munari dedicated himself to all forms of artistic practice, from mobile sculpture to abstract painting, from experimental cinema to industrial design. He also became a very productive illustrator and writer of children's books and a designer of toys and didactic games. As self-taught pedagogist, Munari was influenced by the ideas of active didactics through his relationships with children's author Gianni Rodari and school teacher Giovanni Belgrano, who were both connected to the Movement of Cooperative Education (*Movimento di Cooperazione Educativa*), a secular movement inspired by the pedagogical principles of John Dewey (Panizza 2009).

According to Munari, creativity needed to be taught and encouraged throughout the educational process, by providing school kids with tools that are, on the hand one, essential to their knowledge and, on the other, useful to activating divergent thinking. The educator must supply the necessary tools, explain the basic techniques, and offer as much data as possible to be memorized by the child because, according to Munari, everyone sees what he or she knows. The more we know, the more we see and can develop our creativity. "Do not say *what* to do, but *how* to do it" was Munari's motto (Restelli 2002, 35; my translation). That is, give the pupils the tools and techniques to operate, but not the forms or models to imitate. In other words, he was more concerned with the (hands-on) process than with the (artistic) final result.

Roughly speaking, one can distinguish two types of Munarian hands-on labs: the visual communication experiments and the tactile exercises. The former can be considered "low-tech media labs," in which children are invited to explore the limits of "new media" devices, such as the Xerox machine and the mechanical slide projector (Strauven 2019). The latter are more directly related to tactile or multisensory education, involving applications such as the composition of tactile messages, the reading of tactile pre-books (*prelibri*), and the touching of objects with or without blindfolded eyes. In this regard, Beba Restelli (2002) mentions the touch tub, which was filled with scraps of fabric and furs in which to immerse oneself for a whole-body experience, and the touch carpet, which consisted of a series of square modules on which children could play and discover various types of materials offering different sensations, such as smooth and rough, soft and hard, shiny and matt.

The method of "learning by doing" is typical of Munari's commitment to Dewey's active didactics. Unlike Dewey, however, the Italian designer was less focused on teaching craftsmanship and more driven by the idea of stimulating creativity and activating divergent thinking. As also pointed out by Laura Panizza, Munari adhered to fundamental ideas related to the democratization and desacralization of art. In fact, his educational philosophy found its roots in the Concrete Art Movement (*Movimento Arte Concreta*), which he cofounded in 1948 (Panizza 2009, 15).

It is precisely this mission of demythologizing the sacredness of art that causes Munari's approach to diverge from the Montessori Method. The pivotal concept of Maria Montessori's educational system was children's free choice of activity, allowing them to develop at their own pace and to their own size.[8] Her method focused not only on "learning by doing" but especially on "learning by yourself." This was mainly achieved by practical play and activities with "sensorial materials" (such as tactile letters) that Montessori originally developed for mentally disabled children and that aimed at training the senses by exposure to sights, smells, and tactile experiences. As later followed by Munari, Montessori attributed a decisive role to the educator or teacher, who must give explanations on the materials and their possible usages, so that the child is free to experiment and play with them (Panizza 2009, 4).

In August 2020, on the occasion of the 150th anniversary of Montessori's birth, her great-granddaughter Carolina suggested that Maria would have banned the electronic tablet from the life of children, as they develop intelligence through dexterity and therefore need to explore the world by touching (real) things and

8 The first *Casa dei bambini* (Children's House), which opened in January 1907 in Rome, was designed as a school at the size of children, with lightweight, low furniture that they could move themselves.

 not just their images on the surface of a media device.[9] For the exact same reason, others argue that the great pedagogue and school innovator would probably have admitted touchscreens among children, relying on the principle that "the hands are the tools of human intelligence," whether used for playing with sand or for tapping on a screen (Benedetto 2013).

Evidently, the situation is not that simple. But instead of getting bogged down in the good vs. bad debate, I would like to mention here an educational study conducted in 2012–13 in the Spanish school context concerning the use of the iPad by preschoolers, as I believe its outcomes are revealing in light of Montessori's (and Munari's) legacy.[10] Researchers collected data in two classrooms of a government-funded kindergarten in the suburbs of Madrid, observing children's iPad use in free-choice time (without interaction of the teachers) and comparing their engagement with different educational apps, such as construction or puzzle apps, coloring and drawing apps, and a story-making app, called *Our Story*. The research focused on both communicational and technical skills as displayed by the children involved, that is, the collaborative verbal exchange with their peers, on the one hand, and the individual hands-on dexterity with the software, on the other hand. One of the important findings of the study is that open-ended apps (as opposed to drill-and-practice apps) support high levels of engagement, which manifests itself in collaborative reasoning, thinking aloud, and joint problem-solving. Drawing apps and storytelling apps are open-ended, allowing for multiple "solutions" to each problem, because children can draw or narrate whatever they like in a preestablished space.[11]

9 See radio transmission "Pagina 3," Rai Radio 3, August 31, 2020. Podcast: https://www.raiplayradio.it/audio/2020/08/PAGINA-3-fe219ae6-cb42-4fb9-9d76-a91ff9dc642e.html.

10 See also ongoing research conducted in Italy and Greece on how to implement ICT technologies to enhance "Montessori and Munari based psycho-pedagogical insights" (Miranda et al. 2017).

11 According to the authors, this is especially true for the *Our Story* app as "children exchange ideas related to the functions of the software and the

Conversely, construction and completion apps (e.g., dominos, jigsaws, and other kids' puzzles) are apps with bounded, or specified, success criteria: the puzzle has to be completed, there is a clear and predefined goal, and there is therefore no real openness (Kucirkova et al. 2014).

The notion of openness hints at not only the interactive potential of the app but also the notion of hands-on thinking (or reasoning) that goes beyond merely touching the screen. To be evaluated as a high-engagement educational tool for preschoolers, it seems that the electronic tablet must adopt the features of a programmable, computational toy, functioning thus as something more than a device to access predefined games. The child is then not just touching the games displayed on the tablet's screen but also operating, hands-on, the device's inner processes. Such an operational description of today's electronic tablet evokes the notion of a "dynamic book," or Dynabook, as envisioned in the early 1970s by Alan Kay, in view of providing all school kids with an "intimate computer," the size of a notebook, that might train them, from a very early age, in algorithmic thinking.

Kay developed the Dynabook concept at Xerox PARC in Palo Alto, California, describing its principles in an eleven-page proposal, entitled "A Personal Computer for Children of All Ages" (1972). The Dynabook was thought of as an active "metamedium," incorporating all other media and "respond[ing] to queries and experiments—so that the messages may involve the learner in a two-way conversation" (Kay and Goldberg 2003, 394). It had to be personal (allowing for individual interaction), affordable (for kids to have their own), portable (as a true "carry anywhere" device), networked (ensuring access to all the libraries of the world), with

task of story-writing overall, which corresponds to self-regulated and critical engagement" (Kucirkova et al. 2014, 180). Children can add their own pictures, drawings, and audio files to the database of narrative building blocks. In the Edit mode, they can customize these building blocks by adding captions. A typical situation of joint problem-solving is when children search together for specific letters on a keyboard they are not all familiar with.

 a nearly eternal battery life, and Smalltalk programming language embedded. As for the design and UI, the handheld device would have measured about 23 x 30 cm (9 x 12 inches), being thinner than 2 cm (3/4 inch) and weighting less than 900 grams (two pounds). It would have come with a fixed, embedded keyboard, a touch-based display, and a stylus (Fig. 28a–b). In short, it was a true hands-on educational media device.

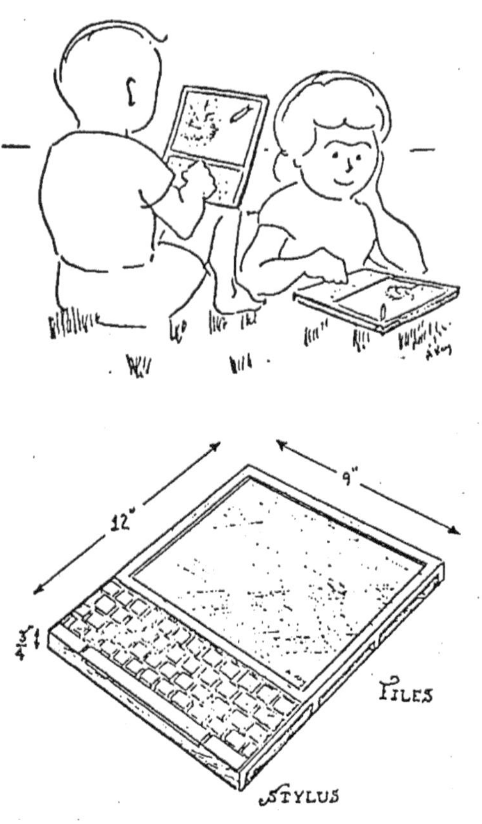

[Figure 28a–b] Sketches for the Dynabook. Source: Kay 1972.

Importantly, among his sources of inspiration, Kay explicitly mentions the name of Montessori as "one of the first to decide that children were much more adept at learning during early years (2–5) than was generally supposed" (Kay 1972, 3). Furthermore, the Dynabook concept is indebted to two men who considered the child "an active agent, a creator and explorer": on the one hand, Omar K. Moore for his concept of the "talking typewriter" as a safe and productive environment and, on the other, Seymour Papert for his work in "teaching kids thinking" (4). Lastly, Kay delves into a discussion of Jean Piaget's developmental stages and the notion of "operational models" that retain the young child's knowledge ad hoc, not necessarily in a logically consistent way. By comparing Piaget's operational model to an algorithm, Kay concludes that "computers are an almost ideal medium for the expression of a child's epistemology"; and crucially for my argument, they allow the child to practice all types of thinking skills "in an environment that is patient, covert *and fun*!" (5).

This final note about fun brings us back to the original concept of the nineteenth-century optical toy as a "philosophical toy," as a hands-on device both for play and education, for entertainment and enlightenment.

[6]

The Image as Screenic Surface and Interface

It's magical and black, but sometimes lots of colors come out of it.
Anonymous

Screen's Cues for Action

To introduce this last chapter, I dive once more into my family archive for an anecdote about my daughter's screenic interactions. It must be said that she grew up in a household without a TV set but with plenty of other media screens, namely a desktop computer, laptops, and tablets. From an early age she became familiar, like many children of her generation, with touchscreen and non-touchscreen operations, that is, typical "Apple gestures" such as pinching and swiping, on the one hand, and mouse clicking, on the other. If I remember correctly, she was about eighteen months old when I first exposed her to YouTube to show her some early Disney cartoons on my laptop. She would regularly point her finger to the images on the screen, reaching out in an attempt to touch them (fig. 29).

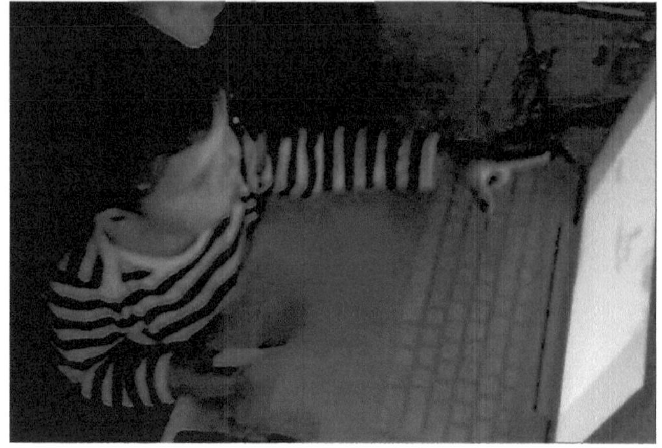

[Figure 29] Watching *Steamboat Willie* on YouTube. From author's personal archive, October 2009.

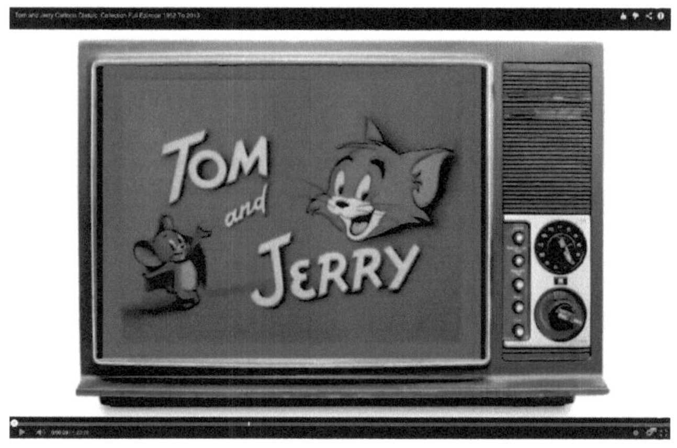

[Figure 30] "Mommy, look, here is your favorite old computer again!" Screenshot from a 1950 *Tom and Jerry* cartoon playing in a decoy frame. https://www.dailymotion.com/video/x39yjmz.

Soon she would understand that the supply of cartoons on YouTube is inexhaustible, that one clip leads to the next by a simple click of the mouse or touch of the fingertip. At a very early age, today's children discover that the Internet provides not only continuous flow but also endless choice. The shorter the clips, the more they want to see. This is how, quite intuitively, they make their own personalized film programs. Obviously, the selection is streamlined by YouTube, or Google, but still, it happens that genres get mixed, that an original *Pat and Mat* animation, for instance, leads to a hard-rock "Hardcore Remix" of its opening theme music. One could say that today's children are indeed improvised film programmers who put together their own digital "cinema of attractions," with the risk of involuntary Kuleshov effects (Tsivian 1990).

When watching YouTube clips on a computer screen, children also become aware of the difference between the screen and the frame, between the screen as display surface and the frame as delimitation of the image interface, that is, the working or viewing space of a specific software program, application, or website. At the age of five, my daughter watched a lot of cartoons online on the screen of a desktop computer. In that period, I had found her a wonderful "vintage" collection of *Tom and Jerry* shows that displayed the clips within the frame of an old-fashioned, obsolete TV set (fig. 30). The first time she saw this decoy frame, she took the mouse and wanted to click it away to go full screen, not realizing that she was already in full screen mode. Sometime later, when she found this collection on her own, rather by accident, she called to me, "Mommy, look, here is your favorite old computer again!"

The click of the mouse, in the case of non-touchscreens, and touch of the fingertip, in the case of touchscreens, are very simple actions that the youngest generation of media users rapidly master and use to manipulate in a direct way the image as screenic surface and interface: to skip ads, to toggle full screen, to point at pictures, to go from one picture space to another.

 Here I like to evoke an anecdote told by Thomas Elsaesser in an article about 3D cinema. Elsaesser narrates how he showed some digitized photos on his laptop to his friends and how one of their daughters tried to click on them with the mouse. So instead of looking at the pictures, she wanted to act upon them, by pointing the cursor of the mouse and clicking on them. "When nothing happened," Elsaesser writes, "she lost interest even though it happened to be a photo of her parents when they were young—that is, before she was born" (2013, 240). It is this "inappropriate" reaction of a seven-year-old that revealed to him the new function of the image, which comes very close to my definition of the screenic image: "The idea of a digital photo as a window to a view (to contemplate or be witness to) had for her been replaced by the notion of an image as a passage or a portal, an interface or part of a sequential process—in short, as a cue for action" (241). The image is not so much something to look at as something that leads, by means of a mouse click, to something else.

The Notion of the Screenic Image

What is an image today? Or rather, what does it mean that an image is no longer a "window to a view," but a "passage or a portal," a "cue for action"? What does this say to us about the changing function of the screen? According to Francesco Casetti, the term "screen" is no longer appropriate to indicate the surfaces of today's media devices, which are "linked to a permanent flow of data" without being necessarily "coupled to an attentive gaze, to a world that asks to be witnessed" (2015, 168). For Casetti, as seen in Chapter 4, the new screen is a "transit point," where images stop for a moment and then take off again; or, even better, it is a display that "simply 'makes present' images" (168). These are images we do not immerse in but grasp and make use of. Or as Casetti puts it, "images that are not necessarily capable of restituting an empirical reality; rather, they are oriented toward supplying data and information" (168).

Whereas Casetti proposes to designate the new screen with the term "display," I would like to suggest that the image is taking over some functions of the screen, both as surface and as interface. I propose to call the new generation of digital images "screenic images," that is, images that only come to full existence as images on a screen. They also exist, of course, as nonimages in the form of digital files, consisting of data and metadata that describe, for instance, image size, color depth, resolution, and date of creation.

I take this basic distinction between the digital image as image and the digital image as file as a starting point for defining the "screenic image" as a new theoretical tool to rethink the relation between the image and the screen. According to Jonathan Crary, many theorists of our field are too concerned with the aesthetics of the digital image (i.e., image as image), thereby missing its operational dimension (i.e., image as file). It seems as if we are still trapped in the predominantly visual regime of the twentieth century. Telling, for instance, was the recurring argument of the loss of indexicality in the many debates about the digital image that took place in the first decade of the twenty-first century and that somehow ignored the numerical, nonvisual operation of previous indexical instruments. As Tom Gunning rightly pointed out:

> Long before digital media were introduced, medical instruments and other instruments of measurement, indexical instruments *par excellence*—such as devices for reading pulse rate, temperature, heart rate, etc., or speedometers, wind gauges, and barometers—all converted their information into numbers. (2004, 40)

But film theory ended up confusing the indexical quality of the photographic image with its iconicity, that is, its truthiness and faithfulness to the referent in *visual* terms. Yet the indexicality of the photographic image resides not so much in the visual picture produced as in its chemical process, that is, in the effect of light on light-sensitive emulsion.

 In *24/7: Late Capitalism and the Ends of Sleep*, Crary observes that "more images, of many kinds, are looked at, are seen, than ever before, but it is within what Foucault has described as a 'network of permanent observation'" (2014, 47). Today's society is a society of sleeplessness, where images are produced, consumed, and discarded without interruption and where our acts of vision are transformed into information. Instead of claiming we are moving toward a post-image era, Crary proposes to consider today's (nonstop) circulation of images in terms of time-management, or rather self-management and self-regulation. It is according to this logic that Crary believes the essence of the digital image is *not* its aesthetic dimension. He writes: "To be preoccupied with the aesthetic properties of digital imagery, as are many theorists and critics, is to evade the subordination of the image to a broad field of non-visual operations and requirements" (47). In other words, today's image is no longer just an image. It is becoming something else, something that goes beyond its merely visual (or aesthetic) appeal.

This is an important point for my two-step definition of the screenic image. Firstly, as I already hinted at, I propose to call "screenic image" an image that exists as image only when it appears on a screen. Whereas a painting on the wall can also become a screenic image when digitized and displayed on a screen, a digital image—like a GIF or a JPEG—only manifests itself as image when rendered (or visualized, if you prefer) on a screen. To put it more simply, all images can become screenic images (when being displayed on a screen), but only digital images are by definition screenic images.[1] Secondly, I prefer not to call the

1 It could be objected that digital image files can also exist as visual images *without* a screen, for instance, when printed out directly from a flash drive. This hypothetical, however, ignores both the composition of images on screen and that digital files almost never bypass the screen. Yet it is worth considering that the digital image resists the traditional meaning of an image being visual. It exists for the computer as image without visualization, that it, as meaningful data that can take any kind of form or expression without being visual to us. As Kyle Stine points out, visuality has its functions

digital image a "post-visual" image, because this term not only connotes a (non-reversal) chronology but also implies a devaluation in relation to the old, non-digital, "purely" visual image. Instead I suggest using the notion of "image+" which is a term I pick up from image processing software programs. I believe that the notion of image+ may help us to think of the screenic image as enrichment, as something in addition to the visual. In short, the image+ is a screenic image that goes beyond its visual appeal by adding an extra dimension. I am referring here to a new functionality that is embedded or inscribed in the digital file.

From Data-Based to Multi-Purpose Image

In some cases, this extra dimension can remain hidden or exist only as code. An extreme case is the raw image file, which contains minimally processed data from the image sensor, before the image is actually processed. So, it is a not-yet-existing image (or, so to speak, an image+ without image). In other cases, the image+ dimension becomes the defining feature of the image. Some obvious examples are the image as clickable icon or hyperlink, as profile picture on social media, as video preview with play button to be put into motion, or the now-dead "living pictures" produced with Lytro's light-field photography that allowed the user to refocus thanks to the interactive depth-of-field (Ng et al. 2005). The notion of image+ is intended to capture the way that screenic images solicit action, either directly or indirectly, after which we might be taken elsewhere, away from the image-as-image, to another image or deeper into the same image (for instance, by zooming in or refocusing). So, what is at stake is the operationality of the image.

for the machine: even if we do not see the image, the computer still does. Referring in particular to integrated circuits, he writes, "The image has been reduced to a processor of data, and data (thought in the Latin sense of 'things given') have been reduced to the simplest form of signification in either being given or not" (Stine 2019, 786).

 Different from the "early touchscreen" interfaces, the image+ operates within the global computerization (or algorithmization) of everyday life. As addressed by contemporary interface studies, the computer is a "power machine" (*Machtmaschine*) that regulates the actively regulating user (Distelmeyer 2017; 2018, 26). More than ever, we are trapped in a Foucauldian "network of permanent observation," because of the data dimension of today's screenic images. These images circulate as nonimages and provide precious information to global corporations about users' clicks. At stake is no longer a simple object–user encounter (as when the child played with the thaumatrope or the lady looked at her panoramic fan) but a complex nexus of agencies and actors that monitor and track our actions.

The image+ as data-based image communicates with the device's inner processes, and as such it is both a surface to be touched or clicked on and an interface, a portal toward the processual data flow or micro-temporality of media. As formulated by Jan Distelmeyer, "clickable or touchable signs are simultaneously linked electronically to the inner processes of the machine, to its interior telegraphy, whose flow of electronic signals connects, among others, the motherboard to the indexical signs of the graphical user interface" (2018, 27). He adds: "This enables us to click/touch them, to start the promised and hidden algorithmic processes, which is why Frieder Nake calls them 'algorithmic images'" (27).

Distelmeyer adopts the term "operative Bilder," coined by German filmmaker Harun Farocki, proposing the translation "operative images" (rather than the more common "operational images") to highlight that "these images are included as efficient components of electronic technical operations" (Distelmeyer 2018, 27). Yet, as Elsaesser reminds us, Farocki's operational images belong to a much larger history of media inscription techniques, constituting one of the "most consequential contributions to media archaeology, as well as an essential part of the prehistory of digital images" (Elsaesser 2017, 219). Referring to *Bilder der Welt und Inschrift des Krieges* (*Images of the World and the Inscription of War*, 1989), Elsaesser points for instance to the genealogy of architectural-military images based on photogrammetrics (*Messbild-Photographie*), a recording and calculating technique invented by Albrecht Meydenbauer in the mid 1850s. In Farocki's work, operational images are ("pre-digital") images that act by recording data and by calculating and anticipating actions.

Defined by Christa Blümlinger as "single-purpose images," Farocki's operational images are technical or instrumental images "produced for a specific operation and destined to be erased, such as military surveillance images which verify the efficiency of a bombing raid" (Blümlinger 2004, 320). The typical operational image, like the military image, is an image that is not meant to be looked at, but that serves as part of a process, a process of executing an operation. In other words, it is already part of the action itself. It does not need to be acted upon in order to be operational. As such it differs from my definition of the screenic image as image+, which offers itself to the digital spectator as a signal for action. Furthermore, most screenic images can be acted upon more than once, so they are rather "multi-purpose images" instead of "single-purpose images."

When displayed on a screen within reach, any type of image, not just the technical or functional image, becomes an image+ inviting further action—even if the promise of revealing its extra dimension is not fulfilled, as for instance happened in the above anecdote told by Elsaesser.[2] When the girl clicked on the digitized

2 Similarly, in his discussion of Farocki's work, Elsaesser advances the idea that all images are in fact operational images. He writes: "One can go even further and claim that operational images—images that function as instructions for action—are the new default value of all image making, against which more traditional images, i.e. images meant merely to be contemplated, to be watched disinterestedly or for their aesthetic qualities are being redefined as specialized instances of operational images—and I'm not even primarily talking about advertising, propaganda or pornography" (Elsaesser 2017, 219).

photo on the computer screen and nothing happened, the two dimensions of the screenic images were nonetheless there: thanks to its digitization, that is, the transformation into digital file, the (analog) photo could be displayed on screen, becoming therefore a screenic image, and as such it also became an invitation for action, even if it led to nonaction. Or as Elsaesser puts it, the girl clicked on the picture on screen, "in the expectation of some action or movement taking place, of being taken to another place or to another picture space" (2013, 241).

Thinking of the image as a "cue for action" turns the traditional notion of the image, and in particular the filmic image, upside down. It means that the image does not end at its borders, that its frame does not "hold" the image and its action, and most importantly, that the image is not there to be looked at. In fact, as suggested above, the image becomes the screen, both as screenic surface of data visualization and as screenic interface of data access or "cue for action." Most notably, in our interaction with touchscreens, we no longer touch the screen alone but instead the images on the screen. Likewise, Casetti in his discussion of the screen as "display" has pointed out the culmination of its features in the touchscreen:

> Here the eye is connected to the fingers, and it is they that signal if the observer is paying attention and, if so, what kind. Touch solicits the arrival of images, but even more so, it guides their flow: it associates them, it downloads them, and it often deletes them. It enlarges them, moves them around, and stacks them. While it is the eye that supervises the operations, it is the hand that guides them. It is the hand that calls to the images and seizes them. (2015, 168)

Concrete actions include confirming an online payment by clicking a button and liking a post on social media to signal that it has been seen.

From Windowed to Screenic Viewing

Here I would like to recall the distinction made by Anne Friedberg in her history of fenestration between the "picture" window and the "display" window. When discussing the introduction of glass as a new architectural building material, Friedberg emphasized its double feature of being able to "keep the outside *out* and at the same time bring it *in*" (2006, 113). Due to its increasing size, the glass window became an interface to look through on both sides. As Friedberg puts it, "Its transparency enforced a two-way model of visuality: by framing a private view outward—the 'picture' window—and by framing a public view inward—the 'display' window" (113). Likewise, today's screen could be said to enforce a two-way model not of visuality but of operationality, displaying screenic images that ask to be acted upon and that take us elsewhere, away from the image-as-image, after we have acted upon them.

For Heidi Rae Cooley, who was one of Friedberg's graduate students at the beginning of the twenty-first century, the relationship between the hand and the device is not unidirectional but reciprocal; she sees the potential of a "dynamic happening" or "innervating exchange" that she proposes to seize with the theoretical notion of "fit," by which the hand "forms" to the device and the device "gives" to the hand, in a mutual molding (2004, 139, 141, 137). Actually, it is from Cooley's seminal article "It's All about the Fit" that I borrow the term "screenic." As already mentioned in Chapter 5, this article looks into the first generation of handheld screenic devices, such as PDAs, flip phones, and digital compact cameras and camcorders, whose embedded LCD screens Cooley distinguishes from both television and cinema screens as no longer functioning as windows or "views onto other worlds" but as forms of "screenic unfolding of the world" where vision becomes an extension of the screen (153).

Already in 2004, Cooley talks about the "shift from window-ed seeing to screenic seeing," which she connects to the idea of tactile vision. Here is a longer quotation from the article:

> Whereas a window distances viewers from what they are looking at, the screen draws them toward the images that are displayed on the screen (not beyond it). In which case, window-ed seeing institutes a detached engagement, while screenic seeing encourages an experience of encounter. Vision, no longer a property of the window and its frame, becomes an extension of the screen. Likewise, that which is being viewed (and perhaps recorded) no longer exists separate from that which is framing it. The object, formerly located on the other side of the frame, converges or fuses with the screen, its physicality becoming the physicality of the screen. (Cooley 2004, 143)

The screenic image refers back to itself, to its physicality on the screen. So, the relationship between the image and the screen is one of convergence, of fusion or even confusion. The image becomes the screen, and the screen becomes the image.

Since 2004 both the consumption and the production of moving images by means of mobile screenic devices have become common practices, also and especially among the youngest media users. Whereas the adult generation might find watching a Hollywood film on a smartphone an alienating experience, because of the smallness of the screen and the grotesque effect of turning famous actors into little insects that can be pinched between fingertips, children are rather comfortable with this way of watching films: it is a viewing regime at their size with close-ups smaller than their own faces. But what is more, this is the way they start watching films as infants and toddlers. Or to put it differently, this is their default cinema.

The iTouch Generation

With the term "iTouch generation" I want to refer to this new generation of media users, who are growing up in a media ecology that significantly differs from the one in which their parents grew up. Already as babies they are surrounded by all types of mobile screenic devices. From a very early age on, they make video calls with distant relatives, often reaching out to the screen to touch the absent/present interlocutor. They watch clips on YouTube before they can walk and talk. They are submerged in a (touch)screen-based moving image consumption, not only at home, but also on the street in their stroller, when their parents let them play with their smartphone to make them stop crying.

Following systems theorist Richard Buckminster Fuller, who in the 1970s claimed that the best "way to see what tomorrow is going to look like is just to look at our children," I have proposed that we pay more attention to today's children and the way they interact with media. By carefully looking at children's media environment today we might get to a different and better differentiated understanding of media. In the "Introduction" to Gene Youngblood's *Expanded Cinema* (1970), Fuller puts it as follows:

> I was seven years old before I saw an automobile, though living in the ambience of a large American city. Not until I was nine was the airplane invented. As a child I thought spontaneously only in terms of walking, bicycling, horse-drawn capability. . . . My daughter was born with cloth-covered-wing bi-planes in her sky and the talkie radio in her hearing. My granddaughter was born in a house with several jet transports going over every minute. She saw a thousand airplanes before she saw a bird; a thousand automobiles before a horse. (Fuller 1970, 31)

And we can proceed along the same lines: Today's children operate innumerable touchscreens before they can hold a pencil or read a book, before they have used a non-touchscreen, before they go to the movie theater, etc.

Another important dimension of this new screenic environment is that children see themselves constantly on pictures and videos, or better on the embedded screens of all sorts of recording devices, which is another indication of the conflation between screen and image. As soon as a picture has been taken, children want to see themselves for themselves, pointing and touching their self-image on the screen. Moreover, many children make pictures and videos of themselves, unbeknownst to their parents, using their smartphones with front-facing camera. As already noted in Chapter 3, today's children are media users and producers before they start learning about media in a more traditional way of (passive) knowledge transfer.

Some of the questions that underlie the remainder of this chapter are: Will their close, bodily contact with the filming (and screening) device have an impact on their way of watching cinema? Will their early touchscreen experiences influence their way of watching film in a traditional setting, that is, at the movie theater? What is the effect of their early familiarization with the phenomenon of cinema's "relocation" (Casetti 2012) for their concept of cinema in general? My aim is not to answer all these questions but to formulate some thoughts about the iTouch generation as the next generation of *film spectators*.

The Neo-Spectators of Relocated Cinema

To this end, I propose to revisit the concept of the "neo-spectator," coined by André Gaudreault and Germain Lacasse in the early 1990s to capture the look of the first cinema spectators, to highlight the fundamental difference of their film reception with respect to ours, in short, to grasp their "foreignness" (*extranéité*). In their article "Premier regard: Les 'néo-spectateurs' du Canada français," Gaudreault and Lacasse use the term to undo the myth of the credulous early cinemagoer who would have run away from the arriving trains onscreen. They ask provocatively: "Who is more naïve, the early film spectator or the historian of early cinema?" (Gaudreault and Lacasse 1993, 19; my translation). The latter, the historian, should take into account his or her own position as retro-spectator, as someone who looks at early cinema from the present, that is, with an eye accustomed to watching "realistic" (or photographic) moving images. The early cinema spectator, on the other hand, was a "virgin" spectator. I quote again Gaudreault and Lacasse: "Essentially, early cinema was most often directed at a 'virgin' spectator, for whom the moving pictures show was a *terra incognita* of which he or she had, at most, only vaguely heard of" (18; my translation).

The virginity of cinema's first spectators is less related to the shock experience to which they had already been exposed through other nineteenth-century attractions, such as, for instance, the "boulevard du crime." The neo-spectator of early cinema is to be considered virgin, according to Gaudreault and Lacasse, in terms of *projected* moving pictures. As discussed in the previous chapter, the phenomenon of mechanically produced moving images was not totally new or unfamiliar to this neo-spectator, considering the popularity of optical toys in the decades before the "official" invention of cinema as public screening practice. The marvel of cinema consisted in the motion of photographic, life-like images, or rather in the transformation of a still photographic image into a moving photographic image, on a "big" projection screen.

Like the early cinema spectator, today's children who have not yet experienced their first theatrical film projection are also not totally "virgin" in terms of moving-image consumption; on the contrary, they are often very accustomed, as suggested above, to the phenomenon of cinema's relocation—from YouTube on the computer monitor to in-flight entertainment displays or portable DVD-players on the road up to the most recent types of mobile screen-based devices. Here I am borrowing Casetti's notion of "relocation," which he uses to refer to "the process in which a media experience is reactivated and re-purposed elsewhere in respect to the place it was formed, with alternate devices and in new environments" (2012, 14). Regarding the relocation of cinema, Casetti writes:

> Cinema: no longer limited to a darkened theater dependent on rolls of film stock running through a projector, but now

> available on public screens, at home, on my cellphone and computer, and still ready, in these new environments and with these new devices, to offer excitement of perception, a sense of proximity to the real, access to fantasy, and investment in that which is represented. (14–15)

I would like to stress that such a definition of "relocation" only works from the perspective of the adult generation of today. Because for the future generation of cinemagoers the classical model of the movie theater is no longer the standard; instead, it has become just one of the possible alternative ways to watch films. Their film experience starts as, or has its origin in, "relocation." And this is precisely the reason why we can consider them as "neo-spectators," for whom the movie theater represents "a *terra incognita* which they have, at most, only vaguely heard of"—to paraphrase the above quote of Gaudreault and Lacasse. In other words, what the historical neo-spectator and the future cinemagoer share is their difference in expectation (or knowledge, or preparation) with respect to the twentieth-century film spectator for whom the darkened theater was (and still is) the classical model of cinema.

One could even claim that it is the exact opposite, that for today's children the movie theater has become a form of "relocation," a place where their experience of watching films is "reactivated and re-purposed" with "alternate devices." Before their first "proper" cinema experience, they have already been film spectators (and even film programmers) of their self-made cinema setting. Indeed, we see that children create their own cinema outside the movie theater, as a form of do-it-yourself cinema.

Do-It-Yourself Cinema

With the notion of do-it-yourself (DIY) cinema, I want to capture two different dimensions of today's spectatorship in relation to children in particular, but in fact also applicable to adults. Firstly, it refers to the practice of creating yourself the "perfect" viewing setting for watching films, which can be for instance your own darkened bedroom, or the construction of a tent on the sofa under which you hide with your friends, or the arrangement of chairs in rows, etc. Even if somehow connected to the tradition of home cinema, the self-made cinemas of today's children are not limited to the home setting. Thanks to mobile viewing devices, such as laptops and tablets, children can take their cinema with them, not only from one room to the next, but also outside the house—which makes it quite different from the TV viewing experience of their parents' childhood. Secondly, today children's DIY cinema is also about the potential for making their own film program, for instance by deciding which DVD to watch over and over again or by clicking from one YouTube clip to the next—a practice in which today's children excel, as already alluded to at the beginning of this chapter. At an early age, they understand the new logic of online cinema that allows them to click through the endless supply of cartoons and to make their own personalized film show, which somehow echoes—as already suggested—the structure of early cinema's film programs because of the mixture of genres, the shortness of the films, and the surprise (or attraction) effects. More strictly speaking, in terms of media genealogy, it is TV on demand in an extreme and immediate form.

After their first visit to the movie theater, at the age of three or four, the practice of creating their own cinema might become more conscious. My own daughter, at the age of five, started to call the highway her "cinema," because that was the place where she was allowed to watch feature-length films on a portable DVD player. Her self-made cinema corresponded to a long journey and, thus, a long film—as opposed to the more regularly consumed YouTube clips. The same portable DVD player was also used to create a little cinema in the holiday cottage of friends, where we spent some nights in the summer of 2014. On a dreadful rainy day of the same summer, but in a different country and a different house, my daughter and two other children prepared drinks and popcorn to watch a TV show projected on the wall of the living room, because the local cinema did not show any interesting kids' movie that week.

In these examples of DIY cinema, the two aspects of setting and programming are combined. Children are rearranging "means at hand," such as portable media devices and pieces of furniture, as well as selecting their film program among the available DVDs or online streaming. It is a form of *bricolage*, or an example of what Casetti half-jokingly proposed to call "IKEA cinema." Without any reference to children, Casetti launched this notion in 2016 in Bologna at the presentation of his book *The Lumière Galaxy* (2015), as an alternative concept for today's relocated cinema. "IKEA cinema" is a cinema that is semi-finished, that you have to compose yourself, by putting together all the separate components. Such a notion of modular (or "composable") cinema is indeed close to my notion of DIY cinema, although I would like to stress the self-*made*-ness of the children's cinemas. Even if they might get some help from adults, my point is that children are actually involved in *making* these improvised cinemas, both as conceivers and as constructors.

But today's children not only make their own cinema settings but also their own little films, with all kinds of mobile devices, such as compact cameras, tablets, and especially smartphones. In most cases, the recording option of these mobile devices is discovered and explored quite accidentally, without explanation from their parents, at preschool age.[3] This is DIY cinema in a very literal sense. For these youngest filmmakers, filming is part of their play, or better, filming is a form of improvised play, or free play (*paidia*). It is a combined act of filming and watching, that is, of making a film and watching the very same film simultaneously on the embedded LCD screen of the photo-camera or the screen

3 To denominate these short digital films made by today's children, Alexandra Schneider coined the term "film-poucet," or little thumb film, inspired by Michel Serres's essay "Petite Poucette" (Schneider 2014; Schneider and Strauven 2017).

display of the smartphone. In general, once the film or video has been recorded, the filmmaking child loses interest in it. While she likes to watch, over and over again, clips taken by parents or relatives in which she appears as protagonist, the child rarely watches her own self-made films. According to José van Dijck, children are very conscious of the power of video footage in creating future memories and even in defining their future public image. This might be true for teenagers, but such a "sophisticated reflexivity" of the recording device is not at stake in the early film practice of preschoolers.[4] In fact, these young filmmakers are not creating future memories (or finished films, for that matter); instead, they are playing the present moment, destroying the stability of perception, and celebrating the camera's (and their own) vertigo. Indeed, children achieve in filming the quintessence of *ilinx* (according to Caillois's categorization of games) through their shaky handheld camera style and brusque body movements during recording. The pleasure lies in making those unfinished, unedited, unwatchable films, that is, in the (dizzy) act of filming itself, which is also a (dizzy) act of looking, of exploring the world.

They explore the world by means of a screen, as a very literal application of the "shift from window-ed seeing to screenic seeing," postulated by Cooley. During the act of filming, they are not looking through the lens or the viewfinder but at the screen that "draws them toward the images that are displayed on the screen (not beyond it)" (Cooley 2004, 143). By exploring the world around them by means of a portable, handheld screen, they create, or rather perform, a new form of cinema—a cinema that is hands-on and that literally fits in the palm of their hands, to be consumed instantly, at the moment of making.

To conclude, I would like to suggest that today's children—through their filmmaking practices and film viewing experiences

4 Van Dijck (2008) tells an anecdote about a ten-year-old girl who would have asked her father to film her and her sister performing karaoke by claiming that one day, when she will be famous, this will be shown on TV.

 originating in "relocation"—are actually reinventing cinema. In a posthumously published essay, Miriam Hansen asked to give the new generation a chance, precisely for this reason, for the rediscovery and reinvention of cinema. Reflecting upon what it means to watch Max Ophüls's films "with a generation of students who do not know a world before computers, cell phones, and videogames," she concludes with an optimistic note:

> Perhaps we should defer cultural pessimism about the digital transformations of experience and publicness for a while and give the generations growing up with these technologies a chance to incorporate them into cultural memory and, along the way, to rediscover and reinvent cinema. (Hansen 2012, 29)

The youngest generations of media users are indeed rediscovering and reinventing cinema by means of screenic images that they both consume and produce, and as such they are challenging traditional notions of "what cinema is" and offering new insights for the future of film theory. Because of the important role of mobile screens and touchscreens in this process, cinema is reinvented as a true tactile practice with the image functioning as a touchable surface and interface.

Conclusion: I Touch, Therefore I Am

It is not enough to say that the world lies "within the hand's reach," to describe our position in the world. We have two hands. We comprehend the world from two opposing sides, which is how the world can be taken in, grasped, intended, and manipulated.
Vilém Flusser

In 2003, *The New York Times* reported on the "affect revolution" that was kicking off in the field of neuroscience thanks to the influence of the Spinozist thinking of Antonio Damasio. Arts reporter Emily Eakin interviewed Damasio and named her article after his motto, "I Feel, Therefore I Am," by which the Portuguese-American neuroscientist counters Descartes's dualist principle that still persists in the so-called hard sciences. According to Damasio, Spinoza was right about reason being intermixed with, or even motivated by, emotion. As he puts it in the interview with Eakin, Spinoza "anticipated one of brain science's most important recent discoveries: the critical role of the emotions in ensuring our survival and allowing us to think. Feeling, it turns out, is not the enemy of reason, but, as Spinoza saw it, an indispensable accomplice" (Eakin 2003).

By rephrasing Damasio's motto as "I Touch, Therefore I Am," I want to suggest that the act of touching is about exploring and understanding the world. If the increase of tactile interfaces in our daily life is not necessarily enriching our tactile perception, this is partly because *to touch* does not mean *to feel*. But it is also because we touch our screens for different reasons than sensory perception: we touch to check out whether or not we are dealing with a touchscreen, to like a post on social media, to put a still image into motion, to zoom in or out, etc.

As I have argued throughout this book, what connects the early film spectator, early museum visitor, early-nineteenth-century child, and today's child of the iTouch generation is a form of hands-on media experience, observed in actions such as hand cranking a viewing machine, grabbing a projection screen, visiting and displacing the objects of the *Wunderkammer*, handling optical toys, and operating smartphones. In all of these cases, I mean literal touching, that is, a physical, concrete "encounter" between, on the one hand, an artwork, a media device, or a toy; and, on the other hand, some part of the body, mainly the fingertips, but also the nose, the elbow, or the feet.

With respect to practices of twentieth-century spectatorship in which audiences looked at the screen from a safe distance, we are now witnessing a change toward (or a return to) tactile spectatorship, which I see as a very material form of spectatorship, grounded in touch. To a certain degree, the emergence of this new type of spectatorship is due to the pervasion of touchscreen devices in our daily life. Yet as my archaeology of the touchscreen has brought to the fore, there exists a long tradition of tactile or hands-on practices related to the moving image and, thus, to being a spectator.

This book has proposed to rethink and historicize both parts of the term "touchscreen," that is, both "touch" and "screen." "Touch" has been understood as an active verb, designating a concrete, hands-on encounter between human and nonhuman actants, a physical contact in the movie theater, the museum, at home, etc. And "screen" has been correlatively understood as a material media surface and interface that not only *can* be touched (screen as touchable surface) but also *must* be touched to bring the media experience to life (screen as touchscreen interface that takes us elsewhere). I have chosen to take as my guide the figure of the rube, the supposedly naïve film spectator of the early days of cinema, who dramatizes the tactile potential of the film medium from the outset and illustrates that the transition to touchscreen media is by no means easy to grasp in terms of innovation and novelty.

My focus has been on the operative side of media, on how screens, toys, and other media devices need to be operated, manually, by a direct or indirect touch. Throughout the long history I have covered in this book, the tactile element has always been an integral part of the media experience and the cognitive process at stake. Today, maybe more than ever, our actions have become tactile actions: we touch screens to vote, to play games, to scroll through news feeds, to buy products online, to book hotels and flights, to be taken elsewhere, etc. As Michel Serres has put it, we access the world by means of our thumbs, to which the will, traditionally correlated with the use of the index finger, has been conferred as well. Thumbing and pointing, scrolling and swiping, clicking and liking, etc., have become the new verbs or "gestures of making" of the twenty-first-century media user. It is through these gestures that we are in the world, or, to say it with Vilém Flusser, that we "describe our position in the world" (2014, 33).

References

Acland, Charles. 2009. "Curtains, Carts, and the Mobile Screen." *Screen* 50 (1): 148–65.

———. 2012. "The Crack in the Electric Window." *Cinema Journal* 51 (2): 167–71.

Agamben, Giorgio. 2000. "Notes on Gesture." *Means without End*, translated by Cesare Casarino and Vincenzo Binetti, 49–59. Minneapolis: University of Minnesota Press.

———. 2007. *Profanations*. Translated by Jeff Fort. Cambridge, MA: MIT Press.

Alighieri, Dante. 2001. *La Vita Nuova*. Translated by A. S. Kline. *Poetry in Translation*. www.poetryinstranslation.com.

Arcagni, Simone. 2012. *Screen City*. Roma: Bulzoni.

Atkinson, Paul. 2007. "The Best Laid Plans of Mice and Men: The Computer Mouse in the History of Computing." *Design Issues* 23 (3): 46–61.

Avezzù, Giorgio. 2016. "Intersections between Showing and Concealment in the History of the Concept of Screen." In *Screens: From Materiality to Spectatorship. A Historical and Theoretical Reassessment*, edited by Dominique Chateau and José Moure, 29–41. Amsterdam: Amsterdam University Press.

Bak, Meredith. 2012. "Democracy and Discipline: Object Lessons and the Stereoscope in American Education, 1870–1920." *Early Popular Visual Culture* 10 (2): 147–67.

———. 2020. *Playful Visions: Optical Toys and the Emergence of Children's Media Culture*. Cambridge, MA: MIT Press.

Bal-Blanc, Pierre, and Mathieu Margerin. 1998. "*Prends garde! A jouer au fantome, on le devient.*" *BLOCNOTES* 15 (Summer).

Baldwin, James Mark. 1911. Ed. *Dictionary of Philosophy and Psychology*. Vol. 1. New York: The Macmillan Company.

Barker, Jennifer. 2009a. "Neither Here nor There: Synaesthesia and the Cosmic Zoom." *New Review of Film and Television Studies* 7 (3): 311–24.

———. 2009b. *The Tactile Eye: Touch and the Cinematic Experience*. Berkeley: University of California Press.

Baudelaire, Charles. 2018. "The Philosophy of Toys." In *On Dolls*, edited by Kenneth Gross, 11–21. London: Notting Hill Editions.

Baudrillard, Jean. 2005. *The System of Objects*. New York: Verso.

Baudry, Jean-Louis. 1974–75. "Ideological Effects of the Basic Cinematographic Apparatus." *Film Quarterly* 28 (2): 39–47.

Benedetto, Renato. 2013. "Ma il metodo Montessori avrebbe ammesso i touch screen? Forse sì." *La ventisettesima ora*, April 28. Accessed September 25, 2020. https://27esimaora.corriere.it/articolo/generazione-touchscreen-e-i-dubbi-dei-genitori-il-tablet-crea-dipendenza/.

Benjamin, Walter. 1978. "Unpacking My Library: A Talk about Book Collecting." In *Illuminations*, edited by Hannah Arendt and translated by Harry Zohn, 59–67. New York: Schocken Books.

———. 2005. "Toys and Play." In *Selected Writings*, vol. 2, pt. 1, *1927–1930*, edited by Michael W. Jennings, Howard Eiland, and Gary Smith, 117–21. Cambridge, MA: The Belknap Press of Harvard University Press.

———. 2008. "A Glimpse into the World of Children's Books." In *The Work of Art in the Age of Its Technological Reproducibility, and Other Writings on Media*, edited by Michael W. Jennings, Brigid Doherty, and Thomas Y. Levin, 226–35. Cambridge, MA: The Belknap Press of Harvard University Press.

Bennett, Tony. 1995. *The Birth of the Museum: History, Theory, Politics*. London: Routledge.

Bergermann, Ulrike. 2006. "Tastaturen des Wissens: Haptische Technologien und Taktilität in medialer Reproduktion." In *"Intellektuelle Anschauung": Figurationen von Evidenz zwischen Kunst und Wissen*, edited by S. Peters and M. Schäfer, 301–24. Bielefeld: transcript.

Blümlinger, Christa. 2004. "Harun Farocki: Critical Strategies." In *Harun Farocki: Working on the Sight-Lines*, edited by Thomas Elsaesser, 313–22. Amsterdam: Amsterdam University Press.

Bolter, Jay David, and Richard Grusin. 2000. *Remediation: Understanding New Media*. Cambridge, MA: MIT Press.

Bottomore, Stephen. 1999. "The Panicking Audience?: Early Cinema and the 'Train Effect.'" *Historical Journal of Film, Radio and Television* 19 (2): 177–216.

Briggs, Asa, and Peter Burke. 2005. *A Social History of the Media*. Cambridge: Polity Press.

Brinkmann, Svenk, and Lene Tanggaard. 2010. "Toward an Epistemology of the Hand." *Studies in Philosophy and Education* 29: 243–57.

Bruno, Giuliana. 2002. *Atlas of Emotion: Journeys in Art, Architecture, and Film*. New York: Verso.

———. 2014. *Surface: Matters of Aesthetics, Materiality, and Media*. Chicago: University of Chicago Press.

Caillois, Roger. 2001. *Man, Play and Games*. Translated by Meyer Barash. Urbana: University of Illinois Press.

Carels, Edwin. 2012. "From the Ossuary: Animation and the *Danse Macabre*." *Tijdschrift voor mediageschiedenis* 15 (1): 25–42.

———. 2015. "Short Notice." *Empedolces: European Journal for the Philosophy of Communication* 5 (1–2): 31–38.

Cartwright, Lisa. 1992. "Women, X-Rays, and the Public Culture of Prophylactic Imaging." *Camera Obscura* 10 (2): 18–54.

———. 2011. "The Hands of the Projectionist." *Science in Context* 24 (3): 443–64.

Casetti, Francesco. 2008. *Eye of the Century: Film, Experience, Modernity*. New York: Columbia University Press.

———. 2012. "The Relocation of Cinema." *NECSUS: European Journal of Media Studies* 1 (2): 5–34.

———. 2014. "Che cosa è uno schermo, oggi?" *Rivista di Estetica* 55 (1): 103–21.

———. 2015. *The Lumière Galaxy: Seven Key Words for the Cinema to Come*. New York: Columbia University Press.

Castellano, Joseph A. 1992. *Handbook of Display Technology*. San Diego, CA: Academic Press.

Christie, Ian. 2016. "The Stuff of Screens." In *Screens: From Materiality to Spectatorship. A Historical and Theoretical Reassessment*, edited by Dominique Chateau and José Moure, 70–79. Amsterdam: Amsterdam University Press.

Classen, Constance. 2005. "Touch in the Museum." In *The Book of Touch*, edited by Constance Classen, 275–86. Oxford: Berg.

———. 2007. "Museum Manners: The Sensory Life of the Early Museum." *Journal of Social History* 40 (4): 895–914.

Cloosterman, Guido. 2002. "Mobiele telefoon doet duim muteren." *Gazet van Antwerpen*. March 24. Accessed March 20, 2020. https://ww.gva.be/cnt/oid185902.

Cooley, Heidi Rae. 2004. "It's All about the Fit: The Hand, the Mobile Screenic Device and Tactile Vision." *Journal of Visual Culture* 3 (2): 133–55.

Crary, Jonathan. 1992. *Techniques of the Observer: On Vision and Modernity in the Nineteenth Century*. Cambridge, MA: MIT Press.

———. 2001. *Suspensions of Perception: Attention, Spectacle, and Modern Culture*. Cambridge, MA: MIT Press.

———. 2014. *24/7: Late Capitalism and the Ends of Sleep*. London and New York: Verso.

Cubitt, Sean. 2013. "Anecdotal Evidence." *NECSUS: European Journal of Media Studies* 2 (1): 5–18.

Davies, Hugh. 2019. "Fanology: Hand-Fans in the Prehistory of Mobile Devices." *Mobile Media & Communication* 7 (3): 303–21.

Da Vinci, Leonardo. 1949. *Paragone: A Comparison of the Arts*. Translated by I. A. Richter. London, New York, and Toronto: Oxford University Press.

De Kerckhove, Derrick. 1997. *The Skin of Culture. Investigating the New Electronic Reality*, edited by Christopher Dewdney. London: Kogan Page.

Deleuze, Gilles, and Félix Guattari. 1987. *A Thousand Plateaus: Capitalism and Schizophrenia*. Minneapolis and London: University of Minnesota Press.

De Rosa, Miriam, and Wanda Strauven. 2020. "Screenic (Re)orientations: Desktop, Tabletop, Tablet, Booklet, Touchscreen, Etc." In *Space Screen Reconfigured*, edited by Susanne Østby Sæther and Synne Bull, 231–62. Amsterdam: Amsterdam University Press.

Derrida, Jacques. 2005. *On Touching—Jean-Luc Nancy*. Stanford, CA: Stanford University Press.

Dewey, John. 1907. *The School and Society*. Chicago: University of Chicago Press.

———. 1916. *Democracy and Education*. New York: MacMillan.

Dickens, Charles. 1853. *Bleak House*. London: Bradbury and Evans.

Distelmeyer, Jan. 2017. *Machtzeichen. Anordnungen des Computers*. Berlin: Bertz + Fischer.

———. 2018. "Drawing Connections—How Interfaces Matter." *Interface Critique Journal* 1. doi: 10.11588/ic.2018.0.44733.

Doane, Mary Ann. 2007. "The Indexical and the Concept of Medium Specificity." *differences* 18 (1): 128–51.

Dulac, Nicolas, and André Gaudreault. 2006. "Circularity and Repetition at the Heart of the Attraction: Optical Toys and the Emergence of a New Cultural

Series." In *The Cinema of Attractions Reloaded*, edited by Wanda Strauven, 227–44. Amsterdam: Amsterdam University Press.

Eakin, Emily. 2003. "I Feel, Therefore I Am." *The New York Times*. April 19.

Edison Manufacturing Company. 1902. *Edison Films* 135 (September).

Eisenstein, Sergei M. 1977. *Film Form*. Edited and translated by Jay Leyda. New York: Meridian Books.

Elsaesser, Thomas. 1994. "Zapping One's Way into Quality: Arts Programmes on TV." In *Writing for the Medium: Television in Transition*, edited by Thomas Elsaesser, Jan Simons, and Lucette Bronk, 54–63. Amsterdam: Amsterdam University Press.

———. 2002. *Filmgeschichte und frühes Kino: Archäologie eines Medienwandels*. Munich: edition text + kritik.

———. 2003. "'Where Were You When...?'; or, 'I Phone, Therefore I Am.'" *PMLA* 118 (1): 120–22.

———. 2004. "The New Film History as Media Archaeology." *Cinémas: Revue d'études cinématographiques* 14 (2–3): 75–117.

———. 2005. "Early Film History and Multi-Media: An Archaeology of Possible Futures?" In *New Media, Old Media: A History and Theory Reader*, edited Wendy Chun and Thomas Keenan, 13–25. London: Routledge.

———. 2006. "Discipline through Diegesis: The Rube Film between 'Attractions' and 'Narrative Integration.'" In *The Cinema of Attractions Reloaded*, edited by Wanda Strauven, 205–23. Amsterdam: Amsterdam University Press.

———. 2013. "The 'Return' of 3-D: On Some of the Logics and Genealogies of the Image in the Twenty-First Century." *Critical Inquiry* 39: 217–46.

———. 2017. "Simulation and the Labour of Invisibility: Harun Farocki's Life Manuals." *Animation: An Interdisciplinary Journal* 12 (3): 214–29.

Engell, Lorenz. 2013. "The Tactile and the Index: From the Remote Control to the Hand-Held Computer. Some Speculative Reflections on the Bodies of the Will." *NECSUS: European Journal of Media Studies* 2 (2): 323–36.

English, William K., Douglas C. Engelbart, and Mervyn L. Berman. 1967. "Display-Selection Techniques for Text Manipulation." *IEEE Transactions on Human Factors in Electronics* HFE-8 (1): 5–15.

Ernst, Wolfgang. 2011. "Media Archaeography: Method and Machine versus History and Narrative of Media." In *Media Archaeology: Approaches, Applications, and Implications*, edited by Erkki Huhtamo and Jussi Parikka, 239–55. Berkeley: University of California Press.

Evans, Caroline. 2011. "The Walkies: Early French Fashion Shows as a Cinema of Attractions." In *Fashion in Film*, edited by Adrienne Munich, 110–34. Bloomington: Indiana University Press.

Export, Valie. 2003. "Expanded Cinema as Expanded Reality." *Senses of Cinema* 28. Accessed March 8, 2020. http://sensesofcinema.com/2003/peter-tscherkassky-the-austrian-avant-garde/expanded_cinema/.

Fineman, Joel. 1989. "History of the Anecdote: Fiction and Fiction." In *The New Historicism*, edited by H. Aram Vesser, 49–76. London: Routledge.

Flusser, Vilém. 2014. *Gestures*. Translated by Nancy Ann Roth. Minneapolis: University of Minnesota Press.

Focillon, Henri. 1989. "In Praise of Hands." In *The Life of Forms in Art*, translated by Charles Beecher Hogan and George Kubler, 157–84. New York: Zone Books.

Foucault, Michel. 1970. *The Order of Things: An Archaeology of the Human Sciences*. New York: Pantheon Books.

———. 2007. *Archaeology of Knowledge*. London: Routledge.

Freire, Rachel, Cedric Honnet, and Paul Strohmeier. 2017. "Second Skin: An Exploration of the eTextile Stretch Circuits on the Body." TEI '17, March 20–23, Yokohama, Japan. Accessed March 20, 2020. doi: 10.1145/3024969.3025054.

Friedberg, Anne. 1993. *Window Shopping: Cinema and the Postmodern*. Berkeley: University of California Press.

———. 2006. *The Virtual Window: From Alberti to Microsoft*. Cambridge, MA: MIT Press.

Fuller, R. Buckminster. 1970. "Introduction." In *Expanded Cinema* by Gene Youngblood, 15–35. New York: Dutton & co.

Gaudreault, André, and Germain Lacasse. 1993. "Premier regard: Les 'néo-spectateurs' du Canada français." *Vertigo* 10: 18–24.

Geertz, Clifford. 1973. "Thick Description: Toward an Interpretive Theory of Culture." In *The Interpretation of Cultures: Selected Essays by Clifford Geertz*, 3–30. New York: Basic Books, Inc.

Ginna, Arnaldo. 1965. "Note sul film d'avanguardia *Vita Futurista*." *Bianco e Nero* (May–June): 156–58.

Giraud, Jean. 1958. *Le Lexique français du cinéma. Des origins à 1930*. Paris: CNRS.

Gomez, Prada, Luis Ricardo, and Aaron Wheeler. 2013. "Hand Gestures Signify What Is Important." *United States Patent and Trademark Office*. Patent #: US008558759.

Graham, Tom. 2016. "The Irresistible Madness of Orson Welles' Don Quixote." *Little White Lies*, April 28. Accessed March 7, 2020. https://lwlies.com/articles/the-story-of-orson-welles-don-quixote/.

Grieveson, Lee, and Heidi Masson. 2018. Eds. *Cinema's Military Industrial Complex*. Berkeley: University of California Press.

Griffiths, Alison. 1996. "'Journey for Those Who Can Not Travel': Promenade Cinema and the Museum Life Group." *Wide Angle* 18 (3): 53–84.

Gruber, Klemens. 2017. "Taktile Medien: Theorien aus der Vorgeschichte." In *Texture Matters: Der Tastsinn in den Medien. Haptisch/Optisch 2*, edited by Jana Herwig and Alexandra Seibel, 207–34. Vienna: Böhlau.

Gruber, Klemens, and Antonia Lant. 2014. Eds. *Texture Matters: Der Tastsinn im Kino. Haptisch/Optisch 1*. Vienna: Böhlau.

Guido, Laurent. 2006. "Rhythmic Bodies/Movies: Dance as Attraction in Early Film Culture." In *The Cinema of Attractions Reloaded*, edited by Wanda Strauven, 140–56. Amsterdam: Amsterdam University Press.

Gunning, Tom. 1991. "Heard over the Phone: *The Lonely Villa* and the de Lorde Tradition of the Terrors of Technology." *Screen* 32: 184–96.

———. 1995. "An Aesthetic of Astonishment: Early Film and the (In)credulous Spectator." In *Viewing Positions: Ways of Seeing Film*, edited by Linda Williams, 114–33. New Brunswick, NJ: Rutgers University Press.

———. 2003. "Loïe Fuller and the Art of Motion Body, Light, Electricity, and the Origins of Cinema." In *Camera Obscura, Camera Lucida. Essays in Honor of Annette*

Michelson, edited by Richard Allen and Malcolm Turvey, 75–89. Amsterdam: Amsterdam University Press.

———. 2004. "What's the Point of an Index? or, Faking Photographs." *Nordicom Review*: 39–49.

———. 2006. "The Cinema of Attraction[s]: Early Film, Its Spectator and the Avant-Garde." In *The Cinema of Attractions Reloaded*, edited by Wanda Strauven, 381–88. Amsterdam: Amsterdam University Press.

———. 2012. "Hand and Eye: Excavating a New Technology of the Image in the Victorian Era." *Victorian Studies* 54 (3): 495–516.

Hansen, Miriam. 1991. *Babel and Babylon: Spectatorship in American Silent Film.* Cambridge, MA: Harvard University Press.

———. 2012. "Max Ophuls and Instant Messaging, Reframing Cinema and Publicness." In *Screen Dynamics: Mapping the Borders of Cinema*, edited by Gertrud Koch, Volker Pantenburg, and Simon Rothöhler, 22–29. Vienna: SYNEMA.

Heath, Stephen. 1977. "Screen Images—Film Memory." *Cine-Tracts: A Journal of Film, Communications, Culture and Politics* 1 (1): 27–36.

Hertz, Garnet, and Jussi Parikka. 2012. "Zombie Media: Circuit Bending Media Archaeology into an Art Method." *Leonardo* 45 (5): 424–30.

Herwig, Jana, and Alexandra Seibel. 2017. Eds. *Texture Matters: Der Tastsinn in den Medien. Haptisch/Optisch 2*. Vienna: Böhlau.

Hirschhorn, Thomas. 2012. *Insoutenables destructions du corps. Entretien avec Hugo Vitrani*. Accessed March 15, 2020. http://www.dailymotion.com/video/xshflo_thomas-hirschhorn-insoutenables-destructions-du-corps_creation.

Hoffmann, Stefan. 2014. "Medienbegriff und Medienwissenschaft." In *Handbuch der Medienwissenschaft*, edited by Jens Schröter, 13–43. Stuttgart: Metzler.

Huhtamo, Erkki. 1996. "From Kaleidoscomaniac to Cybernerd: Towards an Archaeology of the Media." In *Electronic Culture: Technology and Visual Representation*, edited by Timothy Druckrey, 296–303. New York: Aperture.

———. 2004. "Elements of Screenology: Towards an Archaeology of the Screen." *ICONICS: International Studies of the Modern Image* 7: 31–82.

———. 2005. "Slots of Fun, Slots of Trouble: An Archaeology of Arcade Gaming." In *Handbook of Computer Game Studies*, edited by Joost Raessens and Jeffrey Goldstein, 3–21. Cambridge, MA: MIT Press.

———. 2006. "Shaken Hands with Statues. . . : On Art, Interactivity and Tactility." In *Second Natures: Faculty Exhibition of the UCLA Design / Media Arts Department*, edited by Christiane Paul, 17–21. Los Angeles: University of California.

———. 2007. "Twin-Touch-Test-Redux: Media Archaeological Approach to Art, Interactivity, and Tactility." In *MediaArtHistories*, edited by Oliver Grau, 71–101. Cambridge, MA: MIT Press.

———. 2012. "Screen Tests: Why Do We Need an Archaeology of the Screen?" *Cinema Journal* 51 (2): 144–48.

Huhtamo, Erkki, and Jussi Parikka. 2011. "Introduction: An Archaeology of Media Archaeology." In *Media Archaeology: Approaches, Applications, and Implications*, edited by Erkki Huhtamo and Jussi Parikka, 1–21. Berkeley: University of California Press.

Huizinga, Johan. 2006. "Nature and Significance of Play as a Cultural Phenomenon." In *The Game Design Reader*, edited by Kate Salen and Eric Zimmerman, 96–120. Cambridge, MA: MIT Press.

Jackson, Sarah. 2015. *Tactile Poetics*. Edinburgh: Edinburgh University Press.

Jancovic, Marek. 2020. "Misinscriptions: A Media Epigraphy of Video Compression." Dissertation. Mainz: Johannes Gutenberg University.

Jenkins, Keith. 2002. "On Disobedient Histories." *Rethinking History: The Journal of Theory and Practice* 7 (3): 367–85.

Jeong, Seung-hoon. 2012. "The Body as Interface: Ambivalent Tactility in Expanded Rube Cinema." *Cinema: Journal of Philosophy and the Moving Image* 3: 229–53.

Johnson, E. A. 1965. "Touch Display: A Novel Input/Output Device for Computers." *Electronics Letters* 1 (8): 219–20.

Johnson, Geraldine A. 2002. "Touch, Tactility, and the Reception of Sculpture in Early Modern Italy." In *A Companion to Art Theory*, edited by Paul Smith and Carolyn Wilde, 61–75. Oxford: Blackwell.

Jones, Philippa. 2011. "A White Right Hand." *Convergence: The International Journal of Research into Media Technologies* 17 (3): 237–44.

Kaerlein, Timo. 2012. "Aporias of the Touchscreen: On the Promises and Perils of a Ubiquitous Technology." *NECSUS: European Journal of Media Studies* 1 (2): 177–98.

Kay, Alan. 1972. "A Personal Computer for Children of All Ages." Xerox Palo Alto Research Center. Typewritten manuscript available at: https://www.mprove.de/visionreality/media/Kay72a.pdf.

Kay, Alan, and Adele Goldberg. 2003. "Personal Dynamic Media." In *The New Media Reader*, edited by Noah Wardrip-Fruin and Nick Montfort, 393–404. Cambridge, MA: MIT Press.

Kircher, Athanasius. 1671. *Ars Magna Lucis et Umbrae*. Amsterdam: Jansson-Waesberge & Weyerstraet.

Kittler, Friedrich. 1999. *Gramophone, Film, Typewriter*. Stanford, CA: Stanford University Press.

Koeck, Richard, and François Penz. 2003. "Screen City Legibility." *City* 7 (3): 364–411.

Kucirkova, Natalia, David Messer, Kieron Sheehy, and Carmen Fernández Panadero. 2014. "Children's Engagement with Educational iPad Apps: Insights from a Spanish Classroom." *Computers & Education* 71: 175–84.

Kwastek, Katja. 2013. *Aesthetics of Interaction in Digital Art*. Cambridge, MA: MIT Press.

Lant, Antonia. 1995. "Haptical Cinema." *October* 74: 45–73.

———. 2014. "Haptisches Kino." In *Texture Matters: Der Tastsinn im Kino. Haptisch/Optisch 1*, edited by Klemens Gruber and Antonia Lant, 31–67. Vienna: Böhlau.

Latour, Bruno. 1996. "On Actor-Network Theory: A Few Clarifications." *Soziale Welt* 47 (4): 369–81.

Leotta, Alfio. 2018. "Total Cinema: René Barjavel and the Future Forms of Film." *Screen* 59 (3): 372–80.

Leroi-Gourhan, André. 1964. *Le geste et la parole*, vol. 1, *Technique et langage*. Paris: Albin Michel.

Littré, Emile. 1889. *Dictionnaire de la langue française*. Paris: Librairie Hachette et Cie.

Loiperdinger, Martin. 2004. "Lumière's Arrival of the Train: Cinema's Founding Myth." *The Moving Image* 4 (1): 89–118.
Lovink, Geert. 2003. "Archive Rumblings: Interview with German Media Archaeologist Wolfgang Ernst." *Nettime*. Accessed March 2, 2020. http://www.nettime.org/Lists-Archives/nettime-l-0302/msg00132.html.
Malthête, Jacques, Madeleine Malthête-Méliès, and Anne-Marie Quévrain. 1981. *Essai de reconstitution du catalogue français de la Star Film, suivi d'une analyse catalographique des films de Georges Méliès recensés en France*. Bois d'Arcy: Service des archives du film du Centre national de la cinématographie.
Manovich, Lev. 1998. "Towards an Archaeology of the Computer Screen." In *Cinema Futures: Cain, Abel or Cable?*, edited by Thomas Elsaesser and Kay Hoffmann, 27–44. Amsterdam: Amsterdam University Press.
Marinetti, Filippo Tommaso. 2009. "Tactilism." In *Futurism: An Anthology*, edited by Lawrence Rainey, Christine Poggi, and Laura Wittman, 264–69. New Haven, CT: Yale University Press.
Marks, Laura. 1998. "Video Haptics and Erotics." *Screen* 39 (4): 331–48.
———. 2000. *The Skin of Film: Intercultural Cinema, Embodiment, and the Senses*. Durham, NC: Duke University Press.
Mauss, Marcel. 1973. "Techniques of the Body." *Economy and Society* 2 (1): 70–88.
McLuhan, Marshall. 1964. *Understanding Media: The Extensions of Man*. New York: The American Library, Times Mirror.
Meltzer, Marisa. 2011. "When Two Thumbs Down Are a Sign of Approval." *The New York Times*. August 9. Accessed on March 18, 2020. https://www.nytimes.com/2011/08/11/fashion/hand-heart-gesture-grows-in-popularity-noticed.html.
Miranda, Sergio, Antonio Marzano, and Miltiades D. Lytras. "A Research Initiative on the Construction of Innovative Environments for Teaching and Learning. Montessori and Munari Based Psycho-Pedagogical Insights in Computers and Human Behavior for the 'New School.'" *Computers in Human Behavior* 66: 282–90.
Mistry, Pranav. 2010. "SixthSense: Integrating Information with the Real World." *Pranavmistry.com*. Accessed December 29, 2020. https://www.pranavmistry.com/archived/projects/sixthsense/.
Mitchell, W. J. T. 1992. "The Pictorial Turn." *ArtForum* (March): 89–94.
———. 2007. "There Are No Visual Media." In *MediaArtHistories*, edited by Oliver Grau, 395–406. Cambridge, MA: MIT Press.
Monge, Gaspard. 1827. *Géométrie descriptive*. Paris: Bachelier.
Moniker. 2013. "Do Not Touch: Ever-Changing Interactive Music Video." *Studio Moniker*. Accessed March 18, 2020. https://studiomoniker.com/projects/do-not-touch.
Moore, Gerald. 2018. "The Pharmacology of Addiction." *Parrhesia* 29: 190–211.
Morissette, Isabelle. 2002. "Reflexivity in Spectatorship: The Didactic Nature of Early Silent Films." *Offscreen* 6 (7). Accessed December 20, 2020. https://offscreen.com/view/spectatorship.
Mulvey, Laura. 1975. "Visual Pleasure and Narrative Cinema." *Screen* 16 (3): 6–18.
Munari, Bruno. 2004. *The Tactile Workshops*. Mantova: Corraini.

———. 2015. *Speak Italian: The Fine Art of the Gesture. A Supplement to the Italian Dictionary.* San Francisco: Chronicle Books.

Nancy, Jean-Luc. 2008. *Corpus*. New York: Fordham University Press.

Naumann, Francis M. 2003. *Conversion to Modernism: The Early Work of Man Ray*. New Brunswick, NJ: Rutgers University Press.

Ng, Ren, Marc Levoy, Mathieu Bredif, Gene Duval, Mark Horowitz, and Pat Hanrahan. 2005. "Light Field Photography with a Hand-Held Plenoptic Camera." *Computer Science Tech Report CSTR* 2 (11): 1-11.

Obrist, Hans Ulrich. 2011. "Email Interview with Johan Grimonprez." In *Johan Grimonprez: It's a Poor Sort of Memory that Only Works*, edited by Benoit Detalle, 267–72. Stuttgart: Hatje Cantz.

Oppenheimer, Sarah. 2012. "Giuliana Bruno by Sarah Oppenheimer." *BOMB Magazine 128* (Summer). Accessed February 29, 2020. http://bombmagazine.org/article/10056/giuliana-bruno.

Panizza, Laura. 2009. "L'incontro di Bruno Munari con la didattica attiva. I fondamenti pedagogici dei laboratori *Giocare con l'arte*." *Ricerche di Pedagogia e Didattica* 4 (1): 1–19. doi: 10.6092/issn.1970-2221/1547.

Parikka, Jussi. 2011. "Mapping Noise: Techniques and Tactics of Irregularities, Interception, and Disturbance." In *Media Archaeology: Approaches, Applications, and Implications*, edited by Erkki Huhtamo and Jussi Parikka, 256–77. Berkeley: University of California Press.

———. 2012. *What is Media Archaeology?* Cambridge: Polity Press.

Paris, John Ayrton. 1827. *Philosophy in Sport Made Science in Earnest: Being an Attempt to Illustrate the First Principles of Natural Philosophy by the Aid of Popular Toys and Sports*. London: Longman, Rees, Orme, Brown, & Green.

Parisi, David. 2017. "Eine Technik der Medienberührung: Kinästhetische Displays und die Suche nach Computerhaptik." In *Texture Matters: Der Tastsinn in den Medien. Haptisch/Optisch 2*, edited by Jana Herwig and Alexandra Seibel, 152–68. Vienna: Böhlau.

———. 2018. *Archaeologies of Touch: Interfacing with Haptics from Electricity to Computing*. Minneapolis: University of Minnesota Press.

Paul, William. 2005. "Screens." In *Encyclopedia of Early Cinema*, edited by Richard Abel, 573–76. London: Routledge.

Pethes, Nicolas. 2000. "Die Ferne der Berührung. Taktilität und mediale Repräsentation nach 1900: David Katz, Walter Benjamin." *Zeitschrift für Literaturwissenschaft und Linguistik* 30 (117): 33–57.

Plaisant, Catherine. 1999. "High-Precision Touchscreens: Museum Kiosks, Home Automation and Touchscreen Keyboards." *HCIL Archive*. Accessed March 12, 2020. http://www.cs.umd.edu/hcil/touchscreens/.

Poulaki, Maria. 2015. "Featuring Shortness in Online Loop Cultures." *Empedocles: European Journal for the Philosophy of Communication* 5 (1–2): 91–96.

Raymond, Eric S. 2004. *The Jargon File*. Accessed March 17, 2020. http://catb.org/jargon/html/.

Reimer, Jeremy. 2005. "A History of the GUI." *Ars Technica* (May). Accessed March 18, 2020. https://arstechnica.com/features/2005/05/gui/.

Restelli, Beba. 2002. *Giocare con tatto: Per una educazione plurisensoriale secondo il metodo Bruno Munari*. Milan: Franco Angeli.

Riegl, Alois. 1902. "Spätrömisch oder orientalisch?" *Beilage zur Allgemeinen Zeitung* 93 (April): 153–56.

———. 1985. *Late Roman Art Industry*. Translated by Rolf Winkes. Roma: Giorgio Bretschneider.

———. 1988. "Late Roman or Oriental?" In *German Essays on Art History: Winckelmann, Burckhardt, Panofsky, and Others*, edited by G. Schiff, 173–90. New York: Continuum.

Rosenbaum, Jonathan. 2007. "Unseen Orson Welles: A Conversation with Jonathan Rosenbaum." *YouTube*, October 18. Accessed March 7, 2020. https://www.youtube.com/watch?v=jt-8btq7kt8.

———. 2018. "When Will—and How Can—We Finish Orson Welles's *Don Quixote*? (expanded version)." *Jonathanrosenbaum.net*. Accessed March 7, 2020. http://www.jonathanrosenbaum.net/2018/05/when-will-and-how-can-we-finish-orson-welless-don-quixote-expanded-version/.

Røssaak, Eivind. 2009. "Affects and Medium: Re-Imagining Media Differences through Bill Viola's *The Quintet of the Astonished*." *New Review of Film and Television Studies* 7 (3): 339–52.

Rothkerch, Ian. 2010. "Will the Future Really Look like 'Minority Report'?" *Salon*. July 10. Accessed March 8, 2020. http://www.salon.com/2002/07/10/underkoffler_belker/.

Schneider, Alexandra. 2012. "The iPhone as an Object of Knowledge." In *Moving Data: The iPhone and the Future of Media*, edited by Pelle Snickars and Patrick Vonderau, 49–60. New York: Columbia University Press.

———. 2014. "Au delà du dispositif le cinéma (re)trouve son enfance: A propos des films-tablets et films-mobiles d'enfants." Unpublished paper presented at the international conference *Images, Histoire, Langage*. Paris, November 20-21.

Schneider, Alexandra, and Wanda Strauven. 2017. "Children's Little Thumb Films or 'Films-Poucets.'" In *Compact Cinematics: The Moving Image in the Age of Bit-Sized Media*, edited by Pepita Hesselberth and Maria Poulaki, 143–53. London: Bloomsbury.

———. Forthcoming. *Kinderspiel: Media-Archaeological Practices by Today's Children*. Lüneburg: Meson Press.

Sears, Andrew, and Ben Shneiderman. 1991. "High Precision Touchscreens: Design Strategies and Comparisons with a Mouse." *International Journal Man–Machine Studies* 34: 593–613.

Serres, Michel. 1982. *Hermes: Literature, Science, Philosophy*, edited by Josué V. Harari and David F. Bell. Baltimore: The John Hopkins University Press.

———. 2008. *The Five Senses: A Philosophy of Mingled Bodies*. London: Continuum.

———. 2012. "Ce n'est pas une crise, c'est un changement de monde." *Le JDD* (December 30). Accessed March 18, 2020. http://www.lejdd.fr/Economie/Actualite/Serres-Ce-n-est-pas-une-crise-c-est-un-changement-de-monde-583645.

———. 2015. *Thumbelina: The Culture and Technology of Millennials*. Lanham, MD: Rowman and Littlefield.

Shannon, Claude. 1949. "Communication in the Presence of Noise." *Proceedings of the I.R.E.* 37 (1): 10–21.

Shneiderman, Ben. 1991. "Touch Screens Now Offer Compelling Uses." *IEEE Software* (March): 93–94, 107.

Sobchack, Vivian. 1992. *The Address of the Eye: A Phenomenology of Film Experience*. Princeton, NJ: Princeton University Press.

———. 2004. *Carnal Thoughts: Embodiment and Moving Image Culture*. Berkeley: University of California Press.

———. 2011. "Afterword: Media Archaeology and Re-Presencing the Past." In *Media Archaeology: Approaches, Applications, and Implications*, edited by Erkki Huhtamo and Jussi Parikka, 323–30. Berkeley: University of California Press.

Sontag, Susan. 1990. *On Photography*. New York: Anchor Books.

Stafford, Barbara M. 2001. "Revealing Technologies / Magical Domains." In *Devices of Wonder: From the World in a Box to Images on a Screen*, edited by Barbara M. Stafford and Frances Terpak, 1–142. Los Angeles: Getty Publications.

Stallman, Richard. 2002. "On Hacking." *Stallman.org*. Accessed March 2, 2020. https://stallman.org/articles/on-hacking.html.

Stern, Nathaniel. 2013. *Interactive Art and Embodiment: The Implicit Body as Performance*. Canterbury: Gylphi Limited.

Stewart, Garrett. 2007. *Framed Time: Toward a Postfilmic Cinema*. Chicago: University of Chicago Press.

Stiegler, Bernard. 1998. *Technics and Time, 1: The Fault of Epimetheus*. Stanford, CA: Stanford University Press.

———. 2012. "Die Aufklärung in the Age of Philosophical Engineering." *Computational Culture* 2 (September). Accessed September 18, 2020. http://computationalculture.net/die-aufklarung-in-the-age-of-philosophical-engineering/.

———. 2019. *The Age of Disruption: Technology and Madness in Computational Capitalism*. Cambridge: Polity Press.

Stine, Kyle. 2019. "Critical Hardware: The Circuit of Image and Data." *Critical Inquiry* 45: 762–86.

Strauven, Wanda. 2005a. "Touch, Don't Look." In *I cinque sensi del cinema / The Five Senses of Cinema*, edited by Alice Autelitano, Veronica Innocenti, and Valentina Re, 283–91. Udine: Forum.

———. 2005b. "Re-Disciplining the Audience: Godard's Rube-Carabinier." In *Cinephilia: Movies, Love and Memory*, edited by Malte Hagener and Marijke de Valck, 125–33. Amsterdam: Amsterdam University Press.

———. 2006. *Marinetti e il cinema: tra attrazione e sperimentazione*. Pasian di Prato: Campanotto.

———. 2011. "The Observer's Dilemma: To Touch or Not to Touch." In *Media Archaeology: Approaches, Applications, and Implications*, edited by Erkki Huhtamo and Jussi Parikka, 148–63. Berkeley: University of California Press.

———. 2012. "Early Cinema's Touch(able) Screens: From Uncle Josh to Ali Barbayou." *NECSUS: European Journal of Media Studies* 1 (2): 155–76.

———. 2013. "Media Archaeology: Where Film Studies, Media Art and New Media (Can) Meet." In *Preserving and Exhibiting Media Art: Challenges and Perspectives*, edited by Julia Noordegraaf, Cosetta G. Saba, Barbara Le Maître, and Vinzenz Hediger, 59–79. Amsterdam: Amsterdam University Press.

———. 2014. "The Archaeology of the Touch Screen." In *Texture Matters: Der Tastsinn im Kino. Haptisch/Optisch 1*, edited by Klemens Gruber and Antonia Lant, 69–79. Vienna: Böhlau.

———. 2015. "The (Noisy) Praxis of Media Archaeology." In *At the Borders of (Film) History*, edited by Alberto Beltrame, Giuseppe Fidotta, and Andrea Mariani, 33–41. Udine: Forum.

———. 2016. "The Screenic Image: Between Verticality and Horizontality, Viewing and Touching, Displaying and Playing." In *Screens: From Materiality to Spectatorship. A Historical and Theoretical Reassessment*, edited by Dominique Chateau and José Moure, 143–56. Amsterdam: Amsterdam University Press.

———. 2018. "Marinetti's *Tattilismo* Revisited: Hand Travels, Tactile Screens and Touch Cinema in the 21st Century." In *Futurist Cinema*, edited by Rossella Catanese, 69–87. Amsterdam: Amsterdam University Press.

———. 2019. "Media Archaeology as Laboratory for History Writing and Theory Making." In *New Media Archaeologies*, edited by Ben Roberts and Mark Goodall, 23–43. Amsterdam: Amsterdam University Press.

Taylor, Alex S., and Jane Vincent. 2005. "An SMS History." In *Mobile World: Past, Present and Future*, edited by Lynne Hamill, Amparo Lasen, and Dan Diaper, 75–91. London: Springer.

Terpak, Frances. 2001. "Objects and Contexts." In *Devices of Wonder: From the World in a Box to Images on a Screen*, edited by Barbara M. Stafford and Frances Terpak, 143–364. Los Angeles: Getty Publications.

Tissandier, Gaston. 1882. "La Praxinoscope à projection." *La Nature* 492: 357–58.

Trotter, David. 2004. "Stereoscopy: Modernism and the 'Haptic.'" *Critical Quarterly* 46 (4): 38–58.

Trutty-Coohill, Patricia. 1998. "Comic Rhythms in Leonardo da Vinci." In *Enjoyment: From Laughter to Delight in Philosophy, Literature, the Fine Arts, and Aesthetics*, edited by Anna-Teresa Tymieniecka, 185–202. Dordrecht: Kluwer Academic Publishers.

Tsivian, Yuri. 1990. "Some Historical Footnotes to the Kuleshov Experiment." In *Early Cinema: Space Frame Narrative*, edited by Thomas Elsaesser, 247–55. London: British Film Institute.

Turquety, Benoît. 2018. "On Viewfinders, Video Assist Systems, and Tape Splicers: Questioning the History of Techniques and Technology in Cinema." In *Technology and Film Scholarship: Experience, Study, Theory*, edited by Santiago Hidalgo, 239–59. Amsterdam: Amsterdam University Press.

Underkoffler, John. 2010. "Pointing to the Future of UI." *TED* (February). Accessed March 15, 2020. https://www.ted.com/talks/john_underkoffler_pointing_to_the_future_of_ui.

Van Dijck, José. 2008. "Future Memories: The Construction of Cinematic Hindsight." *Theory, Culture and Society* 25: 71–87.

Verbeek, Caro. 2012. "Prière de toucher! Tactilism in Early Modern and Contemporary Art." *Senses & Society* 7 (2): 225–35.

Verhoeff, Nanna. 2012. *Mobile Screens. The Visual Regime of Navigation*. Amsterdam: Amsterdam University Press.

Virilio, Paul. 1989. *War and Cinema: The Logistics of Perception*. London: Verso.

Walton, Kendall. 1978. "Fearing Fictions." *The Journal of Philosophy* 75 (1): 5–27.

Warburg, Aby. 2016. *Mnemosyne Bilderatlas*. Curated by the Mnemosyne Research Group and 8. Salon. Karlsruhe: ZMK and Zurich: Kartoffelverlag.

Webster, Noah. 1900. *An American Dictionary of the English Language*. Chicago: Thompson & Thomas Publishers.

Weibel, Peter. 2007. "It is Forbidden Not to Touch: Some Remarks on the (Forgotten Parts of the) History of Interactivity and Virtuality." In *MediaArtHistories*, edited by Oliver Grau, 21–41. Cambridge, MA: MIT Press.

Weynants. Thomas. 2003. *Visual Media Archaeology: A Historical Window to Early Vintage Visual Media Archaeology*. Accessed March 2, 2020. http://www.visual-media.be/.

Wittgenstein, Ludwig. 1986. *Philosophical Investigations*. Oxford: Basil Blackwell.

Zielinski, Siegfried. 1996. "Media Archaeology." *CTheory*. July 11. Accessed January 21, 2021. https://journals.uvic.ca/index.php/ctheory/article/view/14321/5097.

———. 2006. *Deep Time of the Media: Towards an Archaeology of Hearing and Seeing by Technical Means*. Cambridge, MA: MIT Press.

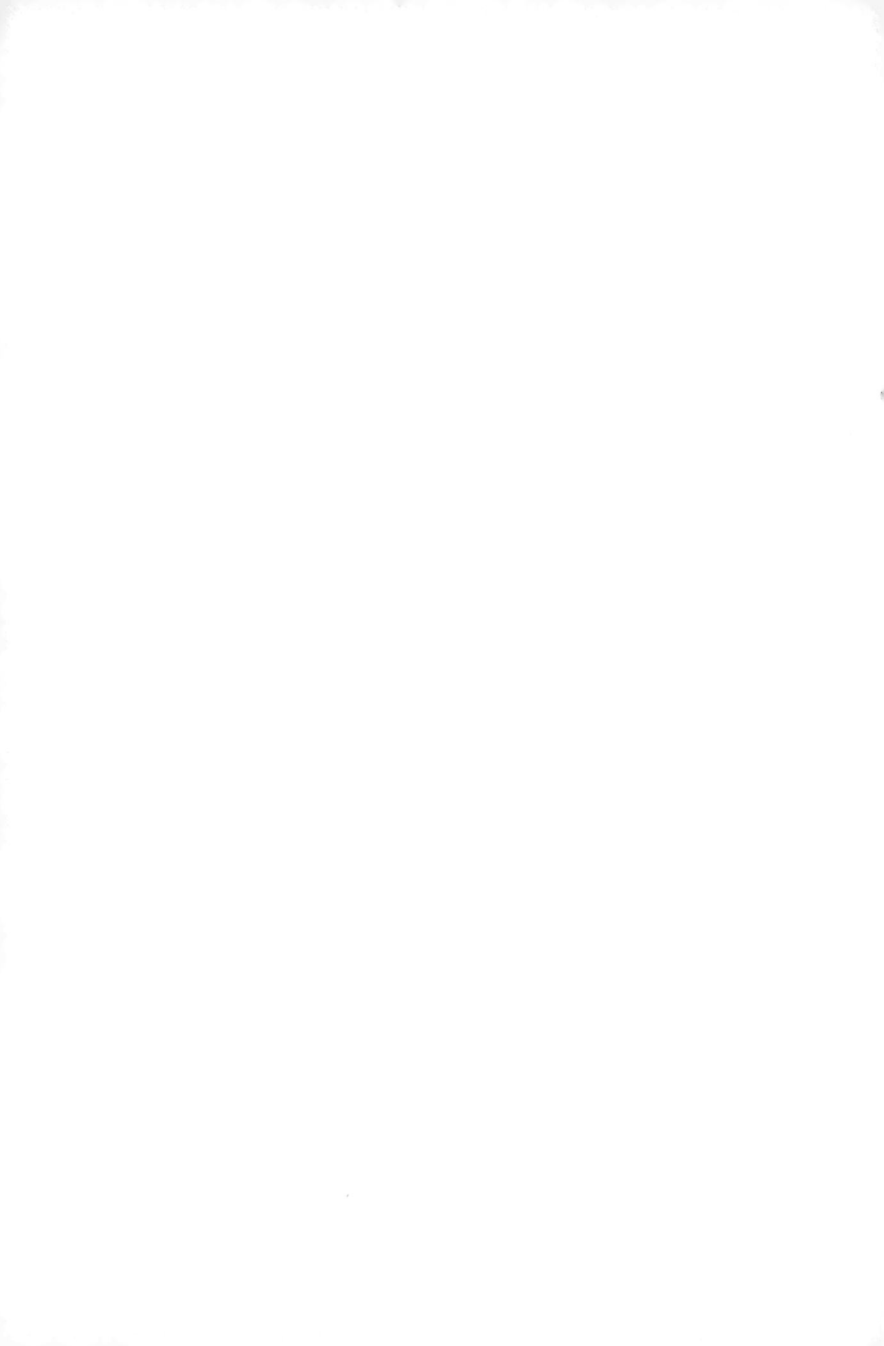

www.ingramcontent.com/pod-product-compliance
Ingram Content Group UK Ltd.
Pitfield, Milton Keynes, MK11 3LW, UK
UKHW041951190726
13854UKWH00005B/1906